This is a wonderful book. It is a model for others to follow because it is so carefully researched. Faculties in our universities need to make inquiries like this. Nancy du Tertre is breaking new ground as she confirms the importance of psychic intuition through interdisciplinary fields. She is on the edge of new thought as she helps us move ahead in the evolution of humankind.

—Severyn Bruyn, sociology professor emeritus, Boston College

If you have ever been interested in the realm of the psychic, then Psychic Intuition *is a must-read. Using her skills as an attorney, du Tertre systematically examines and cross-examines the evidence, the skeptics, and the uses and abuses of psychic tools.*

—Eldon Taylor, PhD, FAPA, *New York Times* best-selling author of *Choices and Illusions* and *Mind Programming*

Nancy du Tertre's book Psychic Intuition *not only fills a void in the theoretical and experiential literature on person-to-person intuition and psychic understanding, but she opens a universe of intuitive sensing for all of us to explore. Treating skeptics and psychics as being equally misled by language and preconception, she asks us in the words of the founder of Gestalt Psychotherapy Fritz Perls—to "lose our minds and come to our senses." In this case, to come to all 40 (or more) of our senses. I particularly enjoyed her step-by-step accounts of how subtle intuitive information comes to her and how it can be so easily dismissed when logic, pragmatism, or ordinary thinking prevail. Here she not only openly reveals her own doubts, embarrassments, and tendencies to reject this information but implicitly provides the reader with both instruction and encouragement to sequester their own hesitations and experiment with intuitive or psychic sensing for themselves. Ms. du Tertre's book reads quick, accessible, richly detailed, and forceful.*

—Ron DeAngelo, PhD, psychologist and director of intuitive training at the Soma-Psyche Institute, New York City

Over the years I have probably read 20 or 30 books detailing the life and experiences of psychics. This book stands above all of them combined. A real page-turner, one cannot help but read it into the wee hours of the morning. Each gripping chapter lays one more piece of the puzzle bare, so that piece-by-piece, a picture emerges. The work avoids trying to explain the origins of psychic phenomena, and instead focuses on the origins of psychic ability. In my opinion, it does so admirably, in a rich and colorful voyage blending the physical and the metaphysical into a unified manifestation.

—David M. Rountree, AES, director, chief science advisor, Scientific Paranormal Investigative Research Information and Technology (S.P.I.R.I.T.)

From the first meeting I had with Nancy to the reading of her incredible book Psychic Intuition, *I've had the great pleasure of hearing her thoughts and ideas, intuition and intelligence. Her book is an awakening for the uninitiated with insights that will give them countless aha's. For everyone immersed in the field there is still plenty to learn and understand. Nancy has a way of exploring and synthesizing that clarifies so beautifully that it needs to be gone over again and again. There is so much value and so much to be gained from her insights, intuition, and intelligence that everyone ever interested in the psychic world needs this book.*

—Nancy Orlen Weber, psychic detective and medical intuitive

If you're curious as to how the brain picks up what we call "psychic, or intuitive information," this book is a must-read. Nancy explains many complex theories in a down to earth way, making the book extremely reader friendly.

—Angela Artemis, clairvoyant and founder of PoweredbyIntuition.com

I admire Nancy's writing style and the openness of the debate it has engendered. On the other hand, I do fear getting embroiled in an "angel on a pinhead" type of argumentation. I find her intellectual prowess delightful, but the direction she is taking it, questionable.

—Dr. Rodolfo Llinás, professor of neuroscience and director of the neuroscience graduate program, department of physiology and neuroscience, NYU Langone Medical Center

PSYCHIC INTUITION

Everything You Ever Wanted to Ask
but Were Afraid to Know

By

NANCY DU TERTRE

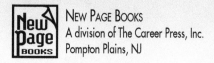
NEW PAGE BOOKS
A division of The Career Press, Inc.
Pompton Plains, NJ

PSYCHIC INTUITION
EDITED BY NICOLE DEFELICE
TYPESET BY EILEEN MUNSON
Cover design by Ian Shimkoviak/the Book Designers and Jeff Piasky
Printed in the U.S.A.

To order this title, please call toll-free 1-800-CAREER-1 (NJ and Canada: 201-848-0310) to order using VISA or MasterCard, or for further information on books from Career Press.

The Career Press, Inc.
220 West Parkway, Unit 12
Pompton Plains, NJ 07444
www.careerpress.com
www.newpagebooks.com

Library of Congress Cataloging-in-Publication Data

Du Tertre, Nancy.
   Psychic intuition : everything you ever wanted to ask but were afraid to know / by Nancy Du Tertre.
      p. cm.
   Includes bibliographical references and index.
   ISBN 978-1-60163-227-2 -- ISBN 978-1-60163-591-4 (ebook) 1. Psychic ability. 2. Intuition--Miscellanea. I. Title.

BF1031.D8 2012
133.8--dc23

                          2012013338

To my husband,

Patrick,

whose favorite expression is

"Only stupid people never change their minds!"

Few people have the imagination for reality.

—Johann Wolfgang von Goethe

CONTENTS

Can a Skeptic Be Psychic?

The answer is yes. But only if you are the right kind of skeptic—a true skeptic, a person genuinely committed to seeking the truth, whatever it may be.

Nancy du Tertre is such a person. As she beautifully and clearly explains in *Psychic Intuition,* Nancy *did not* begin her life as a psychic intuitive. In fact, originally she had "no reason to believe in psychic phenomena because it does not exist" for her.

Nancy's background was grounded in skepticism. She comes from a family of medical scientists, and Nancy received her training as an attorney specialized in securities litigation. Lawyers are educated about the importance of evidence—both physical and circumstantial—and how to draw reasonable inferences based upon the available evidence.

In addition, lawyers are typically left-brained—meaning they are logic-focused. Even if they are representing the defense and questioning the validity, reliability, and/or interpretation of specific evidence against their client, they are doing so (or at least are supposed to do so) within established boundaries of truth and fairness.

So how did a well-trained attorney become a skilled psychic intuitive? In a word, it was first and foremost because of the evidence. Nancy witnessed real phenomena that went beyond her conventional training and then she trained for many years to enhance and develop her psychic abilities. What she experienced over time became replicable enough so that the accumulated body of evidence led her to a controversial conclusion. This conclusion was "beyond reasonable doubt" that the phenomenon of psychic intuition was not only real, but could be developed with training.

This legal standard of "beyond a reasonable doubt" for criminal cases or the lesser standard of "the preponderance of the evidence" for civil cases is enough for most reasonable judges and jurors to make a judgment about reality. Although many hard-core scientists would say this falls short of the scientific gold standard—the scientific method—increasingly, we are beginning to understand that not everything in our universe falls so neatly into our three- or four-dimensional human laboratories. Certain realities, at least for the time being, escape today's precise quantitative measurements.

Like Nancy, I also understand the nature of skepticism. I was well-trained in its philosophy and execution. I was educated in conventional science and received a PhD in psychology from Harvard University. I have been a full-time academic scientist spanning 40 years at Harvard, Yale, and the University of Arizona. During this time, I have received research funding from many established sources including the National Science Foundation, the National Institutes of Health, and the Department of Defense, and I have published more than 450 scientific papers. I share these biographical facts so you can understand that what I am about to share has some serious justification.

I, too, have come to the conclusion that psychic intuition is real and can be trained. I have come to this conclusion first and foremost based upon more than 15 years of laboratory experiments involving more than 30 genuine psychic intuitive and healers. Some of these experiments have been summarized in *The Afterlife Experiments, The Truth About Medium,* and *The Energy Healing Experiments.*

However, I have also come to this conclusion based upon my own personal experience, which has evolved along with my laboratory research. I call this self-science—applying the methods of science to the laboratories of our personal lives.

As I confess in *The Sacred Promise,* even a well-trained scientist like me can have intuitive moments, and I have witnessed them increase in frequency and specificity throughout the years. As a result, I understand what Nancy writes about as she begins to experience the "impossible" partly because I have been privileged to experience the "impossible" as well.

Nancy's approach to explaining psychic ability is based on her observations about how our sensory organs operate and relate to the function of the brain. She brings us on this journey by starting at a place we can all agree upon: our five physical senses. It is no great leap of the imagination for us to understand that our senses provide us with only a very limited slice of reality because they have limited receptors of electromagnetic and chemical data. Nancy explains that recent scientific research has postulated that we don't merely have five senses, but we may have as many as 40 senses or more! Sensory data comes into our awareness through multiple sensory organs, and we are bombarded by more than 11 million bits of sensory information per second and yet retain only 16 bits in our conscious awareness.

Based on this, Nancy concludes there is no such thing as the famous sixth sense. Rather, there is a lack of awareness of the vastness of our existing sensory experience. It is only through training that we can learn how to access this sensory information.

She then explains how language, logic, and reason (all left-brain attributes) corrupt our ability to access this sensory information. She compares psychic ability to certain types of known neurological conditions, such as savantism and synesthesia, where individuals are able to access extraordinary sensory information that is "invisible" to the rest of us. Nancy also demonstrates the difference between psychic sensing ability and sensory hallucinations—so there can be no confusion.

She leaves us with a clear picture of why and how psychic ability is lost during a lifetime, and why skeptics *literally* do not experience the same sensory data as psychics. With this knowledge, she claims, it is not only possible to train oneself to become psychic (as she has done), but she also suggests that we are now on the cusp of a scientific breakthrough that may actually shed light on the mechanics and architecture of extraordinary sensing within the brain.

While appealing to a scientific frame of mind, Nancy also goes a bit further. She talks about what it feels like from the perspective of someone who is now psychic when she experiences these psychic moments. She talks about some of her experiences as a psychic detective, medical intuitive, and medium. Even though skeptics may not be able to identify with these unusual moments, having never had such an experience before, they will find it at least insightful and, perhaps even more importantly, useful in understanding that genuine psychic ability is not some wacky invention by New Age con artists!

Just because we believe or presume that something is impossible does not mean that something is in fact impossible. The history of science provides a wealth of examples of the seemingly impossible becoming established fact—quantum physics is a case-in-point. The key to making discoveries is having an open mind and following the evidence where it takes you. This was the genius illustrated in the fictional character Sherlock Holmes and the real-life person Albert Einstein. All of us can do this to various degrees, and Nancy inspires us to do so.

Nancy appreciates this established history and uses it to our advantage. We are taken on a remarkable journey of discovery and possibility. In the process, we are given practical tips in how to develop our own psychic intuitive abilities. Just as all can be taught to play "Chopsticks" on the piano, and some of us can learn to become professional pianists, all of us can be taught to have intuitive moments, and some of us can learn to become accomplished psychic intuitives.

Psychic Intuition deserves to become required reading in applied intuitive science and evidence-based intuitive living. May you be as enlightened by this book as I have been.

> —Gary E. Schwartz, PhD
> Professor of psychology, medicine, neurology,
> psychiatry, and surgery, the University of Arizona,
> and director, the Laboratory for Advances in
> Consciousness and Health

One day I received an e-mail from a retired police chief. He knew I worked as a trained psychic detective. He told me he was working on a missing person case and wanted to know what I could see about the case using my psychic remote viewing skills. He gave me the name of the woman who had gone missing and an Internet link to the publicly issued police flier. The flier gave only basic information about the woman's description, when she went missing, her age, and when and where she was last seen. I sat down with a piece of paper and pencil, and "imagined" a certain scenario about the missing woman. I felt she had been raped and killed, and that her body had been left near a small stream in the woods. I gave other information, which I am not at liberty to divulge. Some of it made sense and some just seemed like total nonsense. I e-mailed him my response.

Within a day, he got back to me, and, in typical poker-faced law enforcement style, said dryly, "You have described the suspect and the property in question."

He said the detectives wanted to meet with me. They later drove me to the location I had described. It turned out to be the exact place the police had excavated searching for the woman's remains. As of this writing, the case has not yet been solved and so I am not at liberty to give more details—which is always a problem when trying to prove to the general public that psychic work can be a highly useful tool.

Seem impossible? I have learned the impossible is indeed possible. If I can do it, so can you. Don't expect to learn this overnight. It took me more than a decade of apprenticeship and training. I needed to learn how to trust the impossible within myself—and that didn't come easily.

I
N
T
R
O
D
U
C
T
I
O
N

I began my life as a skeptic, not a psychic. I certainly did not see or understand these supposedly colorful displays of electromagnetic energy around the human body known as auras. I did not believe in things such as crystals, dowsing, angels, or energy healing. I figured the healing techniques of American Indian shamans and ancient Chinese medicine were silly voodoo beliefs of primitive cultures. I did not have prophetic visions of the future. I was not fascinated by psychic events because they didn't seem to exist within my life. I never had any desire to have psychic readings or know the future as did many of my friends. Spiritual mediums were presumably theatrical frauds. Despite my efforts, I had never seen a ghost and so could not assume that they existed. I am not nor have I ever been superstitious. So, having black cats cross my path, walking under a ladder, breaking a mirror, the number 13, or other supposedly bad omens just never bothered me.

In short, I had no reason to believe in psychic phenomena because it did not exist for me.

Today I am known as the Skeptical Psychic. This is not a contradiction in terms. It only reflects my belief that we must remain open-minded to accept things that seem impossible while being careful not to engage in wishful thinking. Now I know psychic ability can be trained—well, technically I should say *retrained* because it is a natural human ability that we all disregard during our lifetimes. I know this because I am the living proof. Whether you believe it or not, you are as psychic as I am; you just don't understand what it means.

Why I Wrote This Book

I wrote this book with the specific purpose of trying to logically explain the illogical experience of intuition and psychic ability. I do not try to explain the origin of psychic phenomena.

I wanted to bridge the gap between skeptics and scientists on the one hand, and believers and intuitives on the other. To date, there has been little or no conversation between the two groups. Skeptics have no experience with psychic intuition and therefore no reason to believe in it. Psychics have every reason to believe in it because they experience it, yet they have no ability to explain it in logical terms. So the whole phenomenon rests at a stalemate.

When I started writing the book, I naturally assumed it would be based on psychology. After all, intuition is a psychological phenomenon, right?

I scoured the psychology sections of the book stores and libraries for anything even remotely to do with intuition, and read everything I could get my hands on—which wasn't much.

I was shocked to discover almost no one had dealt with the basic issue of human intuition!

Once in a while, I came across some brave psychologist who gingerly broached the subject of intuition as if it needed special handling with surgical gloves. Typically, they would rename intuition as something else, then reclassify it. Intuition is often described in psychotherapeutic terms as a form of empathy. Empathy, after all, unlike intuition, is a conscious experience of the brain and can easily be invoked at will. Empathy can be sliced and dissected by the scientific method of inquiry. By contrast, intuition is just a loose cannon with no controls.

A theory of resonant empathy was developed by psychologists Basch, Feiner, and Kiersky, to try to logically explain why therapists sometimes have uncanny moments where they have random mental images or emotions that correspond to their client's actual memories or feelings. Of course, this seemingly psychic or telepathic behavior was quickly reduced to nothing more than subliminal clues in the environment or the therapist's personal associations with the client's emotions.

Sometimes intuition is called transference or counter-transference within the clinical relationship between therapist and client. In either case, one party imagines things about the other person that are sometimes startlingly accurate. This is a kind of wish fulfillment based on one's own personal knowledge and expectations. At least, in these circumstances, it could be examined under a microscope as an experience that could be explained by normal facts and circumstances.

But none of this can explain how we can intuitively know things based on zero evidence.

It was becoming obvious to me that the entire field of psychotherapy went running for the hills when it came time to deal with intuition as a human phenomenon. Psychologists did not want to discuss the possibility of human knowledge that might threaten their entrenched belief in the mind-body duality. Psychologists need to believe that individuals have isolated mental systems. Psychology has not, to date, removed itself from its foundation in the philosophy of solipsism. Solipsism basically states that every man is an island. We can never truly understand another person, according to this theory, because we can never be inside his or her brain. We can only speculate about his or her experience in the world. All empathy is a type of mental projection. We can only guess what other people feel.

Well, if psychology couldn't explain intuition, maybe neuroscience could.

I spent the next year pouring over books about neuroscience—more specifically, neurobiology and neuropsychiatry. I began to find fascinating little clues here and there about the possible nature and behavior of intuition from a neurological point of view. But once again, the scientists in the field were demonstrating a very strong aversion to the idea of studying intuition at all. Some of the biggest names in neuroscience, such as Drs. Oliver Sacks, Rodolfo Llinás, and V.S. Ramachandran (dubbed the "Marco Polo of Neuroscience"), are devout skeptics when it comes to psychic phenomena. As with other scientists, I found the neuroscientists unwilling to put their professional reputations on the line in order to explore intuition. Thus, it became clear to me that even these fearless pioneers of the brain and human awareness did not want to touch this topic, either.

What a strange thing! Scientists were refusing to explore phenomena because of their own belief systems. It seemed like the world turned upside down.

At that point, I didn't know quite where to turn to find information about intuition. My research began to explode rather chaotically. I began to read books by and about psychics, spiritual mediums, psychic detectives, military psychic spy programs in the United States and Russia, FBI polygraph research into plant emotions, water crystal formations affected by emotions, crystallography, energy healing, medical intuitives, artificial intelligence experts, NASA consultants, physicists, organ transplant recipients, crop circle designers, medical doctors, psychiatrists, detectives and law enforcement officials, musicians, artists, poker players, exorcists, ghost hunters and paranormal investigators, parapsychologists, and many more.

Then I began to realize that, due to the nature of the beast, intuition must not just be learned intellectually: It must be *experienced*.

I decided the only way I was ever going to really understand intuition was to train myself in the field. So I began to study with a number of well-known psychics, mediums, and psychic healers. After continuously pestering my teachers with thorny analytical questions and a relentless skeptical attitude for many years, I have come out on the other side with a completely new and different understanding of intuition.

After all this research, I confess that the world of intuition began to seem hopelessly huge and unmanageable. But I had learned something very important: Everyone uses the word *intuition* as if it had a common meaning. Actually, intuition means very different things to different people. My goal has been to bring intuition into the common fold of understanding and definition. I am willing to step forward to do this because I have nothing to lose. I have no scientific reputation to defend. I can see the landscape from my bird's-eye view—and, more importantly, I can see the landscape with my third eye.

Lesson #1:

The Impossible Is Real

My First (Memorable) Encounter With a Ghost

Like most people, I had a couple of strange experiences as a child, but quickly shelved them in that dusty brain folder containing weird and unexplainable experiences, and forgot about them. It wasn't until I reached the age of 35 that I had a real psychic experience.

I was an attorney practicing securities litigation and living in Manhattan. I was invited to attend a series of training workshops on intuition for psychologists led by Dr. Ron DeAngelo at the Gestalt Associates for Psychotherapy. Ron is a brilliant, highly sensitive psychotherapist and has been on the forefront of exploring intuition as a psychological phenomenon. I was the only non-psychotherapist who was invited to attend. Dr. DeAngelo knew me personally and felt I would benefit greatly from it.

Here's how a typical workshop would go: Everyone in the group, usually about 10 to 15 people, would sit in chairs arranged in a large circle. Ron would select one volunteer to come and sit in the hot seat. That person's job was to simply sit quietly without displaying any emotion while the rest of us observed him or her. Ron would then ask the group a series of questions that we had to answer silently in our minds before later revealing them to the class. The questions were fairly bizarre, such as "If this person were an animal, what kind of an animal would he or she be?" or "What does the environment look like where this person lives?"

The whole idea was not to spend too much time thinking about the answers. Ron was interested in testing how much seemingly invisible intuitive data could be gathered about a person simply by tiny physical clues such as micro-muscle facial movements, posture, choice of clothes, condition of clothes, colors, body language, and so on. Psychologist Paul Ekman (a protegé of Silvan Tomkins) developed a system in 1976, known as the Facial Action Coding System (FACS), to analytically decipher micro-muscular facial movements on a person's face. He found there are 300 combinations of two muscles; 4,000 combinations of three muscles; and 10,000 of five muscles, although only 3,000 such combinations have actual expressive and emotive value. In the field of psychology, it is assumed that there is a logical reason why we know things about other people even when they are not obvious. Ron adopted this scientific approach toward intuition.

My ghost encounter occurred during one particular workshop. On this particular evening, a woman of Indian descent, with long, flowing, raven-black hair, was in the hot seat. We all did Ron's exercises. At the end of the session, Ron asked this woman several direct questions, and we learned she had led a very sad and tragic life. I remember that there were many suicides in her family, including her brother and her mother. She was a tremendously sad person. This kind of feedback was always helpful because it helped us to compare our images with her personality to see if our intuitions had been accurate.

As usual, Ron's exploration of intuition remained staunchly in the scientific and analytic realm. This particular evening, Ron ended the workshop, thanked us all for coming, and told us he would see us the following week. Suddenly, I felt a very strong urge—I say urge because that is the only way to explain it—to speak. I fought the impulse because I truly did not want to open my mouth, but the urge was greater than my resistance.

"Excuse me, Ron," I said hesitantly, "I'm wondering if I could ask her one more question?"

Ron said, "Sure, go ahead."

"I'm sorry, but you're not going to like my question," I said, apologizing in advance.

Ron looked puzzled. I knew that my question was headed down the murky path of psychic, as opposed to psychotherapeutic, inquiry. Ron always steered clear of psychic proposals. He was strictly scientific in his approach.

"Okay," he responded.

I asked the woman if she knew anyone with the initials "M.S." I have no clue why my brain selected these two letters, but they had popped into my mind and felt not only logical, but *conclusive.* I felt a certainty associated with these letters, but had no idea why. Back in the late 1980s, there were very few books written by spiritual mediums and absolutely no television shows on the subject, so it wasn't the kind of thing I would have seen anyone else doing. I had never done anything like that in my life and wasn't exactly sure why I was doing it then. Moreover, I do not enjoy public humiliation.

The Indian woman looked slightly confused and thought for a few moments before answering that no, she didn't know anyone with those initials. I thanked her, feeling foolish indeed. I would have been perfectly happy to leave it there, but the woman insisted on knowing why I had asked the question. Because I did not know why I had asked such a question, I felt deeply ashamed, especially in such a public display in front of so many people—*especially* professional psychotherapists.

"No, no," I said sheepishly. "Forget it, it was nothing."

But the woman insisted, "No, really, what do you mean?"

So I tentatively ventured further, "Okay, do you know anyone with the initials M.S. whose first name is 'Mary', 'Marie' or 'Maria'?"

"No...no, I don't think so, unless maybe...." She paused for a while. "I think I might have had a secretary a long time ago whose name was Marie, but I don't know what her last name was."

That definitely wasn't it. I was ready to quit.

I said, "Okay, let's just forget it then."

I prayed that we would stop the conversation in which I was feeling more foolish by the minute and we could simply go home. But the woman persisted.

"What makes you ask me that?" she inquired mercilessly.

I realized that I was going to have to bite the bullet and simply explain my bizarre thought process and that there was no going back at that point.

"All right, if you really want to know," I took a deep breath and continued, "I felt a spirit or a presence walk right through here between you and me (I pointed to the roughly 3-feet-wide space between her chair and mine) and I know it's a woman; her initials are M.S. and her name is something like 'Marie' or 'Maria' and so I guess I kind of assumed it was your mother."

I knew her mother was dead from the family history she had already given us. The way I knew a spirit had walked between us (a highly extraordinary claim for one who had never experienced a spirit in one's life before!) was because I felt a distinct cool breeze on my right forearm like a swish of air following in the wake of a person who has just moved in front of you—except cooler than room temperature, making the experience seem unusual. It was about the same sensation as when you open the refrigerator door while you're standing in front of it. (At the time, I was not aware that temperature drops and cold spots have often been associated with the presence of ghosts in paranormal literature.) There were no doors or windows open in the room, no air conditioning, and no physical movement that could have been logically associated with a push of air across the room in that location. It was the sensation of a cool current of air without any corresponding physical source or origin.

I don't know how I figured that the presence was female, but it definitely was. I sensed femininity in a very vague, pre-linguistic way. That also seems like a gross contradiction in terms especially if you can't relate the feminine presence to a visual image of a woman, the sound of a woman's voice, or other typically female sensory attributes. It was a kind of instantaneous, seemingly non-sensory, non-intellectual "knowledge." The odd thing was that I could be so *certain* about this information with absolutely no substantiating sensory evidence in my brain. I "saw" and "heard" absolutely nothing. I was logically disturbed by my explanation for a number of reasons, not the least of which was that it was highly unlikely that any relative of a woman from an Indian background in India would have had a name like Marie, Mary, or Maria. But it was all out in the open then. There was no turning back.

As soon as I told her I thought the presence was her mother, this Indian woman turned absolutely white and her eyes got huge and teary. She began sobbing. This was tremendously shocking for me, because I had no idea what was going on.

Finally, she looked up and said, "No, that was my mother's sister. Her name was Marie (I forget the complicated Indian last name, but it began was the letter S) and she just died about three months ago. She died in England and I couldn't go to her funeral. I felt so bad about that."

Then she began crying all over again. Once again I felt an urge (strangely, without any voluntary desire on my part) to tell this woman that her aunt was present in the room, directly in front of her, standing to my left, and wanted her to know that she loved her very much. So I did. This last comment seemed phenomenally lame to me. I felt stupid for even saying it. It seemed to me that I was simply stating the obvious. What other message would your subconscious mind invent to pass on to a living relative? It wasn't until about 10 years later when I began paying attention to certain psychic mediums on television, such as John Edward, that I realized that is often the exact message that most spirits want to convey. Dr. Eben Alexander III, a neurosurgeon who experienced his own Near Death Experience during a seven-day coma, told me that he was advised by the spirit world to bring back the message of unconditional love. Love, it seems, is a profound spiritual message that isn't heard enough by mere mortals.

It is obvious from this story that if I had followed my logical and normal impulse to keep my mouth shut and not explore my weird impressions, I would never have learned that my strange thoughts were accurate. I would never have permitted myself the opportunity for feedback to see if my weird thoughts were justified or not. They would have remained in that cognitive category of our brain we all refer to as our imagination. I never would have experienced a ghost—just an overactive imagination. This is fairly typical of all of us; we dismiss most of our silly thoughts before they ever see the light of day. So my first advice to those of you who would like to learn how to become psychic is to open your mouth.

Exercise

Every time you walk into a different room or a building, try to feel how the energy of the space feels different from the previous space, and when you walk down the street, look at people and try to imagine who they are, where they are going, and what they do.

Lesson #2:

Don't Ignore Diamonds in the Rough

Our incredible and relentless desire to be *reasonable* is what most often destroys our ability to be intuitive. In order to be sure we are right, we feel a need to rely on *known* facts. But intuition allows us to jump to (accurate) conclusions without the underlying facts. How is that possible?

I would like to share a personal story about intuition. This story shows how our personal memories and collective human memories (what we call "history") are deeply influenced by what we choose to believe. True history is permanently erased when we don't trust our own intuition or that of others.

After I graduated from college, I moved to New York City and tried to find a job as a journalist. As luck would have it, nothing was available because, at that exact moment, all of the writers for the major newspapers had decided to go on strike and were grabbing up all the little jobs that someone like me might otherwise have had a shot at getting. Rather than starve to death in my $80-per-month studio (located in the East Village before it became fashionable), I found three jobs that collectively paid the rent and an occasional splurge at McDonald's. I worked during the day as a receptionist for a Teamsters local. At night, I worked at an uptown restaurant as a waitress. On the weekends, I worked as a researcher for a well-known political *Wall Street Journal* Op-Ed writer and author whose name was Edward Jay Epstein. Epstein had written a number of top-selling books about current events, such as the inside story of the Teamsters Union, the JFK assassination, relations between the CIA and KGB, and the diamond industry.

Edward Jay Epstein, with his graying hair and his perpetual look of intellectual disdain, was a rather stern and forbidding-looking man. He was clearly not interested in me, a lowly researcher, or any of my opinions. He was far more interested in cultivating his relationships with important people such as former Secretary of State Henry Kissinger and their shared passion for exotic orchids (which covered every square inch of his apartment). He told me my job would be to find out as much as possible about the history of diamonds, and come back with as much useful information as possible for his next book, an exposé about the diamond industry.

I dutifully went off to the New York City Public Library every weekend and spent hours and hours in the dimly lit stacks trying to learn everything possible about diamonds. One day, I was researching the history of South Africa, which is home to the world's largest and most prolific diamond and gold mines. I began reading about South Africa's British imperialist "founding fathers." There were really just two founding fathers, both of whom were English immigrants and feuded with each other most of their lives. They were Cecil John Rhodes (for whom the country of Rhodesia, now Zimbabwe, was named) and Barney Barnato. Rhodes eventually became prime minister of South Africa. Barnato became a lifetime member of the Cape Parliament. Both men independently bought up mining claims and parcels of gold and diamond territories in the mid-19th century until both had amassed huge economic interests. The intense competition between the two men to gain control of the crown jewel of all diamond mines—the Kimberley Diamond Mine (which eventually became today's De Beers Diamond Company)—is legendary. By 1889, however, Barnato finally sold out his remaining stock interest in the mine to Rhodes for the astronomical sum of £5,338,650 (the equivalent of $25 million) in the single-largest check that had ever been written in history, making Barnato the richest man in the world.

As I continued to research, I learned from the history books that Barnato (1852–1897) came from very humble beginnings. He was born into a Jewish family in a slum near Whitechapel, outside London. His father was a garment vendor named Isaac Isaacs and his grandfather was a rabbi. Barnato was actually a stage name. He was born Barnett Isaacs, but eventually changed his name after doing a vaudeville act with his older brother Harry when the crowd called out for his participation in the act by shouting "And Barney too!" Barnato's father's favorite bit of advice to his boys was: "If you have to fight, always get in the first blow." Barnato clearly adhered to this counsel. He was a tough, street-wise kid. After pursuing a number of jobs, such as mock-tipsy juggler, professional boxer, scene-shifter at the Cambridge Music Hall, and bouncer in a spit-and-sawdust gin palace (similar to the saloons of the American Old West) owned by his brother-in-law, Joel Joel, Barnato decided to seek his fortune in the Cape Colony in 1871 during the gold rush.

Barnato arrived in Cape Town, South Africa, on a steamer from London with nothing but £30 in his pocket and 40 boxes of defective cigars, which he hoped to sell to unsuspecting diamond traders, and within 10 years amassed a huge fortune and became a multi-millionaire.

According to the history books, Barnato died mysteriously at sea at the age of 44 in 1897, after jumping overboard on a ship bound for London. Most historians claim he committed suicide. According to one noted historian, Barnato had been on his way to England to join celebrations to mark Queen Victoria's golden jubilee. Shortly after his ship called at Madeira, Barnato leapt from his deck chair, cried out "They're after me," rushed to the nearby railings, climbed up and jumped overboard. One of the ship's officers immediately dived overboard. He caught sight of Barnato but the rough sea kept them apart. By the time the lifeboat reached him, Barnato was floating downward. All attempts to revive him failed.

Others speculated that certain dealings with South African gangsters had resulted in his murder after sending him blackmail letters rudely embroidered with skull and crossbones and coffins. Still others suggested strange occult relationships that had rendered him so insane that he jumped off the ship in a psychotic frenzy.

Now, you are probably wondering why I have bothered to tell you this rather long story about a rich, South African diamond merchant. It has everything to do with how we choose to "see" or not "see" intuitive information. How much information do we really need in order to make an intuitive judgment?

After reading about the history of Barney Barnato, I sat pondering my research in the library's main reading room in between the quiet rows of rigid, wooden chairs. A strange thought came to me. Could I possibly be related to Barney Barnato? Of course, this seemed like a ridiculous thought and highly unlikely. No one on either side of my family had South African relatives and no one was even remotely involved in the diamond business. Moreover, there was no family history of this kind of unprecedented wealth or political power. But five little facts got stuck in my craw and I just couldn't get rid of them: Barnato 1) was an Englishman from London, 2) was Jewish, 3) came from a family named Isaacs, 4) had been a vaudeville actor, and 5) he, along with several members of his family, had a double name: Barney Barnato, Isaac Isaacs, and Joel Joel.

I never knew much about my own family origins, especially on my father's side. Neither one of my grandparents on his side, even to their dying days, told me much of anything at all about their family history. It was an accepted void in our family conversations. I always had the faint, unverifiable feeling that they were somehow not proud of their backgrounds, but I never asked and they never told. They had lived a comfortable, but not extraordinary, middle-class life in Brooklyn. My grandfather had been a moderately successful insurance salesman who preferred playing golf to working. My father, a well-recognized medical scientist, never talked about his family, his emotions, or his childhood. He didn't like his parents much. He didn't speak with them for more than 40 years and refused to attend their funerals. There was no love lost there. But here's what I did know:

1. My grandfather's side of the family had originally come from London. My great-grandfather had immigrated to the United States and worked in the tobacco manufacturing business.

2. My grandfather loved to recite poetry and sang popular ragtime ditties from the early 20th century. He came from a large family of 10 children, and they used to amuse themselves by entertaining each other through song and dance. He had a distant aunt named Ada Reeve, who was a famous vaudeville actress in England.

3. My grandparents were Jewish, although this was never obvious to me. They never celebrated any Jewish holidays; they didn't speak Yiddish or Hebrew; they never once attended temple; they didn't own any Jewish artifacts; and they never spoke of Israel or other Jewish matters. There was nothing particularly Jewish about them except their desire for their two sons to become successful doctors. Perhaps their religious indifference is what caused both their sons to convert to Protestantism as young adults.

4. My grandfather's name was Lester Lester.

5. Although neither my father nor my grandparents ever told me this, my mother once explained that my grandfather had changed his last name from "Isaacs" to "Lester." When I asked why, she told me this was to make his name sound less "Old World" (my mother's Protestant genteel code word for "Jewish immigrants") so he could be more successful in the business world. Isaacs is one of the most common Jewish surnames after Cohen, Levy, and Miller.

I immediately felt these five little bits of information connected my family with Barnato. My father's side of the family was originally Jewish, had emigrated from London, and was originally named Isaacs; there was a family history associated with vaudeville in England; and my grandfather had voluntarily selected a double name for himself: Lester Lester. But was that enough information to make such a dramatic leap to the conclusion that I might be related to the once-richest man in the world? I decided to try to verify my strange conclusion.

One weekend, I visited my grandparents at their apartment in Manhattan. I began discussing my research, and decided to ask my grandfather, rather sheepishly, if he had ever heard of a guy named Barney Barnato. I explained Barnato was once the richest man in the world and credited with being the George Washington of South Africa. I was sure he hadn't. I had never heard anyone in my family ever discuss diamonds, the diamond industry, relatives in England, or anything about South African history.

My grandfather looked at me with an expression on his face as if this was something entirely obvious and unexceptional.

"Yeah, sure," he said. "He was my uncle."

Well, I damn near fell out of my chair when I heard that! I couldn't believe my ears. The odds of there being any connection at all between Barnato and my family were so extremely remote as to be virtually impossible. The fact that I had managed to string together five extraneous, unrelated details from the life of a famous historical personage and equate them accurately with my own family was nothing short of a miracle. Even more stunning, as it turned out, was that my own father never knew about our family relationship to Barney Barnato. He couldn't understand how I had figured it out. My grandfather would have taken all this fascinating family history to his grave if I had not fought my impulse not to sound like an idiot!

My grandfather began to tell me stories about Barnato that no historian could have known. He told me how his father (my great-grandfather) was the only one of the three Isaacs children who decided to travel to America. He sought his fortune in the tobacco industry. According to my grandfather, Barney apparently used to send his brother (my great-grandfather) parcels in the mail containing what appeared to be large, rough rocks. My great-grandfather had no idea what these were. Thinking they were nothing more than ordinary rocks, he simply threw them away in the trash can at the post office. In fact, they were huge, raw diamonds!

As if all this wasn't enough of a personal goldmine of information, my grandfather then began to tell me how Barnato had died. This particular bit of information has been one of the great mysteries in the history of South Africa. The official versions of Barnato's death are shrouded in intrigue and mystery. Some historians have argued that Barnato committed suicide by jumping to his death off the side of a ship headed to England. Others believe he was driven mad after receiving strange, demonic messages. Still other historians have suggested that his death was due to a mafia hit. There is no official consensus. *The New York Times* article detailing news of his death in June 16, 1897, contained the following sensational headline:

BARNEY BARNATO'S SUICIDE;
Wrenched Himself from a Man Detailed to Watch Him and
Leaped in the Sea.

MENTAL TROUBLE THE CAUSE
An Officer of the Scot Went Overboard to Save Him and
Recovered the Body
His Death Affects the London Markets

When I told this to my grandfather, he let out a great big laugh.

"No! Not at all!" he explained. "Uncle Barney died because he got into a fight with one of the ship's officers. They got into a big tussle on deck. They were both drunk. They lost their balance and both fell overboard. They were only able to rescue the officer, but not my uncle."

So much for the official version of Barnato's death as a suicide or mysterious mafia hit—and so much for the "courage" of the ship's officer. Given Barney's pugilistic background and fiery temper, my grandfather's story made an infinite amount of sense to me. What a jackpot I had hit! I got excited knowing that I was in possession of information that was completely unknown to all of the historians. I couldn't wait to get home and type up a little summary of the information given to me by my grandfather about Barney Barnato so I could give it to Edward Jay Epstein. He would be able to use information that was hitherto unknown in the annals of history. I would produce something absolutely invaluable to him—better than weeks and weeks of research in the library.

A few days later, I arrived at Epstein's apartment and proudly handed him my single-spaced typed sheet with this extraordinary true-life story about Barnato and my family. He gave a cursory glance at the paper, said nothing, and threw it in the trash can. We never even had the opportunity to discuss it, and I was too young and inexperienced to ever broach the subject again.

I can only guess that he thought I was lying—or maybe worse, fabricating a story to replace good, old-fashioned hard work in the library. Maybe he just couldn't quite accept the fact that a young 23-year-old kid, working only a few weeks on this assignment, could have come up with a piece of information that defied all other historians researching the subject for the previous 150 years. Perhaps that was just too improbable—or maybe it was just too much to ask of a serious author to override more than a century of historical authority.

He did finally write and publish the book on diamonds in 1982. It was entitled *The Rise and Fall of Diamonds: The Shattering of a Brilliant Illusion* and contained the usual historically acceptable information about Barnato. I do know, however, that the information I gave him was not entirely irrelevant to him, because in his book entitled *The Diamond Invention*, published that same year, he devoted an entire chapter to Barnato and Rhodes and described Barnato's untimely death as follows:

Barnato, who by now was one of the richest men in the world, returned to the music hall and acted in a number of amateur productions in Kimberley. Then, in 1897, on an ocean liner headed back to England, he either jumped or fell overboard and disappeared beneath a wave.

At any rate, the reality of my great-great-uncle's life and death will always be denied its rightful place in history because Edward Jay Epstein's personal reality box perspective on what should and should not count in the world of research, in effect, created its own version of "reality" for posterity. This reality box alteration, it should be noted, has to do with our group perception of history and our collective evolution as human beings. This one involves how our modern-day storytellers—historians—alter our understanding of history by virtue of adjusting and eliminating certain facts and data from our collective memory. Our collective reality box begins to shrink by only seeing those events that are socially sanctioned and recognized by our historians, replacing reality with myth.

Intuition, as a means by which one may *legitimately* gather facts, is almost always subjected to this kind of intense doubt. Our collective history has blocked out intuitive information in the same way that we, as individuals, have shunned intuition as an untrustworthy source. So, you must ask yourself: When is enough information really enough to make a judgment? At what point do you feel confident in your data? What would you have done with the five little bits of data that I had about Barney Barnato? Perhaps you would have tossed it in the garbage can of disbelief. But then again, maybe you would have made the same terrible mistake as my great-grandfather by throwing away a large, raw diamond.

Exercise

Ask a family member to tell you a true story about the family. Ask yourself questions about details that weren't described in the story, such as colors, time of day, the type of clothing worn, furniture in the room, and so on. Then imagine the answers. What did you assume from what you already knew? Get feedback.

Lesson #3:

Faulty Questions Produce Bad Answers

I am often asked by skeptics, "Well, if this psychic stuff is truly real, how come it never happens to me?" It's a fair question and deserves an answer.

In 1943, parapsychologist and CUNY professor of psychology Gertrude Schmeidler performed a series of famous ESP experiments. She found that those people who, when surveyed prior to testing, claimed to believe in the occult (she called them "sheep"), actually performed better in psi card tests than those who claimed not to believe in the occult (she called them "goats"). These famous results came to be known as the "Sheep-Goat Effect." This proves again—strange and counterintuitive as it may seem at first—your internal belief system will *actually* and *literally* change the reality "out there."

Skeptics have no reason to believe in psychic phenomena because, for them, it literally does not exist. Why should they believe in something that doesn't exist? Fair enough. However, as I soon learned for myself, if you can open you mind just long enough to explore this kind of seemingly ridiculous and impossible phenomena, your reality will actually change! It is a matter of permitting your brain to reorganize its perceptions. Once it does, reality will *literally* change for you and you will begin to experience things you never did in your entire life.

This is not a question, as many skeptics seem to think, of simply indulging your blind faith or becoming less rigorous in your analytical approach in order to conveniently retrofit reality into your belief system. So, do not fear that you will have to surrender your intelligence in order to become intuitive. What I am proposing is quite different. It involves opening your mind wide enough to capture *additional data about the environment.* The average human brain is only able to consciously perceive a miniscule fraction of the raw sensory data that is received by the body. In his book *The User Illusion*, Danish science writer Tor Nørretranders reveals an absolutely shocking statistic:

> [...] the 1990's is the decade of a breakthrough in the scientific acknowledgment that man is not transparent to himself. The germ of this breakthrough lay in the knowledge that has been apparent for the last thirty years: that the ratio of what we sense to what we perceive is 1,000,000 to 1." (p. 161)

If we only consciously perceive a millionth of what we sense, then would it be obvious to try to tap into the vast reservoir of sensory data that we simply toss away? This is, in simple terms, what "being psychic" is all about. It is the ability to lower the conscious threshold of the mind to access more sensory data. This is not about magic. Psychics are not magical people. However, it requires a different way of thinking and experiencing our senses—what we call "perception."

I will demonstrate, in the next several chapters, why and how the skeptical mind blocks out data and erases critical information about the world. *Skeptics work on the lowest common denominator of data about the physical world.* Skeptics have taught themselves to ignore subtle mental and physical perceptions, which are rich in additional information.

"The time has come," the Walrus said, "to talk of many things."

As I continued to venture into the world of intuition and psychic phenomena, the strange got even stranger. I had to keep an open mind because none of these crazy things ever happened to me and I was convinced they never would.

I read about and interviewed Cleve Backster, a highly respected former FBI polygraph expert and founder of the Backster School of Lie Detection, who has experimented with and documented emotions and precognitive abilities of plant life, human blood cells, and bacteria. I learned about the work of renowned Japanese scientist Masaru Emoto, and his work documenting how human emotions can actually physically alter the crystalline structures found in water and snowflakes. I was invited by Israeli psychic-mentalist Uri Geller to visit his home outside London and watch him bend a metal spoon while barely touching it. Was he manipulating molecules of metal or simply my mind? I spoke with mentalists, psychologists, and hypnotists who are "closet psychics," fearful that if they came out they would be professionally derided and so they pretend their work is merely magic tricks and basic human psychology.

I trained with women who claimed to be transfiguration mediums, a special brand of medium whose appearance will actually change during a séance and begin to resemble the spirit being channeled. They both showed me bizarre photographs. One woman transformed into a man with a mustache and the other woman was shown in a series of photos in which her entire body eventually disappears, leaving nothing but an opaque shadow. Years later, while at a paranormal investigation, I, too, was photographed inexplicably with the face of a man with a red mustache and high cheekbones! I began taking photographs in the pitch blackness of night and began to notice they were loaded with colored balls or orbs of light. What the heck were these? Spiritual beings or dust particles? I read the lab-documented reports in a book by Dr. William Tiller, a professor of materials science and engineering at Stanford University and government consultant on solid state physics, showing how photographs will actually reveal or hide objects depending on the psychic ability of the photographer! Sounds crazy, right?

I found an Englishman who told me he was part of an underground group of artists who operate near Stonehenge in England and surreptitiously create crop circles at night, then pass them off to the general public as the work of space aliens. He insisted he and his colleagues are psychically inspired to create certain images. We visited some of his crop circles.

I interviewed many famous ghost hunters and parapsychologists. Once, at a reputedly haunted castle in Wales, my husband and I even had the occasion to witness (and record on videotape) a table spin and jump several times by itself, fly up into the air, then land softly as if on a cloud of air.

It seemed there was simply no limit to the strangeness of this universe. It was absolutely mind-boggling. It seemed as though I had opened the door just a tiny crack and suddenly everything came flooding in. I interviewed artificial intelligence experts, physicists, neuroscientists, psychics, doctors, alternative healthcare specialists, poker players, artists, famous musicians, psychologists—anyone who I thought might be able to help me get a grip on this bizarre new world that was unfolding for the first time in my life. I interviewed them because I felt they had mastered certain aspects of intuition and possibly psychic ability.

One of the most intriguing people I have ever interviewed was Ingo Swann. Ingo was the creator of the psychic spy program for the CIA. In 1970, a fascinating book titled *Psychic Discoveries Behind the Iron Curtain* by Sheila Ostrander and Lynn Schroeder was published. It was the beginning of a wake-up call to the American public that the Soviet Union had been actively involved in serious studies of psychic phenomena and exploring possible military applications. Suddenly, the U.S. government found itself seriously lagging behind in this new angle of the arms race. No "serious" scientists or military professionals would ever be caught dead exploring psychic weirdness. But they simply had no other option than to try to play catch-up to the Soviets in a field of inquiry in which most people felt acutely uncomfortable and distrustful.

In the early 1970s, Ingo became involved in government-sponsored psychic research at the Stanford Research Institute (SRI) in California. The program received $25 million in research funding during a 23-year period from the CIA, DIA, and Army Intelligence to research various aspects of remote viewing and operational use of these abilities. The program was launched to compete with psi programs already in existence in the USSR and China.

The term *remote viewing* was coined in 1974 by Ingo's scientific colleagues in the program, SRI laser physicists Harold Puthoff and Russell Targ. They defined it, in their seminal book *Mind-Reach*, as: "A human perceptual ability to access, by mental means alone, information blocked from normal perception by distance, shielding, or time." In other words, this was a rather more sophisticated, technical, and refined term for having some kind of psychic ability to "see" things without the use of one's eyes. It is more similar to clairvoyance than ESP or telepathy.

Many books have been written by the people who actually participated in the government remote viewing program. They give countless examples of situations where these trained psychic spies were able to accurately "see" top-secret military or industrial facilities in foreign countries without having any knowledge of what they were looking at beyond being given a pair of encrypted random number coordinates. Some remote viewers even claimed they were able to adversely affect the health of certain world leaders! Talk about black magic! Usually double-blind conditions were imposed on the monitor (the person who conducted the sessions) as well as the viewer. Neither knew the targets, so they were unable to give subconscious or subliminal clues through their body language or conversations. It was an attempt to create double-blind test conditions so the psychic answers would be beyond reproach.

Ingo Swann was not only the star subject of the SRI research program, but he was also highly instrumental in creating a training program for remote viewing for the government. Now in his 70s, Ingo lives a bohemian artist lifestyle in his downtown Manhattan apartment. Ingo, an author and fine arts painter, is an extremely private person and a recluse. It was another strange fluke of fate that I happened to find him in Manhattan with the help of the famed television mentalist the Amazing Kreskin. Ingo's studio, in the windowless basement of his building, is cave-like and filled with huge, haunting, illuminated metaphysical paintings, many open tubes of oil paints, brushes in glass bottles, a few old, ripped chairs, and an office filled to the brim with a huge desk and bookshelves spilling over with books crammed in shelves up to the ceiling.

When I met him the first time, he was dressed casually, much as one would expect of an artist. He ushered me into his cramped, little office, where I squeezed sideways into a wooden chair that was wedged between the desk and the wall. He proceeded to light up a small cigar. He held it with a pair of tweezers in his hand and waited for me to speak. Ingo had the rather confusing look of a European aristocrat puffing away at a marijuana roach from a homemade cigarette holder. Dense smoke permeated the entire small space almost immediately. Attempting to make some pleasant, introductory small talk, I said that my father also enjoyed a good cigar after dinner on the rare occasion. Barely glancing at me, Ingo retorted contemptuously, "I never smoke *good* cigars."

That was quintessential Ingo Swann.

Finding Ingo Swann was, to me, like finding the Holy Grail of intuition. I had read so many of his books, commentaries, and speeches, as well as articles written about him, that I instantly felt as though I knew him already. I was excited because I knew that he was one of the extremely rare breeds of psychics who have both the capacity and the interest in analyzing their psychic abilities. In other words, he was a right- *and* left-hemisphere kind of thinker. I truly hoped that he would be able to supply me with most of the answers I was seeking.

There was something surreal about talking to him. For starters, he has a very unusual kind of a face. He reminded me of a Swedish sea captain with his beard, missing teeth, and crinkly blue eyes sparkling with humor just below the surface. He was unforgiving in his analysis of my questions. If I did not pose a question in exactly the right format, he was quick to reprimand me, telling me that faulty questions produce faulty answers. Ingo was at once quixotic, charming, arrogant, sincere, contemplative, aggravating, funny, and cantankerous. Several times he refused outright to answer my question simply because he didn't like it. I felt like I was back at school again—well, maybe something closer to Hogwarts School of Witchcraft and Wizardry.

I was immediately shocked when he told me that he does not consider himself to be psychic. He appeared to have contempt for those who say they are. Furthermore, we wrestled for a while over the use of the word *psychic*, which he dismissed as so general as to be worthless. From time to time, he would stop the interview, go to his bookshelf, and pull down a large, dusty dictionary and look up a word I had just used to prove to me that it had a slightly nuanced meaning or a history that made it unusable in a particular context. He poured over each page with his oversized magnifying glass under the light emitted by the single, naked light bulb hanging directly over the desk.

Ultimately, I began to realize that Ingo is an acutely logical thinker in the realm of illogical phenomena. In fact, he began his university studies in the field of biology as a bacteriologist before switching over to art. He depends heavily on dictionary definitions and tracing the origins of words in order to uncover their hidden psychological meanings. He is intolerant of inexactitude. I also felt as though Ingo guards his psychic abilities like precious treasure, refusing to take pride or pleasure in them for fear that they will be misunderstood or misappropriated by others. There is a strong secretive aspect to his personality. He explained that rather than using his gifts to give readings to others or for entertainment, he has only used them to try to advance scientific understanding of psychic phenomena. Ingo is one of the few psychics who consistently spent years submitting to be a laboratory guinea pig for parapsychologists and physicists under difficult lab conditions. Most psychics, or really anyone for that matter, probably would have buckled under similar circumstances.

After my initial interview with Ingo, I became friendly with him and had the opportunity to visit him on several occasions. The second time I saw him was even more intriguing than the first. There was something larger than life about Ingo. I couldn't quite put my finger on it. It reminded me of being a little kid when a simple memory of going to get ice cream or visiting the zoo became deeply significant, huge, and memorable—when the streets, houses, and adults all seemed so much bigger. That was what it was like hanging around with Ingo. He had known some of the world's greatest thinkers, psychics, philosophers, scientists, and Nobel Prize winners. He had managed, for a time, to spin the CIA on its head and convinced them that psychic ability could actually be trained. I don't know why Ingo ever agreed to speak to me. I will never understand it. Furthermore, when I went back to visit him, he told me he had decided to stop giving interviews and had already turned down 23 interviews since the last time we had spoken.

During that particular visit, I decided to ask him about a rather unusual phenomenon that I had read about in the psychic world having to do with auras, which refers to the various layers of energy that surround the human body, and can be seen by certain psychics and used to diagnose medical and psychological issues. Usually auras are described as quite beautiful and colorful. I asked him about whether he saw black auras. He understood what I meant, of course. Well-known 20th-century psychic Edgar Cayce and a few others have been able to see black auras around people just prior to their deaths. Ingo called these auras opaque rather than black. He said that every time has ever seen one around a person, that person has died within two years. It is clearly a "gift" that disturbs him—perhaps more in the sense that once having observed this type of aura he is somehow burdened with some unspecified responsibility as to how to deal with this knowledge. Should he intervene? If so, how? Would it matter anyway? In retrospect, it does seem like a terrible gift to be given without some spiritual instruction manual about how to use it properly.

He told me this as we walked on our way to a local Polish diner. He told me (slightly tongue-in-cheek, but it was difficult to know for sure) to use my powers to help clear out the seats at the counter at the place, which was always packed because the food was so good. There were probably no more than 10 vinyl-covered stools along the counter in the very tiny Lower East Side restaurant. We both focused our efforts on that thought. Lo and behold, we managed to clear out nearly half the restaurant! Ingo became distracted as we sat there side-by-side on our counter stools watching the customers come in and out, and the waitress jump back and forth behind the counter and around the short-order cooks. Ingo became heavily silent. I tried to take up some of the slack by talking and telling amusing stories. But absolutely nothing I said seemed to grab his attention.

He nodded in the direction of one of the short-order cooks with a rather florid complexion who was quietly flipping large, greasy wads of scrambled eggs on the grill and said quietly, "There's an example for you. He's not long for this world."

Apparently, the man's aura was somewhat opaque.

After a simble but excellent lunch, we walked back to his studio. On the way, we stopped for coffee in a tiny, gourmet coffee shop. The one woman who was working there seemed a bit overwhelmed by the three or four customers in the shop. She knew Ingo by name (as did at least a half-dozen people we passed in the street) and said hello. For a self-proclaimed recluse, I thought to myself, Ingo sure seemed to know an awful lot of people. He said hello to them in a patchwork of their native languages— Spanish, Chinese, or French.

As we waited for our coffee, I began to talk uncontrollably. I generally play the role of listener, but Ingo's stubborn silence was overwhelming. I felt compelled to fill up the large gaps of silence. Now, he seemed a bit morose. There was nothing I could say that seemed to cheer him up. He seemed to be in a rush to get out of there. The female shopkeeper came over and chatted about how they had run out of some item on the menu and it wouldn't be delivered until the following week. At that point, a couple of men trooped in with a large hand-truck filled with boxes of food.

We left before I had a chance to finish my coffee. As we hurried out, Ingo told me after we had crossed the street that the vibes in the coffee shop were way too depressing and sad. I was certainly perplexed by that, because I didn't pick up anything even remotely sad about the woman or the place.

After lunch, we went back to Ingo's studio. We continued our informal conversation—it wasn't really an interview—in his office. We began talking about various types of psychic phenomena and what seeing things psychically really means. Then after a while, and without any warning, Ingo pulled out a folded-up piece of white paper. It had been folded several times and was no larger than a 2 × 2-inch square. He asked me to tell him what I saw. I said I saw a square piece of paper.

"All right, now tell me what you *see*."

I launched into an immediate, nervous guess: "Cufflinks. Well, either it's nothing or..." I hesitated then quickly added, "Or else it's a pair of square cufflinks."

He shook his head impatiently and told me to stop. I looked harder at the piece of paper. There were no imprints, no bulges, no outlines—nothing to give me any clues.

"Calm down," he said. "You're way too nervous. Just tell me what you see. Close your eyes. You'll see better that way. Just tell me what you see, not what you think it is. Experience it."

His soothing tone did have a brief calming effect on me, until I realized that I was being asked to prove my psychic ability to one of the world's most renowned psychics (even though he hates that word).

I started by trying not to think too much, if at all: "I see two pipes."

"Close your eyes."

I closed my eyes. "I see two pipes."

"Go on."

"Okay, at one end of the pipe is a—it's like a circle."

"Okay, go on."

"Now the circle has kind of morphed into something else. It looks like a sprocket."

Sprocket? I don't even know what a sprocket means. Who the hell uses the word *sprocket* anyway?

"Okay stop," he suddenly commanded.

I opened my eyes. Very carefully, he unfolded the piece of white paper and the object materialized before my eyes. It was a pair of diamond earrings attached to a piece of square cardboard. I was immediately drawn to the beautiful diamonds.

"Oh!" I exclaimed. "Cushion-cut!" (The slightly squared-shape of the stones would explain why I had originally interpreted it as square.) "Cufflinks!" I said, realizing that the overall cufflink concept was very close to the actual item.

"No, these are earrings," Ingo said sternly, as he turned over the little piece of cardboard onto which the earrings were attached so I could see the back side.

"There," he said pointing to the stem of the earring, "is your pipe."

The little fixture that slides on to the stem and holds the earring to the back of the ear was my "sprocket." (I actually looked up the word *sprocket* online the next day because I realized just how ignorant I was of its precise definition. They showed a picture of a sprocket and it seemed to be a remarkably apt word to describe the little back piece of the earring).

Then it became clear to me. In a space of mind where I was not attempting to judge what I anticipated "seeing," I was able to clearly describe the three basic elements of the earring: a pipe (the metal stem), a square at the end of the pipe (the diamond stone), and a sprocket (the fixture in the back of the earring). The words I attached to these things when looking at them non-judgmentally were sort of alien to me. Who would have guessed that, collectively, a pipe, a square, and a sprocket were a right-brain synonym for an earring? I saw the shapes, but had no idea as to their function. I had only a minimal understanding as to their spatial relationship with one another. They only made sense when my logical mind (left hemisphere) was able to compare them, via feedback, to the actual target item in terms I "understood." I realized suddenly that this begins to explain why skeptics are so resistant to the vague imagery in lieu of concrete language proposed by psychics.

In fact, it is a very curious and challenging process of *mental deconstruction*. No skeptic should ever underestimate the grueling intellectual challenge involved in achieving this. We must start at square one: simply experience the world through *perception without prejudgment.* This is no easy feat! There is no knowledge in this realm; there is only observation. Knowledge is a *secondary* operation, not primary, as we normally treat it. This is very similar to the process by which we find meaning in our dreams. Dreams can only be interpreted by first resurrecting the memory of the images or pictures as we try to retrace the pathway of our dreamscape journey. Once we latch on to the pictures, suddenly the meaning of our dream dawns on us. Sometimes the meaning seems to have been staring at us from plain view all along, but we couldn't see it. We were blinded, in effect, by the visual details of our images. Our brain's right hemisphere had a rare moment of global domination before succumbing to the left hemisphere's crushing reorientation into words and logic.

"It's interesting," Ingo commented quietly. "You were drawn to the metal part of the earring and not the crystal."

I was still in awe of the fact that my mental image correlated so nicely with the real item.

"Now," he continued matter-of-factly, "in the world of remote viewing, what you just did would be considered a hit."

I nearly jumped out of my seat with excitement. I had just proven to myself and to the man who developed the CIA's remote viewing program that I could see remotely—and on the first shot! I was ecstatic.

"But don't get too excited...."

I obediently calmed down outwardly, but inside I held self-contained, implosive excitement.

That was my first real lesson in this special brand of clairvoyance.

I was reminded again of my great-grandfather's decision to throw away Barney Barnato's raw diamonds. He threw them away because he thought they were nothing but rocks. He misjudged them. The same is true for intuition. What would have happened if I had thrown away my quirky little description of a sprocket, pipes, and a circle simply because I failed to recognize it as an accurate (but unorthodox) description of a pair of diamond earrings? Intuition amounts to nothing more than a mental reorganization of existing information.

Exercise

Ask a friend to give you a small object such as a piece of jew-elry, a box, or a photo with an interesting history to it. Hold it in your hands and imagine the history, including information about the background of the owner, how they acquired the object, an names and dates that come to you. Get feedback.

Lesson #4:

The Sliding Scale of Intuition Includes Psychic Ability

In 1971, successful New Jersey accountant John List inexplicably decided to brutally murder his three teenage children, his wife, and his mother. He then vanished and, despite all efforts by police and FBI agents, could not be found. Eighteen years later, in 1989, the Westfield police captain managed to convince celebrity John Walsh, from *America's Most Wanted* television show, to air a segment about this cold case murder to see if it would yield any leads to List's whereabouts. The problem with such an old case was that List would certainly have aged in the nearly two decades since his disappearance. Several computer-generated portraits were created, but none seemed particularly helpful. So Walsh contacted a friend, Philadelphia forensic sculptor Frank Bender, to see if he could breathe some additional life into the case by creating a three-dimensional bust of the head and shoulders of an artificially aged List.

Bender accepted the challenge despite the fact that all he was given were a few frontal view photos of List from two decades earlier. Bender did not have the benefit of any three-quarter or side views from which he might determine the overall shape of the face. He used a combination of his creative skills to imagine where shadows might fall on the face in order to create bone definition, as well as his analytic, investigatory skills to research how a person's face ages. For instance, Bender visited plastic and reconstructive surgeons to discuss with them how a mastoid scar, such as the one on List's neck, might ultimately heal and age over time. He met with psychiatrists to discuss whether a man fitting List's fugitive profile might have decided to switch to contact lenses instead of his thick, black-rimmed, 1960s-style glasses from the earlier photos. Bender went to a local antique dealer in Philadelphia and asked if he had any vintage eyeglasses. He rummaged through a large basket of glasses, but didn't feel he had found the right pair. The dealer said he had a few more pairs in the back of the shop. When he returned with a pair of square-shaped, brown, horn-rimmed glasses, Bender grabbed them and exclaimed, "That's the pair! That's it!" In Bender's words, when he works on a case such as this, he "becomes the fugitive." He tries to walk and talk like the fugitive in order to understand every element of the man.

When Bender completed the bust, everyone was impressed with its real quality, but no one knew if it resembled the real John List. The television show aired on May 21, 1989, and featured Bender's bust. Immediately after the show aired, *America's Most Wanted* received more than 200 solid leads in the case—more than the FBI had been able to generate during 18 years with $1 million invested in the case. Soon thereafter, following up on one of these leads, the real John List, who had been living in Virginia under an assumed name, was captured and ultimately sentenced to life in prison. What was extraordinary—one might even say *uncanny*—was not just that Bender had made an almost perfect rendering of the aging List, but that when List was apprehended by police, he was wearing a pair of glasses that were virtually identical to those Bender had selected in the antique shop.

So was this case of luck, skill, hunch, or psychic ability?

Hopefully, it should be clear to you that this is a perfect illustration of how all these different creative, intuitive, and analytic skills mesh together and pushed Bender a little farther on down his ultimate path to breathtaking discovery. Obviously, Bender's analytic background in understanding the psychology of the killer was instrumental in limiting the types of choices that he could *imagine* this man would make. His skill and training in forensic art enabled him to materialize this vision and knowledge. Naturally, he had some plain-old dumb luck by walking into the right antique store that actually had the glasses. And, this is the hardest part for many people to understand: He had a moment of clairvoyance in selecting that particular pair of glasses out of many men's glasses that may have also theoretically fit the bill based on the psychological information at his disposal. His selection was a "guess," but it was not dumb luck. It was too uncannily accurate.

This story perfectly illustrates how creative and analytic skills can be combined and result in something that seems to defy probability. This is intuition operating at its finest level. There are pieces of Bender's intuition that can be explained in terms of his background, psychology, and knowledge, and there are other pieces that cannot be explained by anything at all. So what part was "intuition" and what part was something else? It's not that easy to dissect.

Intuition: Balancing Available Information and Conscious Awareness

Intuition operates on a very broad sliding scale that is controlled by the ratio of *rational to irrational*, and *conscious to subconscious* thoughts. There are many different subtle shades and flavors of intuition along this sliding scale.

The only difference between a smart guess and a psychic experience, under my definition, is the *amount of data* already at your *conscious* disposal. Many people believe intuition is different from psychic ability. I do not subscribe to this belief. For me, psychic ability is simply a different flavor of intuition. It still falls along the intuitive continuum and sliding scale. Once you begin to understand how psychic ability is just a natural extension of our ability to make an educated guess, then you can appreciate that psychic ability is a normal human ability and not supernatural.

The Educated Guess

On the most conservative side of this scale, we have a definition of intuition as a type of *educated guess*. This type of intuition, with which all of us are familiar, involves the creative use of past experience, rational thinking, and judgment calls. It primarily uses our rational faculties to quickly analyze unusual or unanticipated situations.

An example of an educated guess might be: The savvy shareholder accurately anticipated that the market demand for soap would decrease, and by moving his investments into perfume products, he was able to avoid financial ruin. He didn't know for sure the market would collapse, but he made a very informed guess about the future. This kind of prediction is based on underlying rational data. That rational data can then be assembled into a relatively linear thought process to arrive at a conclusion. Rational data can be defined as information that conforms to our preconceptions about how things normally operate, or can be anticipated to operate, in accordance with our understanding of the laws of the universe.

Most scientists and physicians with whom I have spoken seem most comfortable with this definition and explanation for intuitive knowledge that seems to come from nowhere. In their view, intuition can be "explained" by reliance on some degree of pre-existing conditions or subconsciously available data. For these people, reality doesn't exist unless they can see every individual link in the chain of logic.

The Gut Feeling or Hunch

In the middle of this sliding scale is a type of intuition that includes a guess that relies much less on rational inputs. It incorporates a strangely irrational element. This is what we might call a *hunch* or a *gut feeling*.

This implicates previously hidden or unknown emotions, feelings, and physical sensations, and combines them in an unusual way with a few rational thoughts in order to make sense of them. Cognitive thinking begins to take a backseat in this kind of information gathering, as emotions and sensations begin to take center stage. Sometimes these feelings are loosely connected with rational thoughts and data, and sometimes not. The term *gut feeling*, or even having the feeling of butterflies in the stomach, implicates an actual physical sensation in the stomach, just as a sense of heartache seems to emanate from the chest. Thinking is replaced by emotions or physical sensations, which are related to emotions.

The fact that this kind of information is often physically felt in the stomach or heart can be explained biologically. The gastrointestinal tract actually contains more neurons than the brain! It has been referred to as the "second brain" within the medical community because the enteric nervous system, as it is known, contains as many as one billion neurons and can operate autonomously. The enteric nervous system is the focus of the field of neurogastroenterology. This system contains 95 percent of the body's serotonin, one of the major neurotransmitters and mood-elevating chemicals.

This second brain communicates with the rest of the body through two pathways connected to the central nervous system: 1) the parasympathetic system via the vagus nerve and 2) the sympathetic system via the prevertebral ganglia. The vagus nerve is an extremely long neural superhighway extending from the brainstem all the way down, through the neck, heart, and chest, into the abdomen. It is no accident that certain seemingly emotional diseases and disorders express themselves as stomach or intestinal disorders, such as peptic ulcers, irritable bowel syndrome, gastritis, and various forms of colitis. Vagus nerve stimulation (VNS) therapy is currently used to treat epileptic seizures and drug-resistant depression. Thus, it comes as no surprise that a combined thought/emotion/sensation may be first experienced in the gut and not expressed as a "rational" thought within the network of the brain.

Often the basis for these wordless emotional feelings or physical body sensations can ultimately be tracked to subliminal or mostly subconscious influences. We seem to be reacting (physically and emotionally) to information that is unknown to us on a *conscious* level at the time, but may have infiltrated our sensory system on a *subconscious* level.

An example of a gut feeling might be that the wife of an abusive alcoholic has a hunch he will come home early that night. She acts on this impulse and leaves town before he arrives home in a drunken state. In this example, there would not have been any overt signs that he was coming home early (he did not tell her in the morning that he was coming home early, his local bar was not closed that evening, he did not plan to come home early to watch a favorite TV show). However, she might have been alerted to some far more subtle level of information (perhaps she sensed he was starting to have suspicions about her behavior, spent time searching through her belongings, or had strangely "forgotten" his wallet at the house that morning).

For the hunch or gut feeling to operate effectively, a person must be highly sensitized to his or her environment and alert to far more subtle clues about behavior. This kind of predictive ability is based, to some extent, not only on this level of alertness, but also on being able to understand the deeper meanings of things. It permits us to skip one step (or even several) in the chain-linked progression of rational thoughts. The end result appears irrational because there is not a step-by-step connection of thoughts to the conclusion. The skipped steps are not bypassed, but *incorporated* within the assumptions.

Many businesspeople, inventors, and politicians seem to have a comfort level with this definition of intuition. These are people who understand that decision-making is often dependent upon unverifiable factors. They are not looking to justify or support *every* perception with evidence and are content to rely on amorphous sensations when making an otherwise "rational" judgment. Prediction-making among this group of people tends to be a sense or a feeling, not a concrete fact.

Psychic Phenomena

Then we get to the most liberal, far-end of the sliding scale. This is a definition of intuition that includes *psychic phenomena*. Just as educated guesses are based on rational information and processing, psychic phenomena are based upon entirely irrational information. This is where some of you will jump ship. Please attempt to restrain yourself. Psychic phenomena are intimately linked with the natural, biological processes of the human body. Any lack of experience in this type of intuition is, in my opinion, based on nothing more than a failure of conscious recognition.

Naturally, there are many different degrees of psychic information. Let's take an example of a type of intuitive flash that is actually quite common and happens to many people. Let's suppose you suddenly start thinking about someone you haven't thought of in a long time for no reason at all. Shortly thereafter, that person calls you on the telephone. Or, perhaps you somehow "knew" he or she was going to call at that moment. (This happens to me quite frequently.)

Was this psychic? Don't be so quick to answer this question. It may or may not be psychic. The answer really depends upon what information you already had at your disposal and what judgment you could rationally make from it. It could have been just an educated guess if you had recently spoken with this person and discussed getting together on that day. It could have been a gut feeling or a hunch that he or she would probably contact you soon even though you didn't know exactly when. The only variable was when, not if. Or, it may indeed have been psychic if you hadn't spoken with this person for 10 years and had no reason upon which to base this sudden, strange insight. Psychic information is generally based on little or no underlying information at all.

It is difficult to convey this kind of psychic knowledge. It can be felt, but not thought. It is hard to talk about or share any kind of thoughts if they arrive in this kind of incoherent format. It doesn't lend itself to discussion or analysis. It is even easier to discuss what we feel in terms of emotions, because we have been trained to expect that most emotions exist for a "reason." Psychic thoughts do not have a reason for being, and do not come prepackaged in an acceptable, rational format.

Psychological motives are often attributed to this type of intuitive thinking (power, dominance, weakness, insecurity, self-aggrandizement, wishful thinking, subconscious desires, and so on). Intuitive thinking also gets confused with craziness, cloudy thinking, or failure to recognize subliminal influences. Having worked extensively in this area for several years, I now understand that psychic predictions cannot be entirely separated and cut off from the context from where they emanate. The context is the human brain which, like it or not, already contains vast amounts of information. It is impossible to separate the thinking function of the brain from its interpretation of sensory information in the body. Thought and senses are completely intermingled. Please consider this: *Judgments color the facts at least as much as the facts color the judgments.* Assuming, as I do, that psychic information is sensory-based, it would be impossible to separate it entirely from our normal thoughts and judgments based on past experience.

Skeptics dismiss the psychic ability as totally non-existent or nothing but a cheesy hoax. What they fail to appreciate is that psychic ability is more about the *method* than the conclusions. It is simply another way to process normal, human information through different channels. It is an alternative to normal thinking. Because most people don't know how to think psychically, they assume that any accurate conclusions reached by this method must be either magic or a con job. In the early days of my psychic explorations, I tended to automatically distrust any information if it was tainted with actual knowledge. I thought psychic information was supposed to be pure and completely out of the ordinary reach of psychology or rationality—otherwise it must constitute cheating! Since then, I have learned that I simply had a misconception about the word *psychic*. Now I have no problem mixing the various possible and impossible sources of information when I give a reading to someone.

Frank Bender was using all of his skills—cognitive, sensory, and psychic—and he blended them together. True enough, he used his special knowledge about psychology and anatomy, and that undoubtedly influenced some of his more radical choices in making the bust. Most psychics and mediums will tell you that spirit will work with the knowledge, symbols, and senses that already exist within you. In other words, psychic information will acquire meaning by piggy-backing on other stored meanings in your mind. If it couldn't do this, then psychic phenomena would be meaningless. This is why the more you know about the world and the more internal connections you have, the more you will improve your psychic channels.

Psychic insights are usually only accepted by people who have had first-hand experience with them—not by those who need to rationalize them. Professions that accommodate this type of intuition tend to be those that do not claim total mastery of a field, such as artists, healers, and religious leaders.

Exercise

Find someone you don't know. Try to imagine the title of a song that captures the essence of that person, or sing the lyrics that you know. Ask if the words, mood, or spirit of the song means anything to that person.

Lesson #5:

We Can See the Invisible World

Imagine for a second that you are a female frog. You are a Puerto Rican Coqui tree frog that produces a high-pitched chirping sound that sounds like "ko-kee." Anyone who has ever vacationed in this lovely Caribbean country will know exactly what I am talking about. This two-note chirp attains nearly 100 decibels at a foot and a half away! Starting in the early evening dusk and continuing on through the evening, all the male Coqui tree frogs begin their nightly concert of mating calls. With all that background noise, frogs have developed some very intricate systems so that they can learn to hear and recognize their own species.

As an attractive and willing female, roughly 30 percent larger than your male counterpart, and looking for a good sexual mate, you listen intently to these sounds. Like many other females in other frog species, you are silent and do not chirp. You lay in wait, listening to the sounds of the male Coqui frogs and try to select the one with the loudest, most manly chirp. For reasons you don't quite understand, you can tell he is the most aggressive male simply by listening to his chirp. The male's "ko-kee" two-note chirp sound has a dual purpose. The first part of the chirp, "ko," is only heard by other Coqui male frogs and is a territorial chirp designed to let them know the extent and location of his personal territory. The "kee" part of the chirp is purely a mating call intended for the females within his territory. When the other males feel out-chirped by the alpha male's "ko" chirp, their chirps begin to pale in comparison.

The only thing you, as a female frog, can hear every time the male shouts out "ko-kee" is "kee"! That's your entire frog universe of sound. You never hear the "ko" part of his chirp at all! All of the rest of the male chirping, jockeying for best male frog contestant, and battling behind the scenes are completely unknown to you. Your auditory system is so specialized that you can only recognize the calls of your own species, and specifically only that part of the call intended for females! Your auditory system (which, by the way, also includes the lungs, which "hear" by detecting certain pressure vibrations) only operates on a very tiny frequency band. As a result, your world as you experience it is very tiny indeed!

The example of the Coqui tree frog's diminished sensory universe is not hard to understand or appreciate. But now, try to apply the same rationale to your own sensory world.

The Very Narrow Bandwidth of Human Sensory Experience

Understanding the sliding scale of intuition is the first step in understanding how psychic sensing works. Hopefully, I have already managed to convince you that psychic ability lies along the continuum of guesses, hunches, and vague certainties. The next step is in appreciating how little of the world we actually *consciously* experience. The bandwidth of human sensory experience is very narrow compared to what we could potentially experience if our sensory organs were better equipped. You may recall that I said the sliding scale of intuition is based on a ratio of *information* and *conscious awareness*.

In this chapter, you will begin to understand these two factors are intimately related. The capacity of our sensory organs—our eyes, ears, nose, mouth, and skin—to accept information from the environment is indeed very limited. It defines what we think we know. But it doesn't define everything we know. It is merely our *conscious information*.

The human senses have evolved in such a way so as to give us vitally important information about our environment. We need to be able to predict how to protect ourselves in a harsh world. What we *perceive* is a direct result of what we *need to know* in order to survive as a species. However, this does not mean that we are capable of sensing the totality of events that happen all around us and in our universe. There is an invisible world that takes place around us without our knowledge.

Hearing

It is well established that all of our senses operate within very specific frequency bands. The human ear allows us to hear any disturbances in the air that are vibrating between 20 and 20,000 Hertz (full frequency cycle per second). We know there is a universe of activity that exists beyond our sensory recognition. Many species of animals experience a world that is very different from ours and exists beyond our senses.

Ultrasound exists as sound frequency above our range (higher, faster vibrations) and *infrasound* is below our range (lower, slower vibrations).

Bats, dogs, and mice can hear ultrasound (a sound pressure with a frequency in excess of 20,000 Hz.) and elephants, whales, hippopotamuses, rhinoceros, giraffes, and alligators can hear infrasound (a frequency range from 17 Hz. all the way down to 0.001 Hz.). Neither of these two ranges exists at all in our human experience.

High frequency requires a huge amount of energy and so its sounds do not travel long distances. However, low frequency, long waves of infrasound do. Elephant herds and whale pods have been known to communicate with others located miles away using infrasound. Infrasound vibrations are generated by a number of natural geological and meteorological phenomena such as earthquakes, avalanches, wind, meteors, volcanic eruptions, and tornadoes. Creatures have often been observed behaving strangely right before natural geological disasters, often fleeing the area, as was the case in the tsunami triggered by the 9.3-magnitude earthquake in the Indian Ocean on December 26, 2004. More than 300,000 people perished in countries all around the Pacific Rim, and the effects were even felt as far away as Africa. In Sri Lanka, where tidal waters poured 2 miles inland into the island's biggest wildlife reserve, the Yala National Park, which was home to elephants, leopards, deer, alligators, and jackals, many human deaths were reported, but hardly any animal deaths at all. Apparently, the animals knew early enough when to leave the area. The BBC News article entitled "Did Animals Have Quake Warning" by Sue Nelson (December

31, 2004) suggested that animals may indeed have a kind of sixth sense about danger, perhaps stemming from their highly sensitive ability to hear.

The potential for creating a vague sense of something else happening in the human who is otherwise unable to hear these things has not gone unnoticed. Researchers Vic Tandy, a lecturer in international and law studies at Coventry University, and psychologist Richard Wiseman, of the University of Hertfordshire, England, have suggested that infrasound vibrations may result in the human experience of ghosts and other supernatural activity. Tandy, for example, along with psychologist Dr. Tony Lawrence published a paper called "Ghosts in the Machine" in the *Journal of the Society for Psychical Research* in 1998. They expressed the view that infrasound in the apparently haunted Warwick Laboratory had created ghostly apparitions seen by the staff.

After experiencing strange visions that caused the hair on his neck to rise, Tandy realized that an extractor fan in the cellar was emitting ultrasound frequency and made the connection between the psychological experience and the frequency. Two years later, Tandy published another paper, called "Something in the Cellar," confirming that, once again, visions of ghosts by people visiting the 14th-century cellar of the Coventry Cathedral could be attributed to the presence of the same level of ultrasound frequency found in the Warwick Laboratory—18.9 Hz. As he explains, NASA has stated that ultrasound is capable of making humans hyperventilate and the eyeballs roll involuntarily.

Though I have no intention here of addressing the validity of these findings, I bring them up solely to demonstrate that I am certainly not the first person to have considered the possibility that the existence of vague sub- or extrasensory frequencies may actually influence our mental perceptions of what is or is not happening in the world around us—particularly as it concerns the world of the so-called "supernatural." As explained by authors Robert Rivlin and biopsychologist Karen Gravelle in their truly extraordinary book, titled *Deciphering the Senses: The Explanding World of Human Perception*:

> It has even become apparent that some of the supposedly mystical abilities of extra-sensory perception (ESP)—sensitivity to magnetic fields, ability to detect auras, and so forth—could also be explained as the result of still undiscovered sensory systems—either degenerated vestiges of senses found in other animals or

totally human sensory systems that are still evolving into a more so-phisticated form. Five was obviously just not enough to account for the huge range of sensory possibilities of which the human species is capable; seventeen senses is probably a more accurate count." (p. 17)

Thus, our sensory capacities and lack of capacities may indeed provide some significant clues in the origin of intuitive or psychic abilities.

Smell

The sense of sound is not the only sensory input that has a limited, narrow band of frequency in the human experience. The human sense of smell also only reveals a tiny portion of our universe to us. Although smell involves chemical detection, called chemoreception, as opposed to the detection of electromagnetic waves, these odor molecules are translated into nerve impulses and transmitted to the brain. We are capable of detecting the presence of between 4,000 and 10,000 different odor molecules.

By comparison, dogs have about 25 times more olfactory (or smell) receptors than humans, and some species, such as bloodhounds, can detect smells at concentrations 100 million times less than humans. Scientists have even documented dogs' abilities to detect scents at only a few parts per trillion! They are able to detect one tiny drop of blood in five quarts of water by smell alone! They have one million smell cells per nostril. Strangely, insects use their antennae to smell, and sensory neurons inside the antenna generate odor-specific electrical signals called "spikes" in response to odor.

The ability of certain animals to smell things beyond what the average human olfactory range can detect has extraordinary consequences. Once again, it starts to look like supernatural ability.

In the March 2006, issue of the journal of *Integrative Cancer Therapies*, researchers in California revealed that dogs can actually distinguish between people with both early and late lung and breast cancers. Other medical journals have published reports of trained dogs being able to detect melanomas and bladder cancers. There are plenty of anecdotal stories told by dog owners of dogs who are able to alert their owners to the possibility of illness by sniffing skin lesions or even right before they are about to experience an epileptic seizure!

A collaborative study between researchers at the Pine Street Foundation in San Anselmo, California, and the Polish Academy of Sciences, Institute of Genetics and Animal Breeding in Poland, tested the ability of dogs to detect cancer simply by sniffing the exhaled breath of lung and breast cancer patients. Of those tested, 55 had lung cancer, 31 had breast cancer, and there was a control sample of 83 healthy patients. The dogs were trained to give a positive response to the presence of cancer in the breath by either sitting or lying down in front of the test station with the sample container of the patient's breath. The results, as reported in *Science Daily* in an article entitled "Can Dogs Smell Cancer?" published January 6, 2006, showed that dogs can detect the presence of lung or breast cancer with an amazing sensitivity accuracy level of between 88 and 97 percent!

Do humans share any tiny shred of this olfactory experience? Can we also detect illness through smell? The answer is a qualified yes.

Traditional Chinese doctors are trained to use their sense of smell in medical diagnoses and can often diagnose a patient by smell alone. For instance, a fruity smell may be an indicator of diabetes, whereas an ammonia smell could suggest the presence of liver or kidney disease. A rare disease, causing certain people with a defective gene that prevents them from metabolizing trimethylamine (TMA) found in fish, eggs, and liver, causes them to smell like fish. This brings us right to the brink of intuitive information: we may have the sensory capacity to smell illness, but our brain has never made the strong correlation between a distinctive smell and an illness. As a result, we may often overlook valuable sensory data.

Humans, being the innovative creatures that we are, have recently created an "electronic nose," which is a machine with chemical vapor sensors able to detect volatile organic compounds (VOC) and can translate them into a pattern or "smell print." It is currently able to diagnose patients with respiratory infections such as pneumonia, and physicians hope to eventually use it in the diagnosis of lung cancer. According to Dr. Silvano Dragonieri of Leiden University Medical Center in the Netherlands, "A person's breath contains a mixture of thousands of VOCs that may be used as markers of lung disease."

Also, a quick review of the causes of certain odors in perspiration shows a huge number of major diseases result in modifications to the chemical composition of our sweat. Leukemia and lymphoma produce unusual sweating patterns. The lack of certain hormones (during menopause in women and men with hypogonadism or low levels of testosterone) can also cause excessive sweating and hot flashes. Low blood sugar causes hypoglycemia, which can also result in sweating, along with dizziness, shakiness, and nausea. An overactive thyroid (hyperthyroidism) can cause sweating as a result of the thyroid producing too much of the hormone thyroxine. Heart attacks, resulting in low blood supply in the heart, also cause sweatiness, anxiety, and sensitivity to heat.

The U.S. military has long advised soldiers to locate the enemy by smell because different diets and foods produce different body odors.

We unknowingly tend to select our mates depending upon how they smell. In 1986, Dr. Winifred Cutler, a biologist and behavioral endocrinologist, published her co-discovery that pheromones lurk in our underarms in the journal *Hormones and Behavior*. When the sweat was removed, only the pheromones remained! It has been well-documented that pheromones play a significant role in our choice of mate and influence our sexual behavior.

But the strange gets stranger. Certain animals seem to have an uncanny (should we call it "psychic"?) ability to know when someone is about to die! Although cats cannot smell with quite the same incredible range as dogs, they are still better than we are. A cat's sense of smell is 14 times stronger than that of a human. They use their sense of smell to seek out food, find mates, and locate their own and other cat's marked territories.

In the July 26, 2007 issue of *The New England Journal of Medicine,* there appeared an article entitled "A Day in the Life of Oscar the Cat," by Dr. David Dosa, a geriatician at the Rhode Island Hospital and assistant professor of medicine at the Warren Albert Medical School of Brown University in Providence, Rhode Island. The article described the highly unusual behavior of a cat named Oscar who was adopted into the 41-patient dementia unit of the Steere House Nursing and Rehabilitation Center in Providence in 2007. During his stay, he has stood vigil at the bedside of 25 patients at the time of their deaths. According to doctors, nurses, and nursing staff members, Oscar almost always arrives about one hour before the time of death and hops on their bed to stay with them, cuddling and purring. Unless they are actively about to die, Oscar pays little attention to any of the patients—even the ones in poor physical health or a few days away from dying. According to Mary Miranda, the charge nurse on the unit, Oscar has been consistently right in his diagnoses. When some family members, apparently spooked by his well-known presence, lock him out of the patient's room, according to Dr. Joan Teno, professor of community health at Brown and associate medical director of Home & Hospice Care of Rhode Island, Oscar begins to rub "aggressively against the door, paces back and forth, [and] yowls in protest" (Nickerson). As Dr. Teno explained, "Oscar is a normal cat with an extra-normal sense for death. He is drawn to death." The nursing home officials are mystified by Oscar's unusual behavior (none of the other six cats in the facility has this odd ability) and speculate he may be sensing some subtle change in metabolism. Still, they don't understand his apparent attraction to death.

But think about it. If this involved a so-called medium or psychic healer, and not a cat, it is likely that we would hear cries of foul play: "That's just a coincidence" or "They were just picking up on some subconscious clues" or "What a phony!" We would presumably doubt the realness of this talent because 1) it seems to involve the physically impossible, 2) it is unique to one person (or, in this case, one cat out of seven) and doesn't seem to be a universally shared trait, and 3) it cannot necessarily be repeated identically upon demand in laboratory conditions. The ability to detect death and illness, at least as far as humans go, would probably be utterly discounted as a fluke or fraud.

In fact, this kind of death perception is not unique to Oscar or even just to cats. A tiny schnauzer named Scamp, a resident of the Pine Nursing Home in Canton, Ohio, has an even more amazing track record. He shows up to visit dying patients, just like Oscar, and begins barking to sound the alarm and paces around the room when he senses a patient is about to die. According to his owner, Deirdre Huth, a staff member at the Pines, "The only time he barks is when he's trying to tell us something's wrong." According to reports given by the directors of the facility, as of August 14, 2007, Scamp had accurately identified the deaths of 40 patients in three years! Once again, the assumption of his ability is based on smell, although nursing home staff has expressed amazement at Scamp's apparent ability to gravitate toward grieving or sad patients, which isn't sense of smell, but an intuitive/psychological perception. Do dogs even have intuition?

Sight

Our sense of sight is another tightly limited sensory ability. The visible spectrum of light generally lies between 380 and 750 nm (a nanometer is a billionth of a meter long).

Each of the six basic distinguishable colors in the light spectrum, which can be separated by shooting the white light through a prism as demonstrated in Isaac Newton's light experiments in *Optiks*, has its own distinctive wave length range. Thus, the shortest wave length is violet (380–450 nm), then blue (450–495 nm), green (495–570 nm), yellow (570–590 nm), orange (590–620 nm) and finally, the longest wave length, red (620–750 nm). So, within this tiny range of electromagnetic light radiation, we experience our sense of vision. That does not mean that electromagnetic radiation in the form of light photons simply disappears beyond the borders of our perception. It continues to exist and contains valuable information about the environment—for those who can see it!

Beyond the upper limits of our optical spectrum, beyond violet colors, lies an invisible range of color. This is known as ultraviolet (UV) light. It has frequencies shorter than visible light and longer than X-rays. UV radiation is subcategorized according to frequency length. UVA (also known as "long wave" or "black light" radiation) has wave lengths between 400 and 320 nm; UVB ("medium wave") has wave lengths of 320–280 nm; UVC ("short wave" or "germicidal" so named because it is used as a sterilization method to break down micro-organisms, such as viruses and molds in food, air, and water) has wave lengths below 280 nm. Beyond that are VUV ("vacuum" ultraviolet light, which receives its name from the fact that its light waves are so small they are absorbed by the air) with wave lengths between 200 and 10 nm and EUV ("extreme" ultraviolet light) at 3–1 nm.

As most of us know, it is dangerous to sit out too long in the sun without protection because the sun emits UV rays that can damage the skin. UV radiation can actually interfere with biological DNA structures (that's why it's used to kill micro-organisms!), causing skin damage, wrinkles, and cancer. Beyond ultraviolet light is X-ray radiation, which operates at even tinier wave lengths in the range of 10 to 0.01 nm. X-ray "light" is a form of ionizing radiation most often used to permit us to "see" into the deeper structures of objects such as the human body or crystals (radiography and crystallography).

At the very furthest end of this spectrum of high frequency light are gamma rays. These high energy photons have wave lengths of about 100 picometers (a picometer is one trillionth of a meter long) otherwise expressed as 100×10^{-12} meters. The energy for each gamma photon is roughly 10 keV. This type of electromagnetic wave oscillates with a frequency of 3 exahertz (EHz or 10^{18} Hz.) or higher.

Imagine what we might see if we could see the world as illuminated in all these various shades of ultraviolet light. It would be a very different world indeed! We would see that the moon actually shines brighter than our sun if only we could see the gamma rays it emits! A number of animals, such as birds, reptiles, and some insects, are able to see ultraviolet light. Why would they need this acute visual sense? There is data about the world, much of it highly relevant to these animals, which can only be determined using UV light. For instance, bumblebees use their ability to see UV light because a number of fruit and flower pollens are visible this way. This enables the bees to more efficiently locate their food source. Other animals may use this type of vision to identify each other as friend, foe, or food. Scorpions may glow yellow or green in this type of vision, and the plumage of some types of birds may indicate patterns that can only be seen under UV radiation.

Law enforcement and police detectives use machines that can make certain crime scene evidence visible. For instance, certain types of body fluids, such as urine, semen, and vomit, can only be seen in UV light when they are not visible to the naked eye. UV radiation also illuminates a number of geological conditions by enhancing the visible effects of fluorescence and phosphorescence. For example, a number of minerals and gemstones have fluorescent traits. Emeralds, rubies, and the Hope Diamond show a red fluorescence under short-wave UV light. Diamonds actually emit light under X-ray radiation! Crude oil or petroleum will fluoresce in a range of colors depending upon its chemical components. If we had X-ray vision, like Superman in the comic books, we would actually be able to see inside things that had outer, opaque surfaces. We could see the human skeleton or inside closed boxes! If we had the ability to see this world, it would look very different and, more importantly, we would be able to make distinctions between things based on very different characteristics.

In fact, there are certain psychic individuals who seem to have this ability to see inside things *as if* they had X-ray vision!

A 16-year-old Russian girl, Natalya Demkina from Saransk, has reportedly been able to make numerous medical diagnoses of patients' internal organs and structures without the help of X-rays or ultrasound machines.

In an article appearing in the Russian newspaper *Pravada* on January 14, 2004, the teenager explained her gift as follows: "'It's like having double vision. I can switch from one to the other in no time if I need to know a person's health problem," says the teenager. "I see an entire human organism. It is difficult to explain how I determine specific illnesses. There are certain impulses that I feel from the damaged organs. The secondary vision works only in daytime and is asleep at night.'"

She has been extensively tested by medical officials and has been proven consistently correct in her diagnoses. She is apparently often consulted by physicians and has occasionally disproven their diagnoses. In one instance, Natalya found a woman had been incorrectly diagnosed with cancer. "'There was once a lady who had been diagnosed with cancer. I looked at her and did not notice anything like it, just a small cyst. The woman however stated that she had just been diagnosed with cancer.'" Secondary examination however revealed that Natalya had been right.

The British newspaper *The Sun* decided to test Natalya's abilities and flew her to England to examine a 36-year-old woman named Briony who had suffered multiple injuries in a car accident. Before the interview, the woman's leg brace was removed and her clothing hid all clues as to her physical injuries. Briony's testimony about Natalya's immediate "diagnosis" of her medical issues is quite astounding.

Briony, 36, said: "I stood up and let her eyes scan over my fully clothed body. Her pupils dilated and she seemed to go into a trance for a couple of minutes. Straight away she began identifying a pain site at the base of my spine which she called a 'blockage.' In fact I have four healing spinal fractures and some nerve damage. She described my pelvic area as being asymmetrical and pointed to the right side—here I suffered several fractures. *Pointing to my jaw, she reported seeing a 'hard, alien part'—it was exactly the spot where a titanium plate holds my bones together.* The most astonishing moment was when she saw the injuries to my left leg. Both the tibia and fibula bones—the two below the knee—are broken. I was amazed as she identified the two separate breaks and told me I had problems bending my knee joint. Then she said she saw 'traces of several metal pins and screws' which had left their mark on the bone. She could not possibly know, without seeing the scars, that until two weeks ago my leg was held together by half-a-dozen pins and screws. She even said the scars where the screws had been were covered over with new tissue—which is exactly what my last X-ray showed."

Stunned Briony added: "Natalya is amazing. I was very skeptical at first, but after just a few minutes she focused on my major fractures. *I was very impressed. It was as though she was looking at X-rays of me. Only my orthopaedic consultant could have known more.*"

Before you begin to assume this is a one-time fluke type of thing—or perhaps fraud—consider that many such psychic individuals have been found to have this same capability. If a number of different people have this ability (and it is not subject to fraud or delusion), then it must reflect some human sensory capability with which we are not familiar.

I had the opportunity to study with a person who has this ability. Dr. Gregory Antyunhin is a Russian physician who has been living in the United States since 1994. He has been dubbed "Dr. X-Ray" by television journalists because of his ability to medically diagnose internal body injuries and illnesses which are otherwise "invisible" to the unaided eye. His abilities have been tested by physicians and researchers at several medical facilities. His work was showcased on television shows on the English BBC and American TLC networks.

Dr. Antyuhin claims to "see" inside the human body by means of clouds of color, known as auras, associated with the different organs and structures. If, for example, he sees red it means damage, yellow means inflammation, green means healing, and no color means normal. He then interprets these results in relation to their location in the body. He, too, has been proven highly accurate by scientists and physicians who have tested him. People who have this capability, known as medical intuitives, often do not need to physically see the person at all and can perform such diagnoses over the telephone or in a different room.

Of course, I initially thought this kind of X-ray vision was some kind of a joke. However, ironically, I have realized not only is it possible (if you throw out your preconceptions about what the word *X-ray* means), but that I actually have this strange ability!

I was once asked to do a scan of a woman's aura to try to detect any health issues. What I saw in my mind's eye was not the typical electromagnetic colors in her aura, but rather a startlingly clear mental image of her internal bone structure. In my mind, I saw her skeleton, and specifically her pelvic bones, in a kind of layman's simplistic picture—kind of like a Halloween skeleton that my then-9-year-old son might have drawn. I am not a physician and therefore do not know much about the actual placement of the bones. However, I could see that her pelvis was tilted to the left side and the leg bones were uncomfortably asymmetrical. I was actually embarrassed that I seemed to be inadvertently focusing on her pelvis and almost didn't tell her. However, after I mustered the courage to tell her, I was surprised to learn she had been in a car accident and had been told by her doctor that very week that her pelvis was indeed tilted. She was due to see her chiropractor for exactly that issue the following day.

Now, just for the record, I want it to be clear that she was seated the entire time and I could not see any hip issues with my eyes. Nor did I know anything about her background. Furthermore, I was not aware tilted pelvis was a real medical condition because I had never heard of it before.

This X-ray sight ability is not limited to medical diagnoses. I know one well-known psychic who, while undergoing testing by Canadian neuroscientist Dr. Michael Persinger, was able to—strange as this may seem—see through the wall of the room where he was sitting by himself and into the next room where he saw the skeleton shapes of the researchers. Their locations and positions in the room were later confirmed just as he saw them with his X-ray vision. None of the researchers could explain how he could have accurately seen them behind a wall.

Infrared (IR) light is at the other end of the electromagnetic spectrum, beyond visible light, in the very low frequency range. It is also invisible to the naked eye and begins at the point where we can no longer see the color red. The name "infrared" derives from Latin, meaning "below red." IR waves are longer than red visible light and shorter than radio waves. Just as with UV light, IR light is often subdivided into several groups according to wave length. "Near infrared" is the closest to visible light and is used, for example, in television remote controls. "Far Infrared" is the most distant of all the IR radiations, and closer to the microwave spectrum of electromagnetic radiation. IR light is measured in microns (a micrometer, or one millionth of a meter) as opposed to UV light, which is measured in the much smaller wavelength increments of nanometers (one billionth of a meter). Generally, although IR light is invisible to the unaided eye, the longer IR radiation waves are still experienced by us, not as visual light, but rather as tactile sensation in the form of heat. Radiators, sunlight, and flames all emit IR radiation. We have all seen photos taken using the process of thermography, which uses visible colors, such as red, to abstractly represent what the heat sensors pick up about the surface of any object.

This kind of abstract map of thermal heat shows us a radically different perspective of the world. In fact, certain types of pit vipers, notably rattlesnakes, are able to see (or perhaps *image* would be a better word) the world around them as a heat map using IR sensing. This is how they are able to track their prey, usually small, warm-blooded mammals such as mice, in the dark. IR photographic techniques have been helpful in determining otherwise-invisible changes in global warming, climatography, and heat emissions in the solar system. Night vision goggles used by the military use near-IR radiation by amplifying barely visible, ambient photons from the moon and stars, as opposed to thermal images, and converting them into visible color images. IR lasers are also used to provide light for fiberoptic communications systems. IR reflectograms are often used by art historians to see what lies underneath layers of more recent paint on the surface of paintings. All of these uses give us another way to see what we know exists out there but theoretically cannot "see" within the visible spectrum of light. These also represent ways to distinguish objects based on entirely new and bizarre attributes. It is a form of mapping.

Beyond IR radiation are microwaves (ranging anywhere from 1 centimeter long to 1 foot long, the latter being the average size used to heat food in a microwave oven), then television waves, and still further out on the electromagnetic spectrum are radio waves. Radio waves can range from the length of a football to the length of an entire football stadium! Radio waves are used not only to transmit signals to radios, but also televisions, cordless and cell phones, and garage door remotes. There are bodies in the galaxy, such as planets, stars, gaseous clouds of dust, and comets, that emit huge waves of light, up to lengths of 1 mile, which are forms of radio waves. Beyond radio waves, are Very Low Frequencies (VLF), in the range of 300 megahertz (MHz) to 10 MHz, and at the furthest extreme of the spectrum, Extremely Low Frequencies (ELF), all frequencies up to 300 Hz.

Unlike UV light, IR light is non-ionizing. This means that an IR wave does not carry enough energy per quantum to ionize the atoms or molecules and excite them with so much energy that they go into a frenzy and begin to lose electrons. The definition of an ion is an atom that has lost or gained an electron, resulting in a new positive or negative charge. Any type of ionizing frequency will cause all kinds of disturbances in molecules and cells. Because radio waves are non-ionizing, they are believed to pose far fewer dangers to our physical health. However, ultimately, this may be inaccurate because other types of non-ionizing, IR radiation, such as microwaves, have been proven to be harmful to human health. Certainly, microwaves, as a form of IR radiation, can cause damage through extreme heat.

According to the National Association for Amateur Radio/American Radio Relay League (ARRL), in an article published in the April 1994,*QST*, by Wayne Overbeck, entitled "Electromagnetic Fields and Your Health," radio frequencies and ELF frequencies have traditionally been treated as non-threatening to our health because, as non-ionizing frequencies, they do not produce much heat. However, scientists were aware, even in the mid-20th century, that if such frequencies were produced at high enough levels, they could in fact generate enough heat to cause physical damage to the human body. Most household electrical appliances (refrigerators, hair dryers, computers, color televisions, and so on) generate ELF frequencies, as do electrical power lines, at around 60 Hz. There have been increasing concerns that at sufficiently high levels, radio and ELF radiations may still cause "athermal" effects—health problems not necessarily implicating heat, but the electromagnetic radiation effects—such as cancer and leukemia. Strangely enough, if the levels of radiation are high enough, ELF radiation can still result in thermal effects causing health problems such as blindness and sterility.

Scientists have discovered that some levels of electromagnetic radiation can affect living tissue by disrupting vital chemical and electrical signals between cells in the human body. It has been suggested that this may interfere in cell-to-cell communication, resulting in a loss of immunity, especially against diseases such as cancer. Further, certain ELF frequencies, such as those found in electric blankets, have been found to interfere with the production of certain hormones such as melatonin. Clearly, ELF frequencies are still capable of altering body chemistry and harming body function even though we do not seem to experience the physical effects until significant damage has already been done.

I would only suggest here that, although the debate rages on about how much thermal heat constitutes *too much* heat, obviously the human body is capable of being effected and reacting at the molecular level. An increasing number of physicians and scientists are now convinced that cells have a certain level of consciousness. If this is so, then their consciousness undoubtedly expresses itself within the larger human body organism. Or, to make matters simpler, let's get rid of the word *consciousness* and just call it cellular knowledge that comes from experience. That requires memory in that is not self-conscious, but simply records and retains information—kind of like my titanium eyeglasses frame that remembers its original shape even if I sit on it by accident! So, even assuming our cells retain some sort of knowledge, this knowledge becomes absorbed into the overall cellular network of the body. On some level, our body is aware of electromagnetic influences even when our sensory organs are incapable of specifically detecting certain changes. I believe this level of molecular sensing plays a key role in much of what we currently call psychic or intuitive behavior.

Extra-Spectral Data Furnishes the Basis for Psychic Observations

Let me explain why psychic information can be accurate and real, yet doesn't seem to come as a form of sensory knowledge through our five senses.

Imagine, if you will, that all of these electromagnetic frequencies, from gamma rays to ELF frequencies, ionizing and nonionizing, ultrasound to infrasound, as well as smell molecules are passing through your body all the time. Add to that the two other basic senses that I did not mention: touch and taste. It is therefore no real surprise if I tell you that you live in a dense vibrational environment teeming with all kinds of vibrations; let's call them *extra-spectral* data because they lie outside the normal spectra of human sensory capabilities.

Your body reacts to all of these frequencies in very different ways. Mostly, you only recognize events recorded by these frequencies when they pass through the small spectral range of your sensory organs. A leaf is green because our eyes have identified the electromagnetic frequency, or a dog barks because our ears have identified the frequency within our auditory system of capturing such data. What about those gamma rays? X-rays? Radio waves when the radio is turned off? Do they register information in our body? The answer is clearly yes, because in several cases, these frequency assaults can result in bodily illness or physical damage even without our conscious awareness. So what happens to the information they carry? Why doesn't it register in our consciousness?

The reason why they don't leave a sensory imprint in our mind (which would have created conscious memory) is because they do not register with any specific sensory organ. None of our sensory organs seems to be equipped to act as a special receiver for these types of frequencies that fall outside the normal band of electromagnetic frequencies. Yet, they leave some imprint on a cellular level. I would suggest to you that this imprint—pure-frequency-information-carrying data from far beyond our immediate surroundings—is retained and understood by the body itself as knowledge.

So then the question becomes: How does the body, without the aid of its normal sensory imagery, hand this information over to the brain and create awareness? No specialized cells are there to greet them, bring them inside, translate them into acceptable electrical nerve impulses that are sent to the brain, and introduce them to the host body. These extra-spectral frequencies come inside the body, but are unrecognizable as information-bearing frequencies.

The effects of these unseen frequencies can only acquire a "meaning" to the individual person if they arrive in the brain in some kind of pre-packaged sensory format. People who are unusually sensitive and have a vague awareness of this extra-spectral data experience it ambiguously as knowledge without origin. It is neither strictly sensory (because it didn't come in through the ordinary sensory organs) nor is it cognitive, because it has no underlying thought interpretation. It is knowledge without an apparent source.

Now, you can probably see what I am getting at here. Extra-spectral data is starting to sound like intuitive hunches, gut feelings, and psychic impressions. You feel something with absolute certainty, but you don't know why. You know something, but you have no underlying data to support your knowledge. Your conclusions feel irrational yet strangely right. Your information, proven accurate much later, would have to have traveled some extremely long distance in terms of space/time in order for you to have known it. We know gamma rays infiltrate our bodies all the time and come from distant galaxies and the far reaches of the cosmos. Likewise, ELF frequencies can emanate from deep within the earth and have wave lengths miles long. There are clearly reasonable ways to explain "distant" information that comes to us just as we know it comes to other animals.

What is more difficult to explain, from a scientific point of view, is how our brain translates this data into acceptable, comprehensible sensory imagery. In other words, how do we map it within our brain so we can understand it?

Exercise

Sit in a dimly lit room and look at your hands. Try to imagine that you can see the photons of energy flowing out of the tips of your fingers. Once you see a cloud of energy, practice touching energy to energy from the fingertips. Then practice seeing energy in other people.

Lesson #6:

The Sixth Sense Is a Myth

How Many Senses Do We Actually Have?

There is no such thing as a so-called sixth sense. It is a myth—a sweet little story created to explain away a much more complicated mechanism. So, before we even begin discussing psychic sensing, let's start with the really obvious. Let's start with what we know—or at least *think* we know. How many senses do we really have?

If you guessed five, you'd be wrong.

It is true that traditionally we have always accepted that we have five senses (sight, sound, taste, touch, and smell). Since Greek philosopher Aristotle (384–322 BC) first classified our sensory system as having five senses, we have tended follow his rationale quite faithfully. Even Aristotle felt quite firm in his conviction that we did not have a sixth sense, although perhaps he did not mean it in quite the same way that we would interpret a sixth sense today.

However, in recent years, scientists have begun to question the validity of Artistotle's analysis. These days it's just no longer that simple. Scientists now believe we have significantly more senses than we ever previously thought—perhaps upwards to as many as 40 senses!

Even the sense of sight has now been expanded into several sensory classifications. Vision is actually considered by many neuroanatomists to be not one sense but two, possibly, three! It can be broken down in terms of an ability to see color (frequencies of light waves), brightness (energy of light), and possibly depth perception (although this may just be a function of having stereoscopic sight from two eyes).

The authors of *Deciphering the Senses* have suggested that we actually have in excess of 17 senses. Author Guy Murchie Jr., in his book *The Seven Mysteries of Life*, proposed that humans have up to 37 senses, including sense of time and sense of fear.

The problem is that we don't really know because we can't agree on a common definition for the word *sense*. What *is* a sense, anyway? *Dorland's Medical Dictionary* defines the word *sense* as follows: "Any of the physical processes by which stimuli are received, transduced, and conducted as impulses to be interpreted by the brain; they may be classified as either special senses or somatic senses."

Frankly, I was a bit confused by this medical definition of a sense. I had to look up the word *transduce* in the dictionary. The *Merriam-Webster Dictionary* defines it as: "to convert (as energy or a message) into another form <essentially sense organs *transduce* physical energy into a nervous signal.>" Okay, so if I understand this correctly, when we "transduce" stimuli from our environment via our senses, we are changing information that comes to us in one format and converting it into a different format inside our body. But how?

Dorland's separates the senses into two major groups: *special* (vision, hearing, olfaction, and taste) and *somatic*, which are related to the sense of touch (touch, pain sense, vibration sense, pressure sense, temperature sense, tickling, deep body sensibility called *bathyesthesia*, movement sense, muscle sense, posture sense, body sense, the ability to perceive an object by touching it called *stereognosis*, the ability to localize a tactile sensation called *topesthesia*, hair sensibility, and visceral sense). *Dorland's* leaves open the possibility of a third type of unclassified sense: the sense of equilibrium.

By now you are probably beginning to understand why I don't believe in the famous sixth sense. First of all, we have more than six senses anyway.

And secondly, given the existing state of medical confusion on how to define, identify, and classify our senses, it makes little sense to lump all intuitive and psychic observations into the category of an alleged sixth sense. It seems much more reasonable to assume that this kind of psychic sensing ability must arise naturally from our pre-existing, senses, which, at the moment, cannot even be counted!

Moreover, some people have even theorized that our senses may include various aspects of our cognitive brain—and not simply our physical senses. Austrian mystical philosopher Rudolph Steiner (1861–1925) believed in the existence of what he called "higher senses." These included *language, thought,* and *ego.* Obviously we have not yet come close to achieving any type of understanding of the extent or capabilities of these additional senses, assuming they are considered as such.

If we don't know the difference between what we *think* and what we *perceive*, then we are really in no position to be defining what a sense is! The various ways we experience the world and organize our perceptions seems almost endless. Imagine that there are many other types of senses out there that we simply haven't yet identified. This is not difficult to picture, especially when you realize that medicine has managed to identify all kinds of neurological conditions and disorders that indicate a *lack* of a sense. This suggests, in turn, that there must be a corresponding or matching normal "sense" in a state of health. Again, this depends on how you define a sense, but it points out the endless ways in which we experience our reality. The truth is that reality appears so naturally and seamlessly as part of our daily experience—*in a state of perfect health*—that you don't really know it's there until you have lost it.

But once you start dealing with anything less than a perfect state of mental health, you begin to recognize the number of sensing abilities that you simply take for granted. Our ability to sense information is so highly complex that we just don't spend much time dissecting it. During our lifetime, we experience our senses holistically as if they were a symphony orchestra in which all the separate instruments are so highly blended that all you end up hearing is the overall melody. Take, for example, neurological disorders. These cognitive malfunctions actually suggest by their nature that the resulting experience is abnormal.

It occurred to me, while flipping through some medical literature about different types of neurological disorders, that you could actually attribute a sense to almost every neurological condition that results in a loss of any mental ability. Take a look, for example, at some neurological disorders: *acoria* (inability to feel satiated no matter how much is eaten); *amusia* (inability to produce or evaluate musical sounds); *anhedonia* (inability to experience pleasure); *amelodia* (absence of normal variations of pitch, rhythm, and stress in speech); *dyscalculia* (impaired ability to use mathematics); *environmental agnosia* (inability to orient physically familiar places, but able to on abstract representations such as a map); *jamais vu* (sensation of everything being strange and unfamiliar); *dyschronation* (a distorted sense of time); *topagnosis* (inability to localize the site of tactile stimulation); and so on (Dubinweb.com, Appendix II, *Terms of Cognitive, Behavioral and Neurologic Disorders*).

These strange breakdowns in human capacity suggest, at least to me, there must be cohesive sensory mechanisms behind these mental abilities that might constitute some kind of unidentified human senses. Of course, it is extremely difficult to separate out the brain's cognitive functions from its sensory inputs. Sometimes the subtle differences between thinking and experiencing are indistinguishable!

Scientists Identify New Human Senses

Despite the fact we continue to operate on the general assumption that humans have only five senses, the list of other medically accepted, non-traditional senses beyond the normal five continues to grow. These new senses include: a sense of pain (*nociception*); a sense of the body's location space (*proprioception*); a sense of balance (*equilibrioception*); a sense of sex smell based on the VNO organ located in the human nasal septum, which disappears after birth but may be related to our ability to "smell" pheromones without conscious awareness (*vomeronasal*); a sense of temperature or heat (*thermoception*); a sense of direction perhaps based on the vestigial pineal gland located in the brain behind the eyes, which is thought to help with sensing the magnetic orientation of the earth (interestingly, in some reptiles, the pineal eye is equipped with a lens, vitreous humor, and retina just like their normal "eyes"); and a sense of discovery (based on fMRI brain scans of a primitive area of the brain known as the ventral striatim, which lights up when a person is confronted with risk, such as exploration).

Do Humans Share Strange Animal Senses?

In addition to the recent discovery of these new senses in humans, we may share some of the strange and unusual senses that until now have only been attributed to certain types of animals. Ultimately, these may shed light on some psychic abilities in humans that seem so amazing to us now because we cannot explain their origin.

A Sense of Electricity (Electroception)

A number of sea animals, specifically certain types of sharks, eels, fish, and rays, have the sense of electroception. They are able to sense the presence of electrical fields or, in some cases, can generate field patterns of electricity using their bodies. This sense is apparently used not only as a predator's tool, but also to communicate. To me, it is not far-fetched to make a sensory analogy between electroception and the ability of some people to see and feel auras, which are the electrical fields immediately surrounding the human body. The existence of human auras has been shown to exist (not without controversy) in Kirlian photographic techniques (first discovered in 1939) using high-voltage electricity of subjects on photographic plates.

Furthermore, as discussed in earlier chapters, we know that a variety of high frequency electromagnetic waves (cosmic, gamma, X-rays, ultraviolet), and even some visible light are ionizing and can cause ionizing in the human body. This results in disturbances of the bioelectromagnetic balance in the body's molecules and cells by causing the ejection or emissions of negatively charged electrons from the atoms. This effect changes the electrical balance of the cells. This effect, when caused by light bouncing off of a metal surface, is called the *photoelectric effect*. The human body requires about 20 different trace minerals, including iron, zinc, copper, selenium, calcium, potassium, and sodium, and these account for 4 percent of our total body mass. The human body has an enhanced ability not only to conduct electricity, but also to create a photoelectric effect.

Various scientific studies have also proven the human body is indeed surrounded by an electrical field. Moreover, it is common knowledge that the central and peripheral nervous system of the body function by means of tiny electrical impulses exchanged between neurons. It has been estimated, in the brain alone, there are between 10 and 100 trillion electrical synapses (connections between the neurons) that signal information by means of small electrical pulses! Our bodies are conductors of static electricity, depending on levels of atmospheric humidity and our body movements, such as shuffling our feet. Our bodies are thus loaded with electrical activity.

Suddenly, that "crazy" assertion by psychics that they can see a colorful electromagnetic aura surrounding the human body and that it reflects information about the physical health of the individual seems scientifically plausible—well, assuming it can be seen by the human eye.

In 2005, a Japanese company, Nippon Telephone and Telegraph Corporation (NTT), actually developed technology that converts this weak human electrical field into what is known as a Human Area Network (HAN) device. The device, called RedTacton, is worn on the body and can transmit data all over the body's skin. Any area in the body can then be used as a transmitter to trigger other devices in the environment without the use of cables and wires! Thus, you can use your elbow to turn on your cell phone or laptop computer.

Scientists have long known this and have experimented with giving human beings various doses of electricity to alter biological functions and behavior. Around 1945, the United States and the Soviet Union both conducted all kinds of mind control experiments using electrical currents to influence human behavior, emotions, and memory. Certain types of electricity have also been used to promote good health. For example, cranial electrostimulation has been shown to promote better sleeping habits in depressed patients. Electrostimulation using small, pulsing bursts of low-voltage electricity, also promotes tissue and bone healing; reduces swelling, and is commonly used in physical therapy after surgery. It has also been shown to help stroke victims recover motor activity. Certain Far Eastern healing techniques, such as acupuncture, acupressure, qi gong, shiatsu, reiki, and so on, involve circulating or eliminating blocks in the life force (qi) energy of the body, which is perceived to operate very much like a kind of bioelectrical force. Chinese medicine operates on the assumption that emotions are stored in various organs, almost like electrical potential. The success of these experiments and techniques merely underscores the importance of our bioelectrical nature.

A Sense of Directional Sound (Echolocation)

Another type of non-human sense is *echolocation,* which is the ability to sense the environment by means of reflected sound, like sonar. Certain types of animals, such as bats, whales, dolphins, and porpoises, emit clicking noises in order to create a mental map of their environment with echolocation. This mental map contains the size, shape, surface characteristics, distance, and movements of objects. Some can even distinguish between prey and non-prey based on this data. It is really no surprise that these sound maps begin to appear almost as visual maps. Both vision and hearing depend on being able to sense refracted waves of energy. Just as light waves bounce off the surface of an object and are refracted into the eye's retina, creating a visual picture, sound waves bounce off surfaces, creating echos and corresponding mental landscape imagery. Although some scientists feel echolocation is not a separate sense from hearing, others feel it may differ in our sensing capacity.

In recent years, certain blind individuals have popularized the notion of human echolocation, particularly those who have demonstrated that they can see not only the location, but also texture, height, and density of objects in their environment by using clicking noises as a form of echolocation. Thus, echolocation may be a sensory ability or a tool that exists within the human species, but has been left largely unutilized.

A Sense of Magnetic Fields (Magnetoception)

This is another supposedly non-human sense that involves the ability to detect fluctuations in magnetic fields. It has been found to exist in migrating birds and bees. Many animals, such as migratory birds, salamanders, loggerhead turtles, hamsters, dolphins, honey bees, salmon, and even some kinds of bacteria, have been found to be able to sense the earth's geomagnetic field in order to orient themselves. Scientists have discovered that subterranean Zambian mole rats have a certain collection of nerve cells that enable them to process magnetic information. Researchers at the universities of Leeds and Princeton discovered that bats are able to navigate using a magnetic substance in their bodies called magnetite as a kind of internal compass. Magnetite has been found in human brain tissue, leading some to conclude that it may account for a human sense of direction. Interestingly, in recent years, more neuroscientists have begun to explore the effects of transcranial magnetic stimulation (TMS) on the human brain. When weak magnetic fields are applied to particular areas of the brain, sensory perceptions are very often dramatically, and temporarily, altered.

Clearly, we have sensory capabilities that extend far beyond the traditional five senses of sight, sound, taste, smell, and touch. Scientific research has confirmed we have more than five senses and, in all likelihood, we possess still more senses beyond those that are currently recognized! It is pointless to attribute psychic phenomena to some alleged sixth sense when we don't even know how to define a sense or even how many we actually have!

How Do We Know What Experience Comes From Which Sense?

Although we like to think our senses are very different and separate from one another, they are not. We like to think that each sensory organ gives us pure, unadulterated information. Our senses are not isolated receivers and most of them overlap.

What we experience is actually a sloppy mix of data that is interpreted *simultaneously* by different sensory organs, even though it may feel like it is coming through just one sense. Why does this happen? Because the electromagnetic spectrum of each sense shares some overlap with the other senses or even totally non-sensory organs in the body. The cells in the human body, even the body's magnetic aura, are able to respond to vibrations in our environment and, if we are sensitive enough to the way in which the information reaches our brain, we can begin to interpret what these vibrations mean.

Furthermore, we know the human brain has a tremendous capacity for plasticity, which means that if one area of the brain normally reserved for one sense isn't used, instead of remaining dormant and unused, it will be taken over and used for a different sense. For instance, because blind people can't use their occipital region for visual processing, it may get used instead to process auditory information. This also causes sensory overlapping.

Hearing and Touch

The average human ear is capable of hearing between 9 and 22,000 Hertz when tiny hair fibers on its sensitive membrane pick up subtle pressures exerted by atmospheric particles in the air. These vibrations are translated into electrical signals, which are routed to the brain. However, lower and higher audible frequencies can also be experienced through the body through its sense of touch. This process is called *tacitation* (which refers to touch felt as pressure on the skin). Most of us have had the experience of going to a live rock concert when the speakers are cranked up and felt the vibrations in our body. The entire physical body experiences the sound as enormous blasts of physical pressure and vibrations on the skin, and even internally.

Smell, Taste, and Touch

The sense of taste (also called *gustation*) refers to our ability to respond to dissolved molecules and ions called "tastants" in our mouth. The average person has about 5,000 taste buds. There are five taste bud receptors located on the tongue, which account for the sense of taste. They are: salty, sweet, sour, bitter, and the recently discovered umami taste, which responds to glutamic salts and amino acids such as monosodium glutamate (MSG is a flavor enhancer often added to Chinese food and meats). A sixth category of fatty acids has also recently been proposed as a source of taste but is not, as yet, generally accepted. The taste buds are not the only sensory aspect of taste, however. The feel of food can be as important to its overall taste as the flavor itself. The reason for this is because 75 percent of the nerves coming out of the papillae, which form the little bumps on the tongue that are loaded with taste bud receptors, lead to the trigeminal nerve. This nerve connects to pain and touch centers in the brain! As a result, especially to super-tasters, fats may "taste" creamy or the "taste" of ginger root may include a burning sensation. Thus, the sense of touch (and the sense of pain, depending upon whether you believe it has its own sensory classification) and sense of taste overlap.

The sense of smell (*olfaction*) overlaps our senses of taste and touch.

Olfaction plays a major role in the degree to which we are capable of distinguishing between various tastes. The classic test is to cut up some pieces of apple and put them in one bowl and some pieces of potato in another bowl. Then hold your nose closed and take a bite out of the apple and the potato. It is virtually impossible to distinguish between their tastes without the added benefit of smell. We have 25 million primary sensory receptor cells in each 2.5-square-centimeter area of each nostril. It has been suggested the average person can distinguish between approximately 10,000 different odors. This is an obvious improvement on the handful of five basic taste categories we are capable of experiencing using that sense alone!

The olfaction system, like the gustation system, is also connected to the trigeminal nerve, which can determine variations in tactile pressure, pain, and temperature sensations in the areas of the mouth, eyes, and nasal cavity. The sense of smell also overlaps our sense of touch (and pain). Certain chemical trigeminal stimulants can produce effects described as hot, cold, tingling, or irritating. Thus, for example, menthol and eucalyptus actually smell/feel cool!

It has even been suggested that the sense of smell may overlap with the spectrum of electromagnetic radiation. In 1938, G.M. Dyson proposed that our sense of smell may be created by the vibrations of electrons in the chemical molecules associated with certain odors. Many of these vibrations occur in the infrared range of electromagnetic radiation. Infrared radiation (IR) falls into the range of light waves that are longer than visible light waves (we can't see them) and shorter than radio waves (we can't hear them).

Sight and Touch

The color red on the color spectrum has the longest wave lengths of any color, between 625 and 760 nanometers. There is a tiny overlap with IR, which has longer wavelengths (mostly non-visible) between 750 nanometers and 1 millimeter. This might account for why we tend to visualize infrared waves and things that emit heat as red-toned. Normally, infrared vibrations can be interpreted by the human body as a form of heat sensing. It has been postulated that the human ability to sense heat is actually another sense beyond the five senses, and has been called *thermoception*. It refers to the ability of the skin and internal tissues to determine the presence of temperatures either above or below normal body temperature. Vampire bats, as well as certain snakes, such as boas and pit vipers, can literally "see" infrared waves using pits on the side of their head to determine the outlines of heat-emitting animals and gauge their distance. They are able to create mental maps of their environment using this sense alone.

Sensory Data Without Having the Sensory Organ

The last problem with identifying a sixth sense, as I see it, is that even non-sensory organs and tissues in our body are involved in sensing. This has been scientifically documented. So, without being able to identify the port of entry into our body, how do we know it is just one sensory organ or ability that can be credited with receiving sensory data? Our entire bodies are wired like some amazing receiver, and half the time we don't know where or how we are receiving sensory data. But we don't need a sensory organ in order to sense things.

A phenomenon called *blindsight* is a good example of how sensory data somehow leaks into our bodies even without the requisite and ordinary sensory organs being activated. People who suffer from this condition, often as the result of a stroke or brain injury, have perfectly healthy eyes and retinas, but have damage to the primary visual cortex (also known as the striate cortex or "V1"). This is an area of the brain located at the back of the head, which is the first stop in visual processing of retinal signals, considered essential for the experience of seeing, before being assembled by the higher associative visual sections of the brain.

People with blindsight experience blindness in the field of vision that corresponds to the part of the V1 area that has been damaged. This may involve a small hole in the field of vision or the entire field, depending on the scope of the damage to V1. However, it is not absolute blindness. When asked if they see a red ball held up in front of them, for example, they will say no—consistent with their blindness. Yet, when asked to locate the ball, they will point to the exact location without difficulty. How is that possible? How can they see without seeing?

Apparently, this is not an unusual or unique skill. We are all capable of seeing without seeing!

Studies at the University of Texas in Houston have shown that people suffering from blindsight (as well as people with normal vision whose V1 section of the brain is temporarily paralyzed by means of harmless electromagnetic radiation, creating the mental equivalent of blindness) are able to sense the correct shape, color, orientation, and motion of objects put in front of them although they, technically, are unable to see.

Likewise, a team at the University of Wales was able to show that a 52-year-old male subject who had suffered two strokes, leaving him completely blind, although his retina and optic nerves were still healthy, was able to discern whether images of people placed in front of him were happy, angry, or fearful, despite the fact that he was absolutely unable to see objects such as circles, squares, or guess at the gender of faces. His success rate was 59 percent higher when dealing with emotions as opposed to objects, animals, or gender.

Blindsight is thus a form of unconscious sensing not only visually, but emotionally. There are a number of theories as to why this happens. Some researchers believe the retinal signals are rerouted into other visual processing centers and the only thing that remains "blind" is the conscious awareness of the signals.

I was quite amazed to discover, during the course of researching this book, that I have rather good blindsight ability! My normal eyesight is pretty bad. I am very nearsighted (I see at 20 feet away what a person with 20/20 vision can see from a distance of two football fields away!). I have astigmatisms, floaters, some cataracts, and early-stage glaucoma. Because one of the early indications of glaucoma is a decrease in peripheral vision, I am required to take a peripheral visual field test every three months to make sure my peripheral vision hasn't deteriorated. As the disease progresses, one begins to lose peripheral vision, becoming more and more tunnel-like, until finally one becomes totally blind. Strangely, even though my intraocular pressure is high and my retinas are very thin, I still seem to maintain very good peripheral vision. Often, when I take the visual field test, it is almost normal! My ophthalmologist has taken this to mean that my glaucoma is progressing at a very slow rate and is under control. I, on the other hand, have doubts about this.

My fear, however, is that I am cheating when I take these tests!

Let me explain. The visual field test involves sitting with a patch over one eye in front of a large machine and staring into its rounded screen (rather like a satellite dish) at a central focal image such as a dot. The lights are turned off and all that is visible is the dot. Without taking one's eye off the dot, one must click a button on a hand-held clicker every time a pinpoint of light appears anywhere else in the rounded screen. The machine will catch you if try to cheat by taking your eye off the central dot in order to look around at the peripheral space directly.

However, I myself have been shocked by the good results I get on these tests. I actually began to wonder if I weren't somehow "cheating" in a slightly different way—by clicking on my clicker when I didn't quite see the light but thought I *might* have seen it. There were times when my hand seemed to press the button on the clicker almost involuntarily when I (quite honestly) hadn't seen anything at all. One or two such "mistakes" is acceptable—but I seem to do this quite often. What would cause my imagination to be so accurate?

One day I came across an Internet site, *www.serendip.brynmawr.edu*, sponsored by Bryn Mawr College, to promote interdisciplinary discussion on issues relating primarily to the brain sciences and genetics. Dr. Paul Grobstein, a Harvard and Stanford University–educated neurobiologist and professor of biology at Bryn Mawr College, created an interactive test for blindsight ability. Dr. Grobstein and his colleagues propose that *blindsight may not only be a symptom of brain lesions, but of perfectly normal, intact brain function.*

The test immediately reminded me of the peripheral vision tests I take at my opthalmologist's office. The test starts out with a square that is divided up into four invisible quadrants in which small dots will appear at random. You must stare at the spot in the center of the square at all times. After you press a button, a dot appears briefly somewhere in the square and then quickly disappears. You can constantly adjust the speed, radius, and contrast of the dot. You must then use your mouse to point to exactly where the dot occurred. Your answer is registered, but you do not find out the results until the end of the test. After each turn, you must record whether or not you actually saw a dot.

According to Dr. Grobstein, in all cases where you actually saw the dot, the number of times that your mouse accurately identified the location of the dot should be well above 25 percent. Why? Because you have a minimal 25 percent (or 1-in-4) chance of being correct because there are four quadrants in the square and if you actually saw the dot, you can locate its appearance with far greater accuracy within each quadrant. However—and this is the interesting part—what about the cases where you either didn't see the dot or weren't sure you saw it (these are divided into two separate categories), and made a "guess" as to its location? What are the chances of being correct?

The authors say any score higher than 50 percent is strong evidence of blindsight ability. My score was 60 percent. Apparently, I score relatively high for having blindsight—and that made perfect sense to me. Blindsight is a way in which ordinary sensory information leaches into our brain without any conscious awareness of the sensory experience. My fears were confirmed: I was getting credit for seeing what I was not really seeing with my eyes at the doctor's office.

So what then had originally tipped me off to this possibility that I might have blindsight? I had been training myself over several years, through various intuition psychology workshops, psychic development classes, seminars, and reading materials, to trust my instincts and to take action based on nothing but a baseless guess. This takes a tremendous amount of unlearning of techniques that we have all developed throughout a lifetime. We are generally trained from a very early age to distrust and disregard hunches unless they can be reverse-engineered from a logical standpoint. Similarly, according to Dr. Grobstein, increasingly accurate blindsight scores is a trainable skill!

To me, this suggests a further concept—namely, psychic or intuitive ability often *feels* like our imagination or mere guessing because it is based upon sensory inputs that are, for whatever reason, falling below the radar of our conscious brain, but incorporating themselves into our total experience. If blindsight can be learned, then it seems a reasonable corollary that psychic ability, assuming it is based upon sensory inputs, can also be learned. But this is clearly *a new concept of learning where we have no conscious awareness of the data acquisition or method of improvement.* We cannot track our progress except by the results. We cannot reverse-engineer the process.

Total Blindness Doesn't Prevent "Seeing"

What then, you may ask, about people who have actual damage to the retina of the eye and are blind in the traditional sense of the word—can they see things unconsciously somehow? There are numerous examples of this in the annals of parapsychological research. This is called *paroptical vision* or eyeless sight. Generally, people who make the claim they can see without using their eyes are not technically blind. These people are blindfolded before performing these feats. This has led to countless attacks by skeptics and magicians who claim anyone can do this by simply peering down their nose and looking underneath the blindfold.

A 22-year-old epileptic Russian woman named Rosa Kuleshova sky-rocketed to fame in 1963 when it was discovered she had the ability to see without using her eyes. She had normal vision, but had several blind family members and had taught herself to read Braille at any early age. Rosa was apparently able to read newsprint while blindfolded, describe objects in photos, and accurately determine differently colored cards using only her fingertips while holding them inside a black bag. She claimed white felt smooth; red felt coarse-grained; and blue felt wavy. (Once again, this was indicative of a sensory crossover between the senses of sight and touch.)

Rosa was tested by numerous Soviet psychologists and neurologists, and underwent many different tests to determine her ability. To eliminate the possibility she might be sensing the actual textures of the ink or raised print on the paper, a pane of glass was placed over the newspaper she was "reading" with her hands. Under these circumstances she was unable to read the fine print, but could accurately reproduce the headlines if there was bright ambient light. Researchers also used colored lights instead of printed colors. So, for example, in one experiment, they shone a red light on a green book, creating a blue appearance. Rosa accurately described it as blue. When the red light was switched off and the green book assumed a green hue, Rosa accurately state the color had changed. Rosa's psychic ability was scorned by many American scientists, who suggested that Soviet testing procedures lacked sufficient controls and that Rosa was a fraud.

Research by psychic and parapsychology researcher Carol Ann Liaros, in Buffalo, New York, is yielding perhaps even more interesting results because it involves eyeless sight of truly blind individuals. Ms. Liaros had obtained some fascinating results after training groups of blind volunteers to see psychically. This time, such results cannot be assailed on grounds of cheating by peeking around some blindfold. They indicate that there is some unknown leakage in the human system that permits it to acquire information normally only affiliated with visual types of data without the use of sight. The easiest line of attack against her studies is that the results are often subjective and anecdotal.

Ms. Liaros's work began when she was teaching a psychic ESP class at a local YMCA in Batavia, New York. Ms. Liaros launched several pilot studies to investigate psi faculties in blind subjects. In 1973, she began a seven-week pilot program called "Project: Blind Awareness" with 20 blind subjects and 20 trained volunteers to help in one-on-one training. In a series of tape-recorded, photographed, and carefully documented sessions, the blind subjects were asked to place their hands 2 to 3 inches above sheets of colored paper (volunteers assisted them in putting their hands in position) and to keep their eyes closed. These tests were done at the beginning of the course (to establish a baseline ability) and then again after 20 hours of training. The statistical results showed a dramatic increase in the ability of the blind subjects to make accurate predictions about the colors and photos. This tends to confirm Dr. Grobstein's findings that blindsight, like blind-seeing, is a trainable skill.

All this suggests that the so-called sixth sense is really not one single sense, but the ability of the body to receive information from a variety of sensory and non-sensory organs. It also involves the ability of the mind to gather and register extra-spectral information. The collection and reassembly of this kind of information are all done on a subconscious level, and we don't have a clue how much information we are gathering at any given moment. It seems disarmingly magical and mysterious to us to acquire information in this way, so we reject it.

Exercise

Think about a location where you will actually be going in the near future. Imagine what it looks like before you arrive—what you do once you are there, who is there, and how they look. Feel the textures; smell the odors; listen to the noises. Write them down and when you go there, compare your impressions.

Lesson #7:

Like It or Not, Women's Intuition Is Better

Most people will admit that women are generally more intuitive than men. We call it *feminine intuition*. Many theories have evolved about why this should be so. But it occurred to me, assuming this is true, that we might find some clues about the physical origins of intuition by figuring out just why women are in fact more intuitive than men. What is it *specifically* about the female sex that seems to enhance intuitive ability? Are women conditioned this way? Do sex hormones create intuition? Does a biological or societal submissive type of behavior create intuition? Are women more intelligent—or perhaps less intelligent—than men?

In all of the intuitive psychology or psychic workshops, seminars, and training courses I have ever attended, the women always outnumber the men. Women seem to gravitate toward studies of the unknown whereas men generally shun them. Men seem to feel, alternatively, either grossly inadequate when dealing with these subtle skills or totally contemptuous of such ridiculous naïvete of anyone trying to understand what clearly cannot be known! Within the world's greatest religions, while men tend to have a monopoly on the religious leadership, their flocks tend to be mostly pious and dutiful women.

Men tend to be far less spiritual and more pragmatic than women. The world's greatest skeptics tend to be men, not women. Women seem to have developed a tolerance for questionable spiritual information, whereas men seem to view any such belief system as a sign of weakness or vulnerability. One recent study actually showed that high religious involvement actually improves a woman's state of mental health and decreases depression, but it has the exact opposite effect on men! ("For Women, But Not Men").

Generally, "women's intuition" has been attributed to the acute psychological insights and emotional sensibilities of women. These, in turn, are presumed to be a function of their biological need to understand the non-verbal demands of young infants, and manage more powerful, aggressive males by using their powers of observation, persuasion, and manipulation. It has been argued that this accounts for their unusual ability to see what men often fail to see. Moreover, it is claimed that society nurtures a woman's tendency to be emotional and to feel her feelings, both of which probably aid in her ability to be highly empathetic with the feelings of others.

Women are thus permitted by society to be more open-minded, less logical (well, at least that's the positive side of hormones), weaker, reliant, and more whimsical. Men are encouraged to be independent, self-sustaining, non-emotional, targeted, and logical, and are encouraged to remain rather ignorant of the needs of others. The hunter/gatherer biological dichotomy seems to account for the phenomenon of intuition. Although this evolutionary explanation of gender differences is often used to explain the origin of women's intuition, it is oddly almost never used to explain intuition in both sexes. What about the necessity of intuiting the movements of the wild boar in the woods in order to hunt it down for dinner? Wouldn't that require *masculine intuition*?

Are Men's and Women's Brains Wired Differently?

On a strictly neurological level, it has often been said that the corpus callosum accounts for higher levels of intuition. The corpus callosum is the large, flat structure in the brain, loaded with 200–250 million contralateral axonal projections that connect the left and right cerebral hemispheres. It is rather like a vast superhighway running down the center of the brain permitting inter-hemispheric communication between the two halves. The communication between the hemispheres is important because of their vastly different brain functions. The left hemisphere specializes in speech, language, and logical reasoning, whereas the right hemisphere manages more intuitive tasks, such as face recognition, spatial relationships, and reading emotional cues. Many of these mental activities go hand-in-glove. Understanding what someone means when he or she tells you something is not just a matter of listening to his or her words, but also examining his or her facial expression. Thus, the communication between both halves is critical.

In 1992, *Newsweek* magazine came to the conclusion that women's intuition was directly related to the size of their corpus callosum. The article stated it was "[o]ften wider in the brains of women than in those of men, it may allow for greater cross talk between the hemispheres—possibly the basis for woman's 'intuition.'" This conclusion was based, at least in part, on the fact that women are better at multi-tasking (performing several tasks at once) than men and are perhaps better equipped to cross-communicate between the left and right hemispheres, thereby accessing larger amounts of perceptive information.

That sounded logical enough—except that it turned out to be wrong! The published findings in a 1997 issue of *Neuroscience and Biobehavioral Reviews* of a meta-analysis examining the results of 49 studies found that males actually have a larger corpus callosum, regardless of the overall size of their brain. The authors concluded that "the widespread belief that women have a larger splenium [the thickest part of the corpus callosum] than men and consequently think differently is untenable." More recent brain scans have found morphological differences in the corpus callosum of men and women, but no definitive conclusions have yet been drawn as to how this may affect thinking ability.

Women Have More Acute Physical Senses Than Men

I have come to my own conclusions about the origin of feminine intuition. My theory is based on my firm belief that intuition—as I have already suggested—is based largely on our vast network of sensory inputs. Therefore, the bigger the range of your senses or your conscious awareness of them, the greater is your intuitive ability. The more information you have available at your fingertips by which to judge your environment, the better you will be at making quick, intuitive judgments.

So, do women actually have better sensory equipment than men? The surprising (or not-so-surprising) answer is, yes they do! Woman have far greater sensory capacities than men, as a whole, and much of this may be due to the fact that sex hormones often enhance sensory ability.

Women's Sense of Hearing

As for hearing, women typically have a higher sensitivity to higher frequencies than men (Gotfrit, M.). Moreover, studies performed by researchers at the Indiana University School of Medicine in 2000 concluded through brain imaging that women listen by using both sides of their brain, whereas men just use one side. The researchers declined to make any conclusions, however, about the quality of the listening ("Men Do Hear").

In her book *Awakening Intuition*, Dr. Mona Lisa Schulz, a behavioral neuroscientist and medical intuitive, states that women actually use different parts of their brain when listening to words, depending upon where they are in their ovulation cycle. She explains:

> Studies have shown that the left brain is primed for mostly positive words such as "joy," "happiness," "love," and "cheer," while the right hemisphere picks up negative-toned words. It's been found, that before ovulation most women's ability to hear words occurs chiefly in the left hemisphere or the right ear. After ovulation, however, the right brain picks up the tempo. Now the women hear more words such as "grief," "anger," and "depression." This is more than an explanation for PMS. What's happening is that the brain is allowing women to hear things they don't usually want to hear. As they turn inward premenstrually, they may actually be getting more access to matter they need to hear but ignore during the rest of their cycle. Might this be part of intuition? (p. 70)

More recent studies undertaken by neuroscientist Dr. Robert Frisina and his colleagues at the University of Rochester Medical Center and the National Technical Institute for the Deaf in 2004 seem to now indicate that the hormone progesterone is to blame for the fluctuations in hearing ability in women. He compared the hearing of 64 women between the ages of 60 and 86, some taking hormone therapies of estrogen and progesterone, some taking only estrogen, and some control subjects taking nothing at all. His results showed the women taking the progesterone therapies scored significantly worse than both other groups. It would seem, however, the jury is still out as to whether women's ovulation-hearing is still better than men's, regardless of the fluctuations. What is interesting, though, is that women are capable of using both hemispheres for this sensory purpose.

In their book *Brain Sex*, the authors, geneticist Anne Moir and journalist David Jessel discuss various aspects of the sensory differences between men and women. They indicate that one researcher believes infant girls actually "hear" noises as being twice as loud as males do. With regard to auditory sensing, they explain:

> Girls and women hear better than men. When the sexes are compared, women show a greater sensitivity to sound. The dripping tap will get the women out of bed before the man has even woken up. Six times as many girls as boys can sing in tune. They are also more adept in noticing small changes in volume, which goes some way in explaining womens' superior sensitivity to that "tone of voice" which their male partners are often accused of adopting.

Women's Sense of Smell and Taste

Women have a much more acute sense of olfaction than men. This is due in great part to women's hormone fluctuations. The time when a woman's sense of smell is strongest is during her reproductive ages. Her sense of smell fluctuates in direct relationship to the infusion of hormones in her body and varies according to her menstrual cycle. When calculated with Day 0 of the cycle starting at the beginning of her period, the 14th day, which is the start of ovulation, marks the peak of her smell sensitivity. This coincides with the surge in plasma estradiol (in estrogen), which is also increased during pregnancy. It is well known that pregnant women experience all kinds of smell and taste disturbances.

In fact, in a survey of pregnant women reported in "A Longitudinal Descriptive Study of Self-Reported Abnormal Smell and Taste Perception in Pregnant Women," 76 percent of pregnant women reported such disturbances, including 76 percent experiencing increased smell sensitivity. Less commonly, 17 percent experienced qualitative smell distortions, and 14 percent experienced phantom smells.

My own sense of smell became almost unbearably sensitive when I was pregnant with my first child while living in New York City. It was so powerful that I could actually smell when and where a dog had urinated on the sidewalk from all the way across a busy avenue! I began to feel a bit canine myself!

Other studies have shown women use their powerful sense of smell to identify their newborn babies. One study showed that 90 percent of women were able to identify their newborn babies by smell alone after being with their babies for only 10 minutes to one hour. For periods greater than one hour, 100 percent of the women could recognize their baby's distinctive smell (Kaitz, et al).

A woman's powerful sense of smell seems to extend to all phases of her life. Emotions are strongly linked with body smells. In fact, a variety of emotions can be transmitted as sensory information without the need for language or even body cues. Fear, sexuality, and happiness can all be expressed by smell alone. Research has demonstrated, for example, that a panel of women was able to discriminate between armpit swabs taken from people watching "happy" and "sad" films. Men were far less skilled at making accurate smell determinations. Researchers in Austria have shown that women can detect the smell of fear in the armpit secretions of people who have just watched a terrifying movie (Ackerl, et al).

Perhaps even more interestingly, this ability to smell the scents of others—consciously and unconsciously—has a powerful impact on not only our own moods and behavior, but it also influences our physiology! Studies have shown that underarm smell of people can actually influence the moods of others around them (Chen & Haviland-Jones)! Children can distinguish between the smell of their siblings and other children of the same age, just as babies can recognize their mothers by smell alone. Other research has shown that armpit swabs taken from donor women at a particular phase in their menstrual cycle and wiped on the upper lip of a recipient woman (yuck!) can actually advance or delay the menstruation cycle of the recipient so it aligns with that of the donor (Stern & McClintock). Men apparently are sufficiently smell-sensitive to find women more attractive during ovulation and less attractive during menstruation.

If we can tune in, with or without conscious awareness, to the data in the environment that comes from smell, we can then "intuit" illness, happiness, sadness, fear, sexuality, family relationship, and probably a whole host of other traits without having any obvious or logical basis. If women have a more powerful sense of olfaction, then they will be—by definition—more intuitive than men.

As it turns out, not only do women hear and smell better than men, but they also have a stronger sense of taste. In the early 1990s, experimental psychologist Dr. Linda Bartoshuk and her colleagues noticed that certain test subjects seemed to have an especially elevated sense of taste. She labeled this group super-tasters. These people actually experience a far greater range of tastes than the average person. For these super tasters, some of the telltale signs are that the capsaicin burn in chili peppers is stronger; the quinine in tonic water is more bitter; and the salty taste is more pronounced in olives. So far, the tasting ability of humans has been divided into these three groups: 25 percent of the population are non-tasters; 50 percent are medium tasters; and 25 percent are super-tasters. So, here's the interesting statistic: An astonishing 35 percent of all women are super-tasters, as opposed to only 15 percent of men—more than double.

Obviously, if women can taste more subtleties in their food, then they will have more information about items that we eat and their chemical composition. Although this may seem like a miniscule piece of information to have, it can give us vital clues into aspects of our environment. Super-tasters are able to utilize this strange form of "knowledge" to their advantage. So, for example, a super-taster tends to rate fat as creamier than non-tasters and medium tasters because they are experiencing the physical texture as opposed to the taste. They also are more sensitive to the burning sensation created by chili peppers, ginger, alcohol, and carbon dioxide in soda.

Women's Sense of Touch

Did you ever think women were weaker and wimpier than men? Actually, women are literally more sensitive to pain because they are wired to experience more pain! They are significantly more sensitive than men to touch. According to the authors of *Brain Sex*:

At a few hours old girls are more sensitive than boys to touch. Tests between the sexes of tactile sensitivity in the hands and fingers produce differences so striking that sometimes male and female scores do not even overlap, the most sensitive boy feeling less than the least sensitive girl.

Women have a much lower threshold for experiencing pain. They react fast and more acutely to pain even though they have a higher threshold for chronic, long-term pain than do men. This has often been attributed to their female willingness to talk about their pain and not keep a stiff upper lip. However, this has proven to be a false assumption!

A study in 2005 revealed that contrary to popular myths that women are more sensitive to pain because they are not socially encouraged to be tough and stoic like men; they are physically wired to experience more pain. A report by Dr. Bradon Wilhelmi, assistant professor of plastic and reconstructive surgery at the Southern Illinois University School of Medicine, involved a comparison of tiny skin samples taken from the upper cheeks of 10 men and 10 women cadavers donated to science. A microscopic analysis revealed that the women had 34 nerve fibers per square centimeter versus only 17 in the men—double the number of nerve fibers. The researchers concluded that their findings favored a physical rather than psychosocial explanation for more pronounced pain perception in women.

Yet another interesting fact: Women can detect heat more easily than men, according to pain researcher April Hazard Vallerand, PhD, RN, at Detroit's Wayne State University College of Nursing.

Women's Sense of Sight

That gets us to the last of the traditional five senses and, yes, women have a better sense of sight as well.

In terms of blindness, blind adults are divided in half among men and women. However, blind men comprise the younger group—58 percent of those between the ages of 18 and 44, whereas blind women comprise the older group—61 percent of those older than 75. Because blindness often is a function of old age and women have a much longer lifespan than men, the fact that more women are blind when they are older does not come as much of a surprise: There aren't as many men around! The average life expectancy of a woman today is 79 years old, as opposed to that of 72 years old for men.

Women also see color better than men. Eight percent of men and only 1 percent of women suffer from some form of color impairment. However, in an article appearing in the April 28, 2000 *Science Daily* entitled "Map Makers Can Avoid Confusing the Color Blind," it was reported that one in 12 men has at least some color perception problems. Although only 8 percent of men are color blind, they constitute a whopping 95 percent of the 9,000,000 people in the United States who suffer from color-vision impairment! Less than 0.5 percent of women, or only one out of 200 worldwide, are born color blind. Of those people who are color blind, the vast majority (99 percent) are protans (red weak) and deutans (green weak). What this means is that, on average, women literally experience more color—shades, variations, nuances, tones, and distinctions—in their lives than men.

Interestingly, studies of male color blindness led scientists to discover that there exists an entire group of people who actually have *superior* color vision! Roughly 99 million women worldwide, representing 2–3 percent of the total population of women, actually see more colors than the rest of us. Most normal people are *trichromats* because they have three standard color-detecting cones in their retinas for red, blue, and green. These exceptional women, however, are called *tetrachromats* because they have four color-detecting cones. That means they actually see an entire range of colors—theoretically 100 million more shades of color that lie somewhere between red and green—that the rest of us cannot see! These colors cannot be described just as someone with perfect vision cannot describe the color green to a person who is color blind.

This condition only occurs in women and not men because the red and green cones are genetically located on the X chromosome. Because chromosomes often mutate over time, women—who all have two X chromosomes by definition—stand a greater chance of getting a double mutation, and this results in superior color vision. By contrast, men, who always have XY chromosomes and thus only have one shot at getting the vision chromosome right, have a far greater chance of losing a red or green cone, leading to color blindness. Interestingly, many scientists speculate that, in evolutionary terms, humans developed blue-yellow photoreceptors long before we evolved an additional class of red-green photoreceptors in the retina.

Color is more predominant for women in yet another way. Besides actually seeing more color with their retinas, more women see color in their dreams. Researchers have found that although 75 percent of the adult population reports dreaming in color, a much higher percentage of women report dreaming in color. Only 12 percent of the population reports dreaming exclusively in black and white, and recent studies show that number is decreasing. A 2008 report from the British newspaper *The Telegraph* states:

> Only 4.4 per cent of the under-25s' dreams were black and white. The over-55s who had had access to colour TV and film during their childhood also reported a very low proportion of just 7.3 per cent. But the over-55s who had only had access to black-and-white media reported dreaming in black and white roughly a quarter of the time.

Despite the fact that we spend an average of two hours a night dreaming four to six dreams (each lasting between five and 20 minutes), many people are under the misimpression that they don't dream at all! My husband, for instance, rarely remembers dreaming and when he does, he says his dreams are not in color. I, on the other hand, remember most of my dreams, I have a high number of lucid dreams where I am aware I am dreaming during the dream, and they are always in color. Strangely, despite the fact that 75 percent of the population dreams in color, only 25 to 29 percent actually *recall* dreaming in color. More men than women report dreaming only in black and white or having colorless dreams. I find the concept of a "colorless" dream interesting because it suggests the dreamer cannot recall whether the dream was in color or in black and white. This, in turn, suggests we are capable of experiencing the world without the visual element of color. What a strange idea!

Overall, however, I think I have shown that women are biologically wired so that they receive a tremendous amount of sensory information, much of it invisible (and often less important) to men! As a result, it comes as no great surprise that women seem to have a special line hooked into a world that is "invisible" to others. If you toss into this mix, the idea that we have many more than five senses, then it becomes conceivable that women may be more receptive to a whole host of other senses, rendering them more intuitive than men.

Exercise

Test your ability to accurately interpret facial expressions. Women almost always score higher than men on this. There are several Websites you can try *(www.youramazingbrain.org)*.

**C
H
A
P
T
E
R

8**

Lesson #8:

Pattern Blindness: The Antidote to Nonsense

How I First Contacted My Guardian Angel (Or Vice Versa!)

Do guardian angels really exist or are they a fantasy? The answer lies in how you permit your mind to interpret evidence of their reality. Like all psychic interpretations, the answer lies in which dots you choose to connect! You must learn to do it in an untraditional way, connecting seemingly unrelated bits of information, and cause-and-effect connections that seem impossible. Once you learn how to do this, a brand-new picture of reality will emerge—and it will astound you. Your guardian angel may emerge more real than you ever imagined.

I was once apprenticed to a psychic healer named Sue. She claimed to be a nurse and a chemist (although I had my personal doubts). She was a very unusual and strange woman with a high IQ who came from a gypsy heritage in Romania. Sue used to take me with her on her rounds to visit her patients, many of whom were extremely sick with terminal illnesses. I was encouraged to use my energy healing skills, and she gave me the gift of believing in my ability.

One day we got back to her house and she asked me, "Do you know who your guardian angels are?"

I told her, "No. Do you?"

"Sure. I talk to them all the time."

"Where do you see them?"

"You know, everywhere. The mall, shopping, grocery store—sometimes they make me nuts. They are always talking and sometimes I just need to come home for a little peace and quiet. But they know how to find me."

"Really?"

"Yeah, when I get myself something to eat, sure enough, there they are inside the refrigerator," she said gleefully. "They're all lined up in a row, swaying back and forth."

This seemed more *psychotic* than psychic to me, but in a strange world where I was just a toddler, I decided to keep my mouth shut and keep listening.

"Well, I wish I could talk to my guardian angels," I said wistfully.

"You can!" said Sue. "Can you describe them?"

"No."

"Just try."

This was another one of those situations where I felt absurd. How could I describe someone I had never seen or with whom I had never really had any experience? It seemed a bit flaky to me.

"Like what?" I asked carefully.

"What color do you associate with your angels? Are they male or female? What do they look like when you think of them?"

"Okay," I said very uncomfortably. "It's a woman. Her name is Daphne and she likes to wear pale lavender."

This was purely made-up, on-the-spot stuff. It seemed a little silly, but at least it was creative. I was always highly suspicious of people claiming to have the Archangel Michael as their personal guardian angel. It reminded me of people who did past-life regressions and always claimed to have been Egyptian Queen Cleopatra. Far too predictable—not to mention a fairly arrogant assessment of their own self-worth! And, if that's the case, then who were all those slaves and peasants in history who far outnumbered the kings and queens? It just irked my sense of logic. Further, I distrusted people who selected names for their guardian angels with pseudo Biblical-sounding names, such as Ezekiel, Jacob, or Seth, as if that somehow would bolster their standing in the spiritual world.

"What does she look like?"

"I can't answer that," I protested. "And Daphne is a ridiculous name."

I looked around her living room and my eyes fell on the tiny angel statues she had adorning her bookshelves and tables. I didn't think Daphne looked anything like them.

"I don't know anyone named Daphne," I said, "and I can't imagine what she is supposed to look like. The only person I ever knew named Daphne was a fellow student at Princeton. We both lived on the same dormitory floor. She was an African-American girl and played the violin. In fact, she was especially proud of the fact she was the only black person she knew who played the violin!"

"All right, that's good," said my teacher. "So how do you think you would recognize your guardian angel Daphne if you wanted to contact her?"

"I don't know!"

"What do you think?"

I was being pushed up against the wall—a giant wall of nonsense—but I was willing to play along for the sake of argument.

"I think the only association I can make with Daphne is that I would recognize her if she were black—or, maybe if I heard violin music."

"Okay, now you know what to look for."

Well, not exactly. Both of those options seemed pretty unlikely. I was the only white person I knew who claimed to have an African-American guardian angel and that seemed rather odd to begin with. And the real Daphne is, to my knowledge, still alive. Furthermore, I don't particularly enjoy violin music, so the probability of my listening to it was somewhat remote!

I left Sue's house and drove home. On my way home, I decided to turn on the radio and see if my guardian angel Daphne would somehow try to reach me through the airwaves. Not violin music, but maybe disco music reminiscent of the music the real Daphne at Princeton might have listened to in 1973. Now, I hate disco music with a passion. I don't like the relentless beat of the music and the cold, airy, over-mixed sound of the vocals. But I found some commercial radio station that only played disco music and forced myself to listen to it all the way home.

At any rate, I figured if my guardian angel Daphne was going to try to reach out to me in a way I would understand, then she would probably find a way to make the radio station play Sly and the Family Stone's "Dance to the Music." Why? No reason. There was no logic to this. It was the only vague musical association I could make to the real-life Daphne. Because everyone on our dormitory floor was black (with the exception of me and one other white girl because it was during the early days of racial integration at Princeton), we were always listening to loud '70's disco and R&B music in the hallways. "Dance to the Music" was typical of the kind of stuff we listened to. It was just my way of trying to test whether I had a guardian angel.

Naturally, "Dance to the Music" did not play on the radio. I was not disappointed—just annoyed that I had bothered to listen to disco music for a half hour.

When I got home, I turned off the ignition without changing the radio station, and went to bed.

The next morning I had to get up early to do some grocery shopping. I hopped in the car and turned on the ignition, and the radio was still blasting at the previous night's high volume. Except something strange had happened; it was no longer a disco station. Now it was a classical music station and it was blasting an exceptionally beautiful violin solo! I couldn't believe my ears. This was very odd. The chances that a commercial radio station specializing in disco would have morphed into a classical station overnight were pretty remote.

Furthermore, as I drove along, I realized that this particular program was not just playing any old classical music or symphony that happened to include violins. No, this was a program devoted exclusively to violin *solos!* Then I became faintly conscious of the broadcast station. It was WPRB 103.3 FM broadcasting from Princeton University! Princeton is an hour and a half away from where I live by car. Most university stations don't generate enough power to broadcast that far away. I had never heard this station on my radio before. It was just too bizarre.

Four days later, I went for a doctor's appointment and was introduced to his new assistant. Her name was Daphne.

In some very weird way, I figured my guardian angel had spoken. Not speaking in the normal sense of the word. I just needed to make the synchronistic connections in my mind—and that is a form of psychic hearing.

Several years later, I attended my 35th reunion at Princeton University. As I sat at a table by myself under the reunion tent, not recognizing any of my former classmates, I overheard one of two women sitting at the next table refer to herself as Daphne. My ears perked up immediately. I turned and asked her if she was Daphne and if she played the violin. She answered yes. What a wonderful coincidence, I thought, that the one person I would run into at my reunion would be Daphne! I smiled and told her I had actually written a section in my book about her as the inspiration for my guardian angel. I had not seen this woman for 40 years and had only known her for three months in my freshman year. All I knew about her was that she had played the violin. It turns out she is now a psychologist living in Southern California and still plays the violin. When I told her my story, she thanked me and her eyes were deep with gratitude.

Daphne became serious. "Now I want to tell you a story," she said.

"When my mother was pregnant with me, she had a very difficult and long delivery in the hospital. The night before I was born, she was in a lot of pain and in labor. In the middle of the night, a nurse appeared in her room and took care of her all night long. She rubbed her back, talked to her, told her she was going to be okay, and not to be afraid. The nurse wore a nametag on her uniform and it said her name was Daphne. I was born the next day. My mother was so grateful to this incredible nurse that she decided to name me after her. When my mother asked the hospital staff how she could contact Daphne to thank her, she was told there was no such nurse or anyone else on staff with that name. Daphne could only have been an angel!"

In other words, Daphne, the student at Princeton after whom I named my own guardian angel, was actually named after a real guardian angel! I guess choosing the name Daphne wasn't so ridiculous after all!

The point of all this is that when you allow yourself to accept and receive information about people or your environment in a new way, you can discover new meaning. This is a form of re-patterning. It amounts to a radical rearrangement of cause and effect of data that we know is unrelated in strictly logical terms. It is very important to understand how we, as human beings, are deeply unconscious of the patterns that we develop in our sensory and cognitive experiences and that ultimately govern how we experience the world. This is the first step in becoming psychic. You must learn how to re-pattern – and you can't learn that until you have first learned the origin of your own patterning biases.

Sensory Patterns and Relationships

One of the strongest biological drives in the human brain, right up there with pro-creation, is to create reason. It is critically important that we are able to make sense of our world. We need to be able to rationalize and explain phenomena to ourselves so we do not get injured or killed by the dangers that surround us. When we can predict cause and effect in a way that "makes sense," we are better able to make snap judgments and better decisions. It is important for the very survival of the species. This is why we have evolved into highly rational and analytical creatures.

Snap judgments and rational decisions are always based on our ability to remember patterns. For instance, like focusing the lens of a telescope, our eyes are able to distinguish the tawny bits of color of a lion's fur from the surrounding green foliage. We can *hypothesize* that a lion is hidden behind the bush because we are mentally able to guess or reconstruct the parts of the lion's body that are hidden by the bush. This is a kind of pattern-making and it may save our life!

Most of us have no conscious awareness of our addiction to patterns because we have relied on grouping bits of data together a certain way since birth. But the fact remains: Humans are addicted to patterns. We live by patterns. We swear by our patterns. Patterns enable us to make predictions about the unknown. Patterns help us to predict the future and understand the past. *Nothing really has any meaning at all unless and until it can be related to something else. Then you get the first step to creating a pattern. Once you have this, then you have a "blueprint" for future interactions.*

Our very first baby patterns are created by cross-confirming the data from one sense with the data from another sense. This is why infants ly-ing in their cribs looking up at a colorful mobile will try to grab it with their hands even though it is much too far away. They have not established depth perception. Depth perception is only understood by being able to cross-confirm the visual experience of seeing the mobile with a tactile ex-perience of touching it. The more we can cross-confirm our sensory data, the more it becomes an established "fact" in our mind. Think about that. Facts are the building blocks of logic. *Facts depend on cross-modal sen-sory confirmation.* What happens if you can't confirm one sense with input from another sense? Then we consider it to be "fantasy."

Let's suppose I am holding an unknown, alien object in my hands. How do I know what it is?

I begin to explore it with my five senses.

With my eyes, I see the long, green line with multi-toned, oval-shaped, splashes of bright red on one end. I can begin to solidify my sense of this object when I verify its essence with my other senses.

With my hands, I can use the tactile sensation to confirm that the redness that I see with my eyes is actually soft and velvety, and the green line is smooth and rigid.

With my ears, I can hear the sound of the soft red blobs as they brush against one another like pieces of cottony tissue paper, and the crunchy snap of the green line if I break it.

With my nose, I can smell the intense, richly perfumed aroma exuded from the center of the redness. The green hard line has a much more faint smell of vegetable.

With my mouth, I can chew on these colors and come up with a slightly bitter taste of chlorophyll. My senses agree on a single experiential event.

Eventually, I will give this sensory event a verbal name: a *rose*.

As you can see, the very last step in this identification process is to give the conglomeration of the sensory experiences a linguistic name. A single word, *rose*, is used to identify the convergence of all these sensory experiences. After a while, the word—all by itself—becomes a powerful pattern-maker, and, as I intend to demonstrate later, language can actually interfere in our true sensory experience of the rose! As we grow older, we cease to experience the rose with our senses—we merely remember the pattern.

This sensory event that I have called a rose will usually pop up in my brain when I try to recall it as a purely visual image. I see it on my mind's mental screen. This total sensory experience results in a visual image that I call a *mental map*. It is a shortcut tool used by the brain to recall the full sensory experience of the object. It is not a sensory map because it is no longer a product of the senses; it is a product of the mind. The mind has assimilated and cross-referenced all of the simultaneous sensory experiences involved in this event and remembers them together as a unit. The patterns are reflected in a mental image that is not purely visual, but also embodies memories of all the other physical senses.

Patterns That Destroy Psychic Sensing

One of the major reasons why many people don't believe in psychic sensing is because they do not believe it has ever happened to them. Skepticism is rooted in a belief that our senses are the only thing we can trust. It goes back to one of our major animal instincts: *seeing is believing*. We usually trust ourselves a lot more than we trust anyone else. It is extremely difficult to trust someone's experience of a paranormal or psychic nature if it contradicts your own fundamental beliefs about reality.

Speaking for myself, I know that I would probably have to actually experience an extraterrestrial space creature with my own eyes before I could trust that such a thing exists. Because I have no experience with aliens, I have no basis for belief. By contrast, in the last decade, I have had the opportunity to experience ghosts with all five of my physical senses (without any question of hallucination, deception, or mistake), so I have no doubt that ghosts do exist. Prior to that time, even though I had spoken with reputable people who claimed to have seen ghosts and had seen various types of evidence such as photos and EVP (electronic voice phenomena) recordings, I still did not believe in ghosts.

Seeing is believing. Right? The problem with this approach is that you don't realize that your brain can make you *literally* blind.

Four Types of Patterns That Change Our Perception of Reality

There are four major kinds of patterns that *literally* change our perception of reality. They are: 1) sensory patterns, 2) intellectual patterns, 3) memory patterns, and 4) language patterns. Patterns create the equivalent of an optical illusion. Patterns can cause us to think we see things that *don't* really exist or, alternatively, we don't think we see things that *do* exist out there. Psychic phenomena will usually fall under the second category.

Illusions of Sensory Patterns

Scientists generally ignore the study of meaning. It is that pesky subjective stuff that they don't like. They remain largely oblivious as to how it operates and also how it influences their rational experiments.

The one major exception to this general scientific dismissal was the development of the foreground/background theory in Gestalt psychology. Gestalt theory was founded in the 19th century and was developed based on sensory studies, and notably optical illusions. The basic idea was to understand the functioning of the human mind by examining the organizing principles behind human visual perception. The word *gestalt* comes from the German word *gestellt,* which means pattern or configuration. Certain things jump out at us in every situation and become salient, while other things become so unimportant that we literally don't even see them.

Hidden Color-Meanings

The sense of vision is the easiest way to demonstrate how our brain tricks us with its organization of sensory material. Let's start with color perception. Does color *mean* anything at all? Every sensory experience is, by definition, subjective. These color-meanings literally color or influence our impressions of the reality we see. So, how do we acquire meanings for color? Do we all share common color meanings, or are they a strictly personal experience? Are these meanings *intellectual* (such as a traffic code— green is for go, red is for stop, yellow is for yield) or are they more deeply engrained in our animal beings as *sensory* experiences (blue is cool and red is hot)?

I believe that colors feel different in terms of their sensory vibrations (remember the concept of sensory overlap of electromagnetic receptors?), and that we also learn how to associate certain feelings and events with colors. Generally speaking, I believe color-meanings are both sensory and intellectual, but most of us have absolutely no idea how we are being manipulated by our color-associations and their related underlying meanings all the time.

Marketers have long understood that complementary colors are useful for selling their products. Most of us know that every basic color has a complementary color. Red and green, blue and orange, and yellow and purple are all pairs of complementary colors. If you stare at one color and then look up at a white surface you will "see" a retinal afterimage of the complementary color in the same shape. Marketers figured out that if you want to sell your product, the best way is to put it in a color of packaging that is the complementary color of the item being sold. What happens is that the product color is actually temporarily "enhanced" by our retina! Of course, we never realize this is what is happening to us. We simply assume the product is more colorful than it actually is. The color gives it a meaning: richer, fresher, or more desirable. Cuts of red beef are more appetizing and appear fresher to us when displayed on bright green salad leaves. Carrots in blue bags appear more orange to the eye.

Apart from complementary colors, our brains are constantly making judgments about color and meaning. Context will determine color. Most fine artists understand that our brains will determine what color we see. The color will actually change depending on its context. For instance, green will appear brighter if placed on a dark background, grayer if seen at twilight, and bluish if placed on a yellow background. Green in a shadow is not even necessarily still green! Remember the lime green Vincent Van Gogh used for his facial skin color in his famous self-portrait? Colors only stay constant because our brain needs continuity and tells us what to see.

Strangely, the brain does a tremendous amount of color interpretation—which is a form of thinking—very quietly, unnoticed, behind the scenes of our conscious awareness. This is an unconscious *thinking* process. We don't even know we are doing this. One of the brain's most fascinating backstage feats is its ability to fill in missing gaps in our vision or even stimuli that seem like they *ought* to be there, but aren't for some reason. The *ought* is most interesting because it implies something rational and meaningful, neither of which are supposed to play a role in pure sensory stimulation or perception. Our brain regularly fills in gaps detected in our sensory field.

Tinkering With Upside-Down Vision

Did you know that you actually "see" the world upside down? Well, you do. You just don't know it because your brain has fiddled around with your perceptions so that you think you see the world right-side up. This is one of many examples of how the brain rethinks what it sees. It is constantly involved in an interpretative (thinking) function in relation to vision. The brain automatically takes the inverted upside down image presented by the retina of the eye and turns it right-side up so that our vision correlates with our experience of reality.

Fake Color in Our Peripheral Vision

Did you know that your peripheral vision only sees in black and white? Probably not, but your brain has, once again, deceived you without your knowledge. You think you see everything in your vision in color. But you don't.

There are no cones in the part of your retina that takes in your peripheral vision; hence it is a place where we have no actual experience of color. The retina of the eye has about 126 million little photoreceptors that convert light waves into electrochemical signals, which travel to the brain and give us the experience of sight. Of these, 120 million rods (providing brightness sensitivity) and 6–7 million cones (providing color sensitivity) give us the combined sensation of direct and peripheral vision. However, the vast majority of the color-sensitive cones are packed into a tiny area in the center of the retina called the fovia centralis. Around this area is a ring of less-densely packed cones, and around that ring are only rods. The significance of this tiny ringed structure is that we cannot see color in our peripheral vision because there are simply no cones around the outer ring.

Despite this handicap, we regularly experience "reality" has having color in our peripheral vision. This is an outright lie created by our brain!

Phony Vision in the Blind Spot

Still another example of the brain's independent thinking function has to do with blind spots in the eye. There is an area of retina that is obstructed by the optic nerve as it snakes back into the brain from the eye. In this area there are no light sensitive photoreceptors. As a result, everyone experiences a blind spot in their field of vision. The blind spot will show up in our field of vision, in both eyes, roughly 20 degrees to the outer periphery of our field of vision.

Tests using background color, background designs, and movement actually demonstrate that the blind spot will be "filled in" with whatever color or design "fits" the area surrounding it. Thus, the brain intelligently guesses what ought to be in our vision field. It creates the illusion that our visual field is seamless.

Sensory Tricks We Play on Ourselves

It should be very obvious to you by now that the brain has an insatiable desire to make sense of what it perceives. It is so desperate to create logic and order out of raw sensory data that it will actually cheat by cleaning up gaps and holes in our sensory knowledge so that everything appears tidy. The brain is so dead-set on creating order that it will disregard reality and invent an orderly perception.

Optical illusions are a fun way to examine the brain's propensity for making order out of anything. Optical illusions put the brain's parlor tricks and guessing games on obvious display so we get to actually watch our brain creating order and rationality. Optical illusions reveal the brain is thinking without language or conscious control. The thinking process gets laid out bare on the table.

Illusions of Intellectual Patterns

What is interesting is that the brain treats words (or what I call *thought-units*) in the same way that it treats sensory data. By this, I mean that the brain's compulsive patterning behavior spills over into the realm of our intellectual data as well as our sensory data. The brain fills in linguistic gaps in order to create a cohesive meaning, the same way it fills in sensory gaps to create a seamless experience of reality.

Over time, the brain becomes extremely adept at ignoring, adding, or modifying linguistic material so that the entire linguistic experience, verbal or written, will make sense. The analogy between sensory gap-filling and linguistic gap-filling is quite extraordinary. In both cases, the ultimate goal is for the brain to create an artificially seamless, coherent reality. Just as German philosopher Immanuel Kant defined, in 1781, the process of thinking as talking with oneself, *you could just as easily define sensing as thinking with oneself—minus the language in which to think!*

There are a number of brain games equivalent to optical illusions that illustrate this point. I will call these *cognitive illusions*. Try taking this test. Count how many times the letter F appears in the following text:

> FINISHED FILES ARE THE RE
> SULT OF YEARS OF SCIENTI
> FIC STUDY COMBINED WITH
> THE EXPERIENCE OF YEARS...

How many did you get? Most people count three, and the rare person can count four Fs. However, the correct answer is six because the brain has difficulty processing the word *of* in this context.

This task is obvious and extremely simple—yet we consistently fail! This is not a matter of intellect or vision; it is a matter of pattern-making. The brain has decided to only count the letter F when it appears in a sufficiently important word such as *finished*, *files*, or *scientific*. The lowly and common word *of* is treated with the characteristic humble invisibility of a domestic servant.

The brain organizes the world according to its expectations
of what it expects to find!

Try another classic test. This one may be a little easier now that you've been tipped off as to how to read. Is there anything wrong with the following phrase?

A

BIRD

IN THE

THE HAND

If read rather quickly, most people simply don't see the word *the* in the fourth line of the phrase. After having learned how to read in grade school, we all tend to assume that the word *the* is attached to a noun and will appear together with it. This assumption overrides the visual information that the word has already appeared in the preceding line.

In other words, the brain desperately wants to make sense of the sentence and has no qualms about ruthlessly and flagrantly eliminating a word just to satisfy this goal.

Within the written language, there is apparently sufficient redundancy of information that the brain is quite happy going along with the function of reading and understanding even with what might appear to be, at first blush, significant gaps in the written information. For example,

"You u_ders_and w_at is _rint_d her_ even _houg_
ever_ fift_ lett_r has _een r_move_, righ_?"

This little exercise, as pointed out by science writer Tor Nørretranders in his epic on consciousness, *The User Illusion* (p. 71), shows that the brain can function quite effectively even with the loss of every fifth letter. Because there is a "rule" to how and when a letter goes missing (every fifth letter), this means it will strike randomly on a given word. This suggests, in turn, that the brain probably has not been able to figure out some logical rule to this puzzle because every word will have a hole in a different location, although it may be able to piece together unrelated principles of basic grammar and word construction.

Without a context, the brain cannot make intelligent guesses about sense and experiences the data as raw sensory data. This is where a closed system of complexity reaches its maximum capacity to handle new, absent, or inconsistent data. It overloads and collapses at this point because its organizational rules cannot tolerate too many exceptions and possibilities. They are being pulled in too many different directions, making it impossible to create a coherent pattern. It then plunges into a helpless free fall of chaos. This is where "disorder" subsumes "order."

But then, let's take a slightly different example of written chaos. Is it possible to decipher what this text is saying?

I cdnuolt blveiee taht I cluod aulaclty uesdnatnrd waht I was rdanieg. The phaonmneal pweor of the hmuan mnid, aoccdrnig to a rscheearch at Cmabrigde Uinervtisy, it dseno't mtaetr in waht oerdr the ltteres in a wrod are, the olny iproamtnt tihng is taht the frsit and lsat ltteer be in the rghit pclae.The rset can be a taotl mses and you can sitll raed it whotuit a pboerlm. Tihs is bcuseae the huamn mnid deos not raed ervey lteter by istlef, but the wrod as a wlohe. Azanmig huh? Yaeh and I awlyas tghuhot slpeling was ipmorantt! If you can raed tihs sned it to yuor fiernds.

In this amazing little "nonsense" paragraph, which circulated for a while on the Internet, Cambridge University researchers discovered we can still make sense out of the text with words containing jumbled-up letters—as long as the first and last letters of the word were in their correct positions. I call these letters the "anchor" letters. They act as guideposts for determining what the other letters ought to be.

Strangely enough, the human brain is capable of re-scrambling the letters at lightening speed in order to make sense of the words. Just as it does when viewing an optical illusion, the mind has a fantastic ability to spontaneously restructure reality in a way that is meaningful according to its prior expectations of meaning.

How does this relate to psychic intuition? It should be increasingly obvious by now that psychic ability is not tainted by logic. But it should also be apparent that as we age and become more intelligent, the brain begins to hijack our perceptions. The brain applies logic where none exists and creates rationality where none exists. The brain seeks patterns in order to help us understand our disorderly impressions. This is how we unwittingly unlearn psychic ability during a lifetime.

Illusions of Memory Patterns

There is another reason why human beings are so addicted to patterns: It makes it much easier to remember an event if you can condense it into a pattern. The brain's natural facility for making patterns and superimposing them on reality makes the item, object, or experience much more *memorable*. If we didn't have patterns such as language or causal relationships, we wouldn't remember anything. Life would be one, long, endless blur of unique and incomprehensible events.

So, after the brain has created some nice patterns from reality, these events are stored as small, sensible chunks of data, such as strings or networks of words, and are committed to either short- or long-term memory depending on the perceived utility of the pattern. Our memory capacity is highly related to our brain's ability to make sense of phenomena and package them into tidy patterned nuggets that are easily recognizable. These pre-packaged meanings can then be dredged up from memory with relative ease because they are not intolerably complex.

What happens to the rest of the stuff that was too complex to fit into nice neat packages? We simply throw it away. It might actually surprise you to know the mind-boggling amount of information you receive through your five senses that is disregarded by your brain and lost forever. We are totally unaware and unconscious of this vast wealth of information that we have in our body.

Neuroscientist Antonio Damasio, known for his pioneering research into the more subjective realms of the mind, such as emotions, expressed his amazement at the pure enormity of the goldmine of information contained in the human brain that never makes it to the light of the conscious mind. These are the things we are doomed never to remember because they were never conscious to start with!

Our conscious minds are able to recall or remember only those things of which we were *already conscious* when we recorded them in our memory. That narrows the field significantly. In *The User Illusion*, Tor Nørretranders states that during any given second of the day, we consciously process only a handful of bits of sensory information. We remember only between 16–40 measly little bits of sensory information out of the grand total of 11 million bits that invade our conscious awareness every second! It is mind-boggling!

The irony in all this is that we may actually *know* more than we *think* we do. The trick is that the less we try to *understand* it, the more we know.

Of course, there is a practical reason why we try to be rational. There is a biological advantage to retaining such a small amount of information in our conscious mind. The brain and conscious awareness, according to Nørretranders, act as a kind of filter that allows us to function without being completely confused by all the data we have available to us. Think about how difficult it would be to store all that information in our memory banks! Our memory and consciousness are nothing more than a survival mechanism for our organism. Our brain decides what should or should not be significant enough to rise to the level of awareness. Memory is intended to help the localized needs of the individual and is not concerned with the larger picture of humanity or the environment.

According to Dietrich Trincker, a German physiologist, in a lecture he gave in 1965 at the University of Kiel, our consciousness filters out information so it can focus on one thing at a time.

Of all the information that every second flows into our brains from our sensory organs, only a fraction arrives in our consciousness: the *ratio* of the capacity of *perception* to the capacity of *apperception* is at best a million to one. That is to say, only *one millionth* of what our eyes see, our ears hear, and our other senses inform us about *appears in our consciousness*.

Metaphorically, consciousness is like a spotlight that emphasizes the face of one factor dramatically, while all the other persons, props, and sets on the vast stage are lost in the deepest darkness. The spotlight can move, certainly, but it takes a long time for all the faces in the chorus to be revealed, one after the other, in the darkness. (Nørretranders p. 126)

Psychics have learned how to "spotlight" the invisible characters and props that lie hidden in the dark backstage of the human theater of consciousness. They do this by lowering the threshold of their conscious sensory experience and intentionally rotate the spotlight onto areas that are less illuminated. They have learned how to remember information retrieved in the murky realm of the subconscious mind. Both of these abilities are trainable.

Most psychics and mediums find it difficult to remember what they have said during a reading. The reason for this is that they are generally in some degree of an altered state of consciousness. Some mediums go into a full-blown trance state and perform what is known as trance channeling during which they lose all conscious awareness. Others go into a light trance state—similar to self-hypnosis. Speaking for myself, I generally go into a light trance state, although I am fully conscious during a reading. I often find it very difficult to remember what I have said. Any loud sensory distractions will pull me out of this state. I often do not have words to describe what I see or feel. Without the benefit of language or familiar symbols, it is very difficult to capture the experience in a memory.

When exploring this state of mind for data, psychics and mediums cannot rely on the usual methods of memory "chunking." At this level, they permit themselves to experience and capture raw sensory data that has not been pre-processed or pre-patterned by the conscious brain. Without the benefit of pre-processed, "chunked" units of memory, it is *very* hard to remember what you say in a psychic reading. This is why psychics develop very unique, individualized, and other highly unorthodox methods and symbols in order to remember what they have sensed.

Chunking Memory

In order to understand how psychics memorize and retain data differently than the rest of us, you need to first understand the basic mechanics of how the brain controls memory. Try a little memory test. Attempt to memorize the following 12 letters by looking at them for no more than a couple of seconds. Then cover them up and try reciting the letters from memory:

CI APH DSO SIB M

In all likelihood, you weren't able to able to do it. Short-term, working memory generally has a small storage capacity of no more than five to seven items and allows for recall for several seconds up to one minute. The original research in this area was conducted in 1956 by George Miller at Bell Laboratories and led to the development of the easily remembered seven-digit telephone number system. However, a simple rearranging of the spaces between the letters creates "meaning" and dramatically improves our ability to remember:

CIA PHD SOS IBM

In this new arrangement, we have four chunks of memory: a spy agency, a doctoral degree, a distress call, and a computer company. Now we have mental images (pictures) we can associate with the otherwise-meaningless letters. This is a process known as *chunking* information. It involves sorting otherwise-meaningless data into groups which are more meaningful and therefore more memorable. If it's not meaningful, chances are that even though we experience it and have the capacity to remember it, we won't! Whatever is deemed "meaningless" becomes invisible to our conscious mind—and ultimately, forgotten.

We Remember Only What Makes Sense

The most fleeting type of duration of a memory is that of a sensory memory. Usually these occur within the initial 200–500 milliseconds of observing or perceiving the item with our five senses. Studies have shown that the retention capacity of sensory memory is only about 12 items, and the ability slips away almost immediately within a few hundred milliseconds. This becomes a terrible chicken-and-the-egg problem. The less we re-member, the less will be recognized as meaningful in the future. The less we see as meaningful, the less we remember. And so on. The end result is that our sense of the world is diminished.

The reason I bring this up is because it begins to explain the process of how only those things that already meet our expectations will be remem-bered. *We have an extremely low tolerance for remembering pure nonsense.* We have a much better shot at remembering the experience if we can or-ganize it into neat little comprehensible chunks based on already-digested, symbolic information.

Psychic and intuitive data often arrives in the brain in a *nonsensical* format that is, as raw sensory data that has never been reviewed by the brain. Consequently, it is more prone to be forgotten because the brain lacks the capacity to organize it according to recognizable memory chunks. Whatever is not remembered is deemed by the brain not to exist—and this is why psychic observations cease to exist for most people.

Illusions of Language Patterns

Language is really the mother of all patterns. Language takes what we have sensed, thought, and remembered, and puts them into symbolic form, called words, so we can communicate with each other. Communication by means of language makes us feel as though we have shared real experiences and understood one another. By the time we graduate from high school, a typical English-speaking person will know between 45,000 and 60,000 words. The more precisely we can communicate our experience, the better our vocabulary, the more information we are able to convey, the better the other person will understand us. This is how information is transmitted between human beings.

Of course, as we all know, language is only one of several forms of communication. It does not constitute communication between human beings in its totality. It is only a small subset. Other types of communication include body language, emotional language, sign language, written language, computer language, and non-verbal noises. Ironically, language, like consciousness, acts more as a limiting filter of experience than a magnifier or enhancer of experience. Language can only express a small piece of reality. One's *native* language defines, to some extent, what we think and feel. That is why, in my opinion, it is so essential to learn a second language. It allows us to understand the limitations of our own language by forcing our brain to relearn and re-sense what each word means. Loan words (for example, pajamas from Hindi, iceberg from Dutch, flamingo from Portuguese, safari from Swahili, talc from Persian, penguin from Welsh) come into our language from other languages because our native language has no way to express something. As adults, we tend to forget that language is nothing but an artificial construct. Language becomes an invisible structure. It is like the old joke about the fish who, when asked to describe everything in their environment, named everything except the water that surrounded them.

Each language carries a certain re-positioning (for lack of a better word) of one's experience of the universe. The nuance of a similar word in another language may be shaded slightly differently. Very often, the syntax, the placement of the word in a sentence, the use of a reflexive verb, the absence of a word that is normally used in your own language, will all *ever-so-slightly* alter your experience of reality. Generally, you never notice your own sense of reality until you are forced to speak in a foreign language, where you suddenly notice that you can't express some things at all and yet there are other things that have meaning in the second language that you can understand and yet cannot express in your native language.

The English Language

My native language is English. I am fluent in French and consequently am capable of understanding a fair amount of Spanish and Italian (although I cannot speak those languages). While in college, I also studied Middle and Old versions of English and French, which are virtually separate languages in their own right. I studied German (so I can also understand, but not speak, bits and pieces of Dutch and Yiddish) and Thai for several years. In law school, I rather unexpectedly got a good dose of Latin as well. Years of looking up words in the dictionary has also given me some basic concepts of Greek derivations.

The Spanish Language

In Spanish, the word for the subject of the sentence (you, me, we, they) is eliminated and replaced with a particular vowel on the end of the verb. (For example, the verb "to eat" results in *como* for "I eat," *comas* for "you eat," and *coma* for "he eats.") Technically, this is an example of what is known as a pro-drop (pronoun-dropping) language, where pronouns are eliminated and must be inferred from the context or verb conjugation. Suddenly, for an English-speaking person, the sense of self and of being present in your language and your self-narrative seem to slip away and disappear.

In psychological terms, it reminds me of my mother, a deeply shy woman despite her outward gregariousness, who will talk up a blue streak but won't reveal a thing about herself. She is absent from her mental monologue. She frequently drops the pronoun "I" from her sentences as if to make herself invisible to others. She will say things like, "Went to the store today. Had a great time. Love to you, dear." Her internal sense of being in the world is thus reflected in her use of language. Without a pronoun, most English-speaking people feel somewhat unimportant and lost. That is an example of an alteration in one's sense of reality.

The French Language

French has always been called the language of diplomats. As I have learned through many years of business dealings in France, as well as living there and communicating with my French husband's family and friends, the formation of thoughts within the framework of the French language is very linear. Sentence structure favors an expression of thought where you don't really know the full extent of the communication until you arrive at the last word in the sentence. Because the language is so long and linear in its construction, the expression of one's thoughts is often long, a bit pedantic, and flowery. For the average American who is used to getting down to business as rapidly and frankly as possible, doing business in the French language can seem almost intolerably long-winded, pompous, and somewhat artificial. The French take their time to express themselves to the fullest extent possible. For example, a typical example of an ending phrase in a French business letter prior to signing one's name—the equivalent of "Yours truly" or "Sincerely yours"—would be *"Dans l'attente de vous lire, je vous prie d'agréer, Messieurs, l'expression de mes sentiments distingués."* This translates roughly into: "While waiting for your response, I beg of you to agree, gentlemen, to the expression of my distinguished sentiments." The end result is that the French version feels different. It feels flowery, a bit theatrical, and uncomfortably insincere.

The German Language

The German language, by contrast, has always been considered the language of science. The most striking aspect of the German language is the incredible density of the words and, consequently, the density of thought. No wonder some of the world's best philosophers have been German! The German language has mastered the ability to put together a literally endless possible group of words to create new compound words. The way this is done is usually by gathering together all the adjectives, nouns, and verbs you intend to use in your sentence, then putting them all in front of the main object. This generally results in the creation of a massive, compact, and unique word.

Currently, the longest official German word (although there is really no such thing as the longest word because almost any German word can be continuously modified by adding additional elements) has 62 letters:

Rindfleischetikettierungsüberwachungsaufgabenübertragungsgesetz
Literally, it means: "Cattle marking and beef labeling supervision duties delegation law." New words are the hallmark of the German language. It makes sense that science, with its ever-changing repertoire of technical terms, would be embraced by this language. By contrast, the longest recorded English vocabulary word is a mere 45 letters by comparison with the longest German word, and is also a scientific term referring to a type of lung disease: *Pneumonoultramicroscopicsilicovolcanokoniosis.*

As an English-speaker, I have always felt that, when speaking German, my thoughts must be almost thought out in advance—the exact opposite of speaking French. My sense of reality while speaking German is compressed, condensed, and focused.

The Thai Language

The Thai language creates a completely different sense of reality altogether. As an Asian language, it simply does not share any of the traits or have the familiarity of most other Indo-European languages. Linguists believe that this mostly monosyllabic and tonal language falls under the "Ka-Tai" group of languages, which is believed to have originated in the area of southern China that borders on Vietnam. However, the origins of this language are largely unknown. The written aspect of the language, which utilizes an alphabet derived from the Khmer alphabet (อักขระเขมร), is modeled after Brahmic script from the Indic family (which includes Sanskrit).

The issue of pitch and tonality tortured me throughout my Thai language lessons. I lived in the perpetual fear of saying a perfectly ordinary and useful word (at least in Thailand) such as "water buffalo" with the wrong intonation, which would have turned it into a particularly nasty obscenity. (My husband apparently has similar apprehensions in English and is terrified of saying certain things in English with his thick French accent, such as: "Hand me that shit of paper please" or "Let's go for a walk on the bitch.")

As English-speaking people, we are constantly using inflection in our voices to express meaning. Our tone goes up to express surprise, down for disapproval, flat for lack of interest, up for a question, and so on. But you absolutely cannot do this when speaking in Thai, because it will wreak havoc on the meaning of your sentence. If you lift your tone at the end of sentence to indicate a question mark, you may actually change the meaning of the word itself! One of my earliest grammar book translation exercises went something like this (of course, this is the Anglicized version of the Thai alphabet):

> "May may may may.
> May may may may."

No kidding! This is not the written version of someone stuttering uncontrollably. This is a real sentence in Thai and translates roughly into:

"Is the new silk burning?

No, the new silk is not burning."

As this example illustrates, the word *may* can be translated not only a subject (silk), adjective (new), verb (burn), but also an expression of negative (no) and also an actual word used in lieu of a question mark or English upward inflection. Thus, the entire meaning hinges on the proper tonal inflection. One false move, an involuntary query, or momentary hesitation can change the entire meaning of your sentence. Scary stuff! Unlike German, the Thai words themselves are so short and simple they feel almost infantile to a Western speaker.

Another odd sensation when speaking Thai is the difference in time. Thai verbs do not change form in different tenses, such as past, present, or future. There are no words to express the past or the future. For instance, a Thai person would say "Yesterday I come." Different tenses are conveyed and understood through the use of adverbs, expression of time, or the overall context of the sentence. This was a rather shocking discovery for me. I had no way of saying, at least in a way that I thought would convey my meaning, something in the future like "I *will* go to the store." Somehow it had to be implied by other stuff I was saying within the same context, like "I need clothes. I go to store," or alternatively, "I go to store at two o'clock."

Do Thai people have a different understanding of time because of their language? Do they not have any idea of what the future is? Is the future or past not really important to them? Do they live perpetually in the present? I don't think so—although I profess I have never been inside the mind of a Thai person. They seem to appreciate the nuances and distinctions of time as well as any Westerner. At any rate, I believe this aspect of their language ever so slightly colors their *sensation* of time. When you speak Thai, you feel as though your launching pad, so to speak, is always from present time.

As these examples of Spanish, French, German, and Thai show, we may *think* we have our world totally under control, but really once you begin to explore other languages, you learn that your own *sense of reality* has been deeply shaped by your native language.

Exercise

Study optical illusions. See how fast you can find the second image and once you find it, see how long it takes to find the first image again. Go back and forth as fast as you can.

Lesson #9:

Beware the Double-Edged Sword of Words

Language is our most lateralized brain function. This means it is the brain function that is the most confined to a single hemisphere. For 90 percent of all people, language ability is located in the left hemisphere. (The remaining 10 percent is split equally between those who have it exclusively in their right hemisphere and those who use both hemispheres.) Language looms large over any attempt we make to sense reality in its purest state. It enforces certain set meanings and messages. It makes sure we see things the way the language sees them, and stamps out and eradicates any alternative interpretations. The double-edged blade of the linguistic sword is that it can shrink reality as much as it can enhance it.

Blue Pearls and Spiritual Truth

Let me give you an example of how I began to teach myself to un-pattern my senses, rearrange my perceptions, and, most importantly, find new words to describe my experiences so I could communicate them.

For many decades, I have experienced a tiny visual disturbance involving tiny, bright-blue pinpoints of light. It's difficult to say if they are visual or mental disturbances. They seem to lie somewhere in between the two. This happens only occasionally and is not obtrusive in any way; nor is it particularly memorable. The flashing blue lights appear on my mental screen with the faint ephemeral quality of a wisp of smoke. They usually last no longer than a fraction of a second. I spent most of my life vaguely realizing that I saw these little flashes of light but basically denied their existence. I never paid any attention to them. No one ever mentioned having a similar experience, so I just assumed they didn't really exist. I assumed (or rather, my rational, conscious, linguistic, left-hemispheric self, assumed) they were part of my quirky mind playing mental/visual tricks on me.

At some point, after beginning to study intuition and psychic phenomena, I thought I might try to identify these strange flashes of blue light because I was learning how to identify all kinds of other nebulous sensations. I thought perhaps they might be related to auras that psychics claim to see. I asked the members of my psychic workshop if they ever saw this kind of thing when they saw auras. No one had a clue what I was talking about, so I quickly dropped the subject.

I tried to mentally catalog these flashes of blue light in relation to other types of visual/mental lights. I knew they were not the same thing as the bright flashes of light, brilliantly shimmering scotomas, like those I have sometimes seen during a severe migraine episode; nor were they retinal afterglows from staring too hard at bright colors; and they were not the little scintillating white lights that occasionally appear when one stands up too quickly or digests lots of sugar on an empty stomach. They are most certainly not the same as drug-induced hallucinations; nor are they products of the imagination, because my blue spots of light are somewhat opaque and actually overlay the visual landscape. However, they can be seen in both light and dark surroundings, lending support to the idea that they are more mental than visual. They seem to appear sporadically and not in relation to anything identifiable in the environment or the physical body. They were somewhat baffling, but they did not rise to the level of a "real" experience for me. They remained in the twilight zone of seemingly imaginary projections.

One day I came across a passage in a book called *The Biology of Transcendence* by Joseph Chilton Pearce that absolutely astounded me. Pearce had apparently himself experienced something similar to my little blue flashes of light and he actually had a name for them!

A couple of weeks later, as I sat quietly at home, musing over what might be next in this marvelous adventure, I felt a stirring within me and felt for the first and only time an audible inner voice. As clear as if it came from someone sitting right next to me, I heard from my heart the words: *Will you give up all support systems and follow only me?* Instantly and emphatically some deep part of me all but shouted "Of course!" as though it would be ridiculous to consider anything else. I felt rather left out of the discussion going on within me, but with those affirmative words *Of course!* I experienced an explosive and ongoing shower of what in Siddha yoga is called the Blue Pearl, a tiny point of intense, electric blue light that just appears at random in our visual field.

Until I met Mukananda I had never heard of, much less experienced, such a visual effect—it is referenced in American Indian ceremonials, as I found out, as an affirmation of or granting of spiritual blessing. (p. 186)

Apparently, these seemingly random, internally generated mental flashes of blue light had actually acquired a meaning in other cultures. I have since read these flashes of light are quite common among people who meditate or are clairvoyant. The Swami Mukananda (1908–1982), an Indian saint and guru who brought the practice of Siddha yoga to the United States in the 1970s, discusses the significance of the Blue Pearl in his book *Does Death Really Exist?* He claims the blue dot, as he often calls it, is a sign of an awakened Kundalini and dwells in the crown chakra of the head where it resides as the source of all consciousness.

I was more surprised to read on a spiritual Website called *www. souledout.org*, the author of the site had grown, with time and repeated experience, to acquaint his own experience of these Blue Pearls with an affirmation of a spiritual truth. The author describes how he came to relate this phenomenon with a certain meaning. He clearly equates the process of giving the experience a label as the starting point for being able to understand its significance. It was only at this point that he began to equate the blue lights with specific situations.

Once I could name the experience of seeing the blue light, I started to notice when it came. It would come of its own accord. One doesn't invoke it. The blue sphere appears as both inner and outward, with eyes-opened visions. Sometimes it will come when I'm meditating or working in a group situation like a healing. Other times it will flash in my consciousness for no seemingly apparent reason. I see it in my head and with my eyes open. One never knows when the Blue Dot will come or whether it will appear to be inside or outside the head.

Now that I've been working with it for some cycles, I see the Blue Dot as an affirmation of a truth and that something spiritually significant has happened, or that I'm on target with my thinking.

I also had begun to notice, prior to reading about Blue Pearls, the instantaneous flash of blue light would occur immediately during or right after I had had a rather intense, serious, and generally spiritual kind of a thought. I began to notice that I also had red flashes of light from time to time; they were basically the same thing—instantaneously appearing like a small, whirling pinpoint of light—but in red. (I have never read anything that would explain the existence of these red flashes, but my hunch is they are related to highly charged or tumultuous emotional moments.) This was also a phenomenon I had experienced very faintly for many years, but never acknowledged to myself.

Interestingly, since reading about Blue Pearls, I have read that certain flashes of light called *phosphenes* can be generated in the occipital cortex when a person is subjected to a particular type of transcranial magnetic stimulation (TMS) involving single or paired pulses of electromagnetic stimulation to the brain. It occurred to me that our thoughts—by themselves—may be capable of generating tiny electromagnetic fields within the brain, causing neurons in the neocortex to depolarize and discharge an action potential, or a spike of electrical charge across a cellular membrane, just as they do under TMS. This would tend to confirm the theory that when altering our thoughts, we can actually see and sense things that would have been otherwise invisible to us. Moreover, it would allow us to reverse-engineer an intuitive realization by recognizing that a particular flash of light, for example, was related to a particular type of thought. Maybe this is why in our language we refer to a sudden intuition as a flash of insight. But this is only speculation.

My point here is that this phenomenon did not exist at all until I found a name for it. Giving a phenomenon a corresponding label, a linguistic flag, meant I could keep the experience alive in my consciousness through memory of the word itself. I was able to attribute an actual meaning to something that I could easily have gone through my entire life not seeing at all!

Most psychic experiences, because they are so confusingly subtle and contradict our "known" reality, never get a proper word or name to describe the experience. On the flip side, those that do get assigned a word, often have connotations that only confuse the communication.

Learning Language Like Helen Keller

In the last chapter, we discussed how language patterns control the logic of the brain. Language controls our experience without our awareness. Language is a double-edged sword; it can breathe life into a sensory perception that was previously invisible just as much as it can also limit the scope of a sensory perception and make it smaller than it is. *Language controls our reality and psychic observations are notoriously illiterate!*

Most of us don't remember *how* we learned our language. Perhaps the most outstanding example of how this process works was the famous interaction between deaf-blind-mute Helen Keller (1880–1968) and her teacher, visually impaired Anne Sullivan.

When Anne Sullivan, as the new tutor, arrived at the Keller's Alabama home in March 1887, she began to teach Helen sign language with her fingers. On April 5th, Anne took Helen outside to the water pump. She pumped water over Helen's hands and then spelled out the word "water." The sharp contrast and immediacy of the sensory experience (sudden wetness, coolness, and liquidity) was then equated with the inputting of the symbolic word. The connection between real and representational was made in that instant. The process of equating a unique experience with a universal symbol was not an obvious conclusion, but a learned, intellectual one. Helen recounted her experience in her autobiography, *The Story of My Life*:

As the cool stream gushed over one hand she spelled into the other the word water, first slowly, then rapidly. I stood still, my whole attention fixed upon the motions of her fingers. Suddenly I felt a misty consciousness as of something forgotten—a thrill of returning thought; and somehow the mystery of language was revealed to me. I knew then that "w-a-t-e-r" meant the wonderful cool something that was flowing over my hand. That living word awakened my soul, gave it light, hope, joy, set it free! There were barriers still, it is true, but barriers that could in time be swept away.

I left the well-house eager to learn. Everything had a name, and each name gave birth to a new thought. As we returned to the house every object which I touched seemed to quiver with life. That was because I saw everything with the strange, new sight that had come to me.

Thereafter, Helen went into a virtual frenzy, dragging Anne around the entire house, demanding to know the words for everything she could touch. Interestingly, although we tend to think that sign language for the deaf as being a visual and spatial skill that would likely be processed in the spatially oriented right hemisphere of the brain, it is in fact processed just like spoken language in the left hemisphere (*A User's Guide to the Brain*, p. 276). Moreover, studies on deaf and blind Japanese people have shown the brain processes language in separate auditory and visual regions.

In a sense, we are all like the young Helen Keller. At our birth we are deaf and mute to abstract thought and symbolism. We experience the world as raw sensory data without prefabricated meaning of words—with all the disorder and nonsense because language has not yet become the middleman to sensory experience. The difference between Helen Keller and the rest of us is that she remained a cognitive newborn until the age of 7, whereas most of us made that transformation soon after birth and quickly lost all recall of what life felt like prior to that time. Before language, there is only raw sensory experience.

What Color Is "Grue"?

Grue is green/blue combined. Some cultures, such as the Japanese and Welsh, cannot see the difference between green and blue, and have only one word in their language for these two colors. For years, researchers wondered whether these people saw color differently because their eyes had differently shaped retinas or they lived in a part of the world where ultraviolent waves traveled differently. Scientists have now discovered that we are all able to see green and blue as the same color! How is that possible?

In February, 2006, researchers discovered that our perception of color is actually influenced by the name we give the color. They found that subjects would routinely identify a swatch of color as either green or blue when it had the name of the color written under it—but only when it appeared on the right-hand side of a circle of color swatches where the left hemisphere of the brain was interpreting the color. Because the left hemisphere is the seat of language, it was completely influenced by the label given to the color. Strange as it may seem, these tests prove that perception is governed by language, not the converse! We tend to think that our senses always tell us the truth—but obviously this is not true. Our sensory experience can be manipulated, even altered, by the mere use of a word!

Scientists have long known that the left and right cerebral hemispheres literally and simultaneously think very different thoughts inside the same person. The fact that we all seem to have a single set of sensory perceptions, thoughts, or feelings is really just a fantastic illusion. Every human being is a complex internal battlefield of competing elements. The final victor ultimately represents what we tell ourselves to believe. We never really get to know the defeated perceptions. We are only aware of the winners. Everything else remains hidden behind the veil of consciousness.

This strange human dichotomy was made exquisitely clear by the famous so-called "split brain" studies done in the mid-20th century by Nobel Prize Laureate, neuropsychologist Dr. Roger Sperry. When Dr. Sperry tested his famous patient, N.G., a housewife who had surgery done to sever her corpus callosum to alleviate her epileptic seizures, she was able to see and identify the image of a cup when it was flashed on the right side of a projection screen. Yet, she strangely saw nothing at all when it was flashed on the left side of the screen. How was that possible? It became clear that the left hemisphere (controlling what the right eye saw on the right side of the screen) was able to see the cup because it could identify the object with the word cup. The left hemisphere houses the linguistic-processing and speech-making parts of the brain. These are known as Wernicke's and Broca's regions. The right hemisphere, on the other hand, saw nothing, presumably because the object (the cup) was linguistically unidentifiable (and therefore could not be verbalized). As a result, the image of the cup became indistinguishable from its background—invisible!

Other studies arising out of the split brain studies have revealed some of the most bizarre behavior ever exhibited by human beings. An example of this was demonstrated by a female patient of Dr. Kurt Goldstein (1878–1965), a German neuropsychiatrist. Dr. Goldstein noted that his patient seemed normal in all respects except for one small thing: Every once in a while, her left hand would fly up to her throat and she would try to strangle herself! During these episodes, she did not appear to be in control of her own hand. Sometimes Dr. Goldstein would witness a terrible struggle as his patient attempted to control and subdue her own unruly arm. Sometimes she had no choice but to sit on it in order to stop it from trying to kill her! It was not until after her death that it was discovered she had suffered damage to her corpus callosum from a previous stroke that had resulted in a condition similar to that of split-brain surgery patients. Because the two halves of her brain had very different ideas about whether she wanted to live or die, she literally fought with herself to the death!

How does all this apply to psychic phenomena? Once you begin to realize that we are not consciously aware of all that we experience because our left brain monitors our conscious reality with its verbal mafia, then you begin to understand what we are missing. Psychic ability is consistent with a right-brain reality that is able to escape and finally see the light of day.

The Brain's Frankenstein's Monster: Language

After we have had enough similar sensory experiences, a word-label takes precedence in our memory and we actually begin to forget the reality of the sensory experience. *Language begins to assume a life of its own.* Language, being the trusty tool and "right hand man" of the left hemisphere of the brain in which language is comprehended and created, is like a large, muscle-bound, bone-crushing, mob enforcer. Language does all this while giving us the warm and fuzzy feeling that it is our helpful friend, enabling us to label, categorize, and understand our confusing reality. It also pretends to give us confirmation that we have actually been able to communicate with other human beings and can know their very soul by talking to them when, in fact, we may not even be talking about the same thing! It grips us by the collar, threatens us with total confusion, tells us how much we owe if we want to survive, and must continue to pay out in the future. In short, language is nothing but a thug.

Despite its great power over us, I would like to show you the poverty of language when it really comes to describing reality.

Imagine a dog, for instance. What does the word *dog* look like? Try to see the word *dog* on your mind's visual screen. It is impossible to pin down the specifics of what a dog looks like because every time we do, the image will ever so slightly metamorphose into something different. The word *dog* represents every dog I have ever experienced with my senses or learned about cognitively from others. The word *dog* combines all the black, spotted, brown, white, golden, long-haired, short-haired, large, small, long-eared, short-eared, friendly, unfriendly, smart, and stupid dogs I have ever met in my life. It is simultaneously all-of-the-above and none-of-the-above. This is a physical impossibility in the real world. The word *dog* is only an abstract concept—a symbol—and refers to nothing real. The word dog is a mental spread sheet or summary of experiences, and can only be visualized in the mind as a creature with the characteristics common to *all* dogs—four legs, a tail, fur, mammal, nose, two eyes, usually under 3 feet tall, eyes on each side of the head, and so on. The variables, such as the color, softness, and length of the fur, length of the nose, color of the tongue, drool, running or walking, and so on, are eliminated from the image of dog.

What we have done is effectively condense all of our sensory experiences and memories of those experiences into a few very non-descript characteristics or traits. We no longer really remember the true total experience of dog.

By contrast, autistics seem unable to meld their sensory experiences under a single word. For them, the experience of "dog," for instance, remains strictly a sub-heading and does not contain intrinsic meaning. In her book, *Thinking in Pictures*, Temple Grandin, a well-known, gifted, autistic animal scientist, describes how her brain compiles the concept of *dog*.

> For example, my concept of dogs is inextricably linked to every dog
> I've ever known. It's as if I have a card catalogue of dogs I have

seen, complete with pictures, which continually grows as I add more examples to my video library. If I think about Great Danes, the first memory that pops into my head is Dansk, the Great Dane owned by the headmaster of my high school. The next Great Dane I visualize is Helga, who was Dansk's replacement. The next is my aunt's dog in Arizona, and my final image comes from an advertisement for Fitwell seat covers that featured that kind of dog. My memories usually appear in my imagination in strict chronological order, and the images I visualize are always specific. There is no generic, generalized Great Dane. (p. 28)

In Grandin's world, a dog is not an abstract collection of features that together comprise the concept of "dog." Rather it is an enormous and continuously growing picture catalog, or expanding PendoFlex file if you will, of unique dogs which she must review one-by-one in order to make a mental connection and comprehend the meaning of "dog." Like other autistic savants, Grandin appears to have difficulty dumping out useless information. Grandin maintains an increasingly huge mental library of every unique and literal event or object she experiences.

From the point of view of sensory accuracy and memory, Grandin's approach is incredibly rich. There is knowledge to be gained from studying her intriguing ability to hang on to very specific perceptions and observations about her environment—but it uses up a tremendous amount of memory storage capacity. From the point of view of synthesis and analysis of these perceptions, Grandin's thought process is greatly hindered by her massive collection of literal information. It slows down her ability to prioritize her observations.

If you want to learn how to improve your psychic ability, then you need to start by viewing every perception as a unique, one-of-a-kind, wordless event. Try to imagine that you no longer understand easy vocabulary words and can only understand the world literally. Force yourself to re-evaluate every experience as if it had never happened before. Practice remembering things without using words to describe the objects or events. Don't assume or attach any meaning to anything at all. Try to experience the world as if you were blind and deaf, like Helen Keller, or autistic, like Temple Grandin. Go back to the infantile experience of absorbing raw sensory data as if everything were a novelty. Pretend you are a baby lying in your crib, looking up at the shadows moving on the wall and trying to understand what shadows are made of or how they move. Don't assume you understand anything at all—because chances are, you really don't! Practice undoing your brain's patterns. Create mental anarchy. Only at this point does psychic ability begin to emerge.

The Under-Articulated World of the Senses

Physicist Brian Greene has said: "Experience informs intuition." But as I have shown you, our experience is dictated by the outer limits of our language. Our words transform what we actually perceive. Words can shrink or even change what we experience. The grue color studies prove this fact. This suggests a simple syllogism. Logically speaking, if *language informs experience* and *experience informs intuition*, then *language must inform intuition*. This seems all backward. Shouldn't our intuition inform our language? Shouldn't language be a slave to our sensory and emotional experiences? Unfortunately, the sad fact is that our poverty of language limits our sense of reality and, therefore, our psychic ability.

If we can see one million colors, why don't we have a language for all these colors? Think about the largest crayon box sold in the art store and you have almost the sum total of all color names in the language! In 1998, the largest box of Crayola Crayons had 120 different colored crayons. That year, the manufacturer added 24 new colors, beyond the normal rainbow spectrum, with unusual new color names such as Fuzzy Wuzzy Brown, Outer Space, Manatee, and Almond. Can you visualize these colors in your mind? Probably not. They are not part of our normal color language.

The industry standard for printed colors, called the Pantone system, originally had 504 colors, but has recently been increased to a somewhat measly 1,012 colors for three-color matching systems (RGB, based on red, green, and blue elements; or HSL, based on hue, saturation, and luminance), and roughly 3,000 for four-color matching systems (CMYK, based on cyan, magenta, yellow, and black elements). These colors are given identifying numbers, not names. Still, this does not even begin to approach the actual number of colors we see with our eyes.

Similarly, the spectrum of smell is as vast and equally, if not more imprecise as our understanding of color. As I mentioned previously, the average person can distinguish up to 10,000 odor molecules. There are seven basic categories of human smell. They have been loosely subdivided into the following major groups: camphoric (mothballs); musky (perfume/aftershave); floral (roses); pepperminty (mint gum); etheral (dry cleaning fluid); pungent (vinegar); putrid (rotten eggs). But these are enormous categories and seem hopelessly inadequate to truly express the range of smells we actually experience. Moreover, the words for the sources of the smell (such as mint gum) are most often used to describe the abstract smell itself; so smell and source of smell become merged in the mind. As a result, our personal experiences will dictate how we find a word to describe a smell.

A pioneering biophysicist and researcher of primary olfactory reception and prediction of odor character, Luca Turin is familiar with the nonverbal vastness of our olfactory experience. As a scientist and also author of a leading authority on perfumes called *Parfum: le guide* and *The Secret of Scent,* he has spent much of his career trying to create not only a verbal (highly subjective) language to describe smells, but also a scientifically established (highly objective) chemical lexicon. His well-documented struggle to bring verbal identification to the field of olfactory perception is well-documented in a fascinating book by Chandler Burr called *The Emperor of Scent*. Turin explains in the book:

> "It makes everyone nervous, smelling," he says re the vial, "because smell is such a strong sense." Turin gives talks on smell to scientific audiences, and the squeamish reaction pisses him off. The intellectual squeamishness, too. People will say, "But isn't smell totally subjective?" And I'll say "What the hell does *that* mean?" It's not more subjective than color or sound. (p. 11)

The problem of subjectivity of how we experience data through our senses is often disregarded by scientists whenever it suits them. Most scientific researchers are perfectly happy to make arbitrary distinctions in electromagnetic ranges to describe our senses—these ranges are, however, purely subjective cut-off points. This is actually a blind prejudice in the scientific world.

Take the example of the color green. We don't really bother breaking the wave lengths for green (which range between 500 and 578 nanometers) into even smaller units (for argument's sake, let's say we break it down to 500–523, 524–567, and 568–578 nm) to create "sub-greens." Green is green is green. We don't have word labels to describe any other more subtle variations of a *different* color within that range. Isn't this really part of the problem underlying the paradox of the color grue? We become illiterate and speechless when we try to talk about these very subtle distinctions.

Auditory sound suffers a similar fate. People from the Occidental world who are accustomed to the diatonic musical scale, for example, do not spend a whole lot of time considering the wave lengths of possible musical notes that might exist between the semi-tones in a typical 12-tone octave (C, C#, D, D#, E, F, F#, G, G# A, A#, B). Musical notes have been arbitrarily divided according to what frequency ratios appeal to our innate sense of harmony. We prefer to break up the infinite realm of musical sound waves into mathematical ratios of frequencies called harmonics. Thus, middle C on the piano vibrates at 264 Hz. whereas the next C one octave higher vibrates at exactly twice that speed at 528 Hz. The major fifth note in the C-scale is G (396 Hz), which has exactly a 2:3 ratio with middle C. And so on! All of the frequencies in the harmonic series of the octave are integer multiples of the fundamental note (C, in our example). We would never distinguish any non-integer multiples—such as a 3:1.7 ratio. There is no name for that "note." Those musical sounds that lie outside our neat and tidy little system of identification constitute our musical scale. It's the stuff that's there that we simply don't differentiate, don't label, and don't recognize as separate.

At least with the electromagnetic range, it can be broken down numerically, even if our ranges within it are artificial. The problem with smell is that there is no way, at least today, to even break it down into a numeric range.

However, with smell, it is a different story because it is based on chemical compounds in the air, and we have no common agreement on what to call or label certain quantities of blended chemicals. We have no mathematical or *quantitative* way to divide up types of smells into different categories. There is no equivalent of an industry-sanctioned color wheel or standard Pantone color chart to use as a basic starting point. There are no relational systems, such as ranges of light wave lengths, to use when describing smell. There is no tonal scale, as there is in music, equated with the number of vibrations per second.

If you can't agree on how to identify basic smells, then you have no way to prove or disprove how smell is received or transmitted to the body. There is no "tape measure" by which to distinguish between the smell molecules.

In 1996, Turin found this out the hard way when he tried to prove his vibration theory of smell perception based upon differing molecular frequencies. His fascinating theory suggests smell is created, at least in part, by the minute electrical vibrations emitted by the molecules of chemicals evoking smell. He proposed that electrons are exchanged upon contact and tunnel their way into the receptor sites in the nose.

His theory, which received an icy cold response in the scientific community, opposes the traditional shape theory in which different smells are presumed to be detected by the human body due to the chemical composition (shape) of a molecule that is capable of unlocking certain receptors in the nose, like a key in a lock, and then sending electrical signals to the brain, evoking the experience of a particular smell.

Turin's theory was that it was a catch-22. In order to propose a new method by which smell can be identified, you need to be able to identify (label) different smells. The problem was that when Turin tried to prove his vibration theory, he was unable to get his scientific colleagues past the starting gate of agreeing on what constituted certain smells! He had to show—in some agreed-upon convention—that similarly shaped molecules with different molecular vibrations have different smells, and, conversely, differently shaped molecules with similar molecular vibrations have similar smells. But he could not get other scientists to categorically agree that certain smells were different! The vicious problem of subjectivity had raised its ugly head again! He smelled the difference, with his finely tuned nose, but they did not.

In one of his early letters, he wrote to a colleague about his observation that the perfume conglomerates' smell laboratories he visited in Europe were unable to scientifically discuss smells because they lacked words for the smells.

I leave, struck by the dearth of collective intelligence in perfume composition owing to the lack of words: they can't really discuss things with each other, tremendous waste of intelligence. Amazing that the rate-limiting step in a field should be mere words, never thought of it, though I guess in science we're minting them all the time as we go along. (Burr, p. 121)

Words, as Turin astutely noted, form the basis of our collective communication of reality. Without word-labels, we have no science. Science is absolutely dependent upon some basic agreement as to how we describe our sensory experience in terms of quantity, and these quantities must be first subjectively determined and agreed upon. Without words, there can be no discussion, and without a discussion there is indeed a "tremendous waste of intelligence."

Psychic sensing has suffered a similar fate. Words just don't adequately describe the experience. Without words, psychic phenomena will remain forever relegated to the world of subjective experience. Science will continue to ignore psychic phenomena because it is not part of our verbal/linguistic reality. Scientists cannot make the fine distinctions in language necessary to evaluate psychic phenomena because they do not have the ability to recognize such distinctions in their own experience. The deeper problem, however, is that scientists are not even faintly curious about psychic phenomena because, for them, it does not exist. They cannot even identify or recognize the subtle distinctions in sensory experience that require words.

I love the comments of author Bill Choiser, a middle-aged man who suffers from a neurological condition called *prosopagnosia,* better known as face-blindness. Like other people who have this condition, he is unable to distinguish between people except by details such as clothing, beards, or hair length. To him, human faces all look alike. Human faces are as indistinguishable and generic as the faces of wolves, mice, or groundhogs. As a result, he is not interested in most television shows because he cannot distinguish between the actors and thus cannot follow a simple story line. He prefers not to watch TV because it doesn't make sense to him—rather like scientists who express no interest in psychic phenomena because they do not share the same level of sensory sensitivity.

As he has said so simply and profoundly in his writings: "Few people are going to be interested in the things they cannot distinguish."

Exercise

Practice giving words and names to phenomena that have no name (a certain color of daylight, the texture of water flowing over rocks, a telephone static noise, the feeling of just waking up). Find ambiguous things and name them.

L esson #10:

Skeptics Ignore Hidden Biases in Logic

The Birthday Paradox

My husband and I once had dinner in Manhattan at the apartment of some dear friends. Antoine and Beverly are both extremely intelligent people and highly successful in their respective businesses. Antoine worked in the software technology sector but had also founded his own investment banking firm, worked with many capital management firms, and was formerly chairman of the board of Loehmanns Holdings, Inc. and Eye Care Centers of America. His wife, Beverly, an economics major and Harvard Business School graduate, who has written a book about time management, is chairman of the board of Big Brothers Big Sisters International and was a former top-level vice president of Citibank. In other words, Antoine and Beverly are both down-to-earth, pragmatic types!

During this dinner, I began talking about intuition. Antoine surprised all of us by recounting a story about what had recently happened to him at the dentist's office. I had always assumed he was a die-hard skeptic and non-psychic. But he said he had gone for dental cleaning on one particular occasion. A new hygienist came into the room and introduced herself to him. He had never seen or met her before. Before she said anything, he had a sudden impulse to tell her that he thought he knew her birth date. He didn't know why he had this impulse or why he felt so strangely correct. The hygienist seemed a little taken aback. When he told her the date, she confirmed that he was right. He gave the month and the day, but not the year.

Our dinner conversation then quickly turned to the probability and odds of having guessed this woman's birthday correctly. Skeptics almost always dismiss any accurate psychic observation as mere coincidence or luck. Everything can be explained, so they argue by the law of probability. Beverly began explaining that Antoine's lucky "guess" was not so unthinkably unusual or impossible. After all, she explained, there are only 365 days and 12 months in the year. That immediately reduces the "amazing" quality of the information to something much more probable.

Anyone who has studied the field of statistics and probabilities will undoubtedly run across the famed birthday paradox. It is a textbook exercise that shows how probabilities are calculated. The bottom line is that if you gathered 23 people in a room (*assuming* no one has a birthday in a leap year on February 29th because that adds an additional day to the list of possible days in a year), the odds of finding two people with exactly the same birthday is strangely high at 50 percent! This high probability seems bizarrely counterintuitive. If you get 100 people in the room, the odds of two people having the same birthday are almost an absolute certainty—3 million to one!

But these odds contain all kinds of hidden assumptions. For example, if you change the rules of the game ever so slightly, the odds will change dramatically. If you have 23 people in a room and you want to know the odds of anyone else having *your* birthday, the odds drop from 50 percent all the way down to a measly 6.1 percent, or less than one chance in 16. In order to achieve a 50-50 chance of someone having your exact birthday, you would need to fill the room with at least 253 people. In other words, you would need 230 more people in the room to achieve the same 50-50 odds as in the previous example. Something about this just rubs us naturally the wrong way. It seems counterintuitive.

Those of you who are familiar with the laws of probability understand that what can sometimes seem like magic can often be explained by the normal rules of the universe. Although I will not venture to explain to you exactly how these probabilities function, they are all based on matching up potential pairs of the 365 days and 12 months within the given universe of the number of people in the room. But as these counterintuitive odds demonstrate, the seemingly miraculous ability to find the identical birthday pair in a group of people is really not all that miraculous after all. Beverly argued along these lines in trying to show that Antoine's lucky guess of the woman's birthday was really not that astonishing after all.

I, however, argued a different line of logic to my friends. I started out by explaining that if Antoine's initial "universe" of potential variables was limited to 365 days and 12 months, then perhaps Beverly would have a valid point. However, Antoine's potential universe of things that he could have mentioned to the hygienist was not limited: It was virtually infinite! He could have chosen to say anything at all—that she owned a white poodle, suffered from high blood pressure, was going to win the lottery the next day, was the middle child in a family of 10 children, had no prior experience as a hygienist. You get the idea. But Antoine's brain selected, out of this infinite range of possible subjects, a birth date. And his guess was accurate.

Many people, after seeing a psychic reading or listening to a spiritual medium's message from those who have died, dismiss the information as generic or obvious. Having tried this stuff myself, I understand how difficult it is just to get the information that is even good enough to seem generic or obvious. Getting something correct *at all* is not as easy as one might think.

This is all a very long way of explaining that psychic phenomena cannot be dismissed as nothing but wishful thinking or a desire to control the underlying random behavior of the universe. It is not so simple. We usually fail to take into account all of the hidden assumptions in a given situation and this erroneously tilts the equation in a certain direction. More importantly, our failure to really flush out these hidden assumptions is usually rooted in our own strong cognitive biases. These biases generally run so deep within us that we no longer recognize them at all.

Hidden Prejudices

Traditionally, scientists have always steered away from any research involving the evolution of "meaning." A "meaning" is the end result of a process of making judgments—and, God knows, this is subjective. This is a field of study that, as Dr. Oliver Sacks has pointed out in his writings, has long been neglected in neuroscience. There are no locations in the brain or neurological events, such as blood flow or electrical activity, that would suggest the brain has discovered meaning at a given point in time or place; maybe other things happen, such as decisions and judgments, but not meaning itself.

Meaning doesn't exist out there in the world. Meaning only exists in our minds. However, psychologists have assembled impressive lists of the ways in which human beings act compulsively to create patterns and organization out of random events, thereby generating a kind of *artificial meaning* to situations. This is how we organize the world and give other-wise-random or senseless events a meaning. Let me put it another way: The brain selects only certain bits of data from any given event. Then the brain sees a pattern or a shape from the data it has pre-selected. In this way, we generate a *meaningful* experience out of random events. These are known as *cognitive biases*.

Although I will not attempt to list the hundreds of biases that have been identified, I will mention a few that I believe are relevant to this discussion. These have a direct impact on the way in which we permit our-selves to experience sensory data. These biases are human tendencies to perceive the world around us a certain way that results in inaccurate con-clusions. These judgmental or cognitive biases were first introduced and developed by Amos Tversky and Daniel Kahneman in 1972, and devel-oped in their subsequent work, during which they explored the psychology of irrational decision-making.

1. *The Backfire Effect.* A tendency to strengthen our stated be-liefs when we are confronted with disconfirming evidence. A Republican might respond to a Democrat who accuses former President Bush of having lied to get us involved in the Iraq War by saying that the Iraq War was the only way to combat terrorism and ultimately it was the right decision. (Fails to ad-dress the initial complaint and only strengthens his position.)

2. *The Bias Blind Spot.* A tendency not to compensate or adjust for our personal cognitive biases or prejudices. A police officer states his belief that police officers need to receive higher pay-checks so they can entice more recruits to join the police force. (Fails to recognize his own self-interest in making a general policy statement.)

3. *The Confirmation Bias.* A tendency to seek or evaluate information in a way that confirms our own preconceptions. A scientist structures a scientific experiment to test whether Lyme Disease is a real health threat to the population by only examining urban dwellers who do not have any contact with tick-infested animals or plants. (Fails to create a truly objective experiment so she can confirm her own belief that Lyme Disease is not a real threat.)

4. *The Congruence Bias.* A tendency to only analyze or examine the most attractive hypothesis without testing other alternative hypotheses. The detective decides to focus his attention on the husband of a murdered woman as the sole suspect because the husband was having an affair with another woman, rather than examining the fact that muddy footprints left by the suspect were not the husband's shoe size. (Fails to test the alternative hypothesis that the husband might not have committed the murder.)

5. *Framing.* A tendency to employ an overly narrow approach to a problem by framing the issues too tightly to be representative of the reality. A cancer patient asks his physician if he got cancer because he ate processed foods instead of organic, whole foods. (Has framed the question of causation too tightly and fails to consider other likely influences such as the environment, genetics, lifestyle, and so on.)

6. *Illusion of Control.* A tendency to believe we can control or influence outcomes in situations even when we cannot. A gambler playing the blackjack tables in Las Vegas believes she can influence the dealer's hand simply by wishing for bad cards. (Fails to recognize that she cannot control the cards that have already been randomly distributed in the deck.)

7. *The Mere Exposure Effect.* A tendency to prefer what is familiar to us already and to dislike those things that are not. The mailman delivered the mail on his typical route, in which he knew the houses, dogs, one-way streets, and pathways, and automatically decided he would not like to take the route that would involve taking the highway, but would get him to his

destinations faster. (Fails to make an objective evaluation of his postal route because he already feels comfortable with the one he knows.)

8. *The Need for Closure*. A tendency to seek definitive answers because the sense of ambiguity is too uncomfortable for us. The woman decided she hated all tattooed, leather-jacketed bikers because they were violent, including one such biker who kindly offered to take her home when her car broke down and she was stuck without a ride. (Fails to change her beliefs about bikers even in the face of evidence because the result would mean she might have to accept that some bikers are actually good people!)

9. *Selective Perception*. A tendency to allow our expectations to affect and alter our perceptions. The student attended a lecture by a professor who was world-famous in her particular field of mathematics, and he was dazzled by the professor's knowledge, even though she failed to sufficiently answer many questions raised by his fellow students. (Fails to allow the reality that the professor is not that knowledgeable interfere with his admiration of her.)

10. *The Ambiguity Effect*. A tendency to avoid options that will lead us to unknown or ambiguous conclusions. A biblical historian refuses to consider whether the Bible's references to the Nephilim or Fallen Angels might have actually referred to extraterrestrials that came to earth in UFOs. (Refuses to consider a theory that might destroy or confuse existing biblical doctrine.)

11. *Anchoring*. A tendency to rely too strongly upon one's own beliefs when judging new information. The NASA space shuttle experts insisted that the heat tiles on the exterior of the shuttle could never have fallen off the shuttle during flight, causing it to disintegrate from extreme heat on re-entry into the atmosphere. (Fails to recognize the true cause of the disaster due to over-reliance on their well-established technology.)

12. *The Attentional Bias*. A tendency to neglect relevant data when making judgments due to a failure to refocus one's attention on the new situation. The public relations aide to the president of

the Fortune 500 company insisted to the media that the president was well-equipped to answer all questions by the media at a conference later that day, even though the president had just drunk an entire bottle of scotch at lunch and was passed out on the sofa. (Fails to recognize that, although the president is normally well-equipped to handle the press, his recent decision to get drunk would entirely change this situation.)

13. *Availability Heuristic.* A tendency to make a biased prediction by focusing on the most salient, emotionally charged outcome. Because the woman's son had begun smoking marijuana, she predicted that he would soon die of a heroin overdose. (Fails to understand the role of her emotions and then jumps to a conclusion that may or may not be relevant to his use of marijuana.)

14. *The Clustering Illusion.* This is the tendency to see patterns where none exist. A mother praises her child for always sharing his food with his little sister when in fact sometimes he accidentally drops food in her plate, he gives her food he doesn't want, or the little sister doesn't eat her own food. (Perceives a pattern of child's good behavior where none exists.)

All of these biases interfere with our unfettered ability to experience life in its ultimate richness. They represent internal patterning techniques that we use in order to make sense of the world. These prejudicial mental operations have the effect of honing down our total input into smaller, more manageable packets that tend to conform to our pre-existing ideas. They also give us a way to justify what we see.

In 1960, an English cognitive psychologist named Peter Cathcart Wason (1924–2003), who studied why people consistently make errors in logical reasoning, created his well-known "2-4-6 Problem," which demonstrates very clearly how human beings *seek* and *justify* patterning. Wason presented his subjects with three consecutive numbers (2, 4, and 6) and told them the three numbers conformed to a particular rule. He asked them to figure out this rule by generating their own groups of triplets. Few people ever correctly guessed the rule, which was: "Any ascending sequence of three numbers." More often than not, his subjects proposed rules that were far more difficult and complex. *Apparently, this rule was too "obvious" to be considered a rule!* Moreover, and relevant to our discussion of psychic phenomena, the subjects almost always only tested triplet sequences that they believed would conform to their hypothesis; *they rarely tested unlikely sequences*. This is an example of the Congruence Bias.

In fact, most scientific experiments are rigged to simply test a preferred hypothesis. This conserves time, money, and energy—and usually generates more government grants for future experiments. Open-ended experiments are far less common. Skeptics and doubters of psychic phenomena fall under this category and usually remain blissfully ignorant of their own bias. They rarely test for unlikely causal connections, such as those that are generated by psychic observations, and thus never confirm them. It is a vicious cycle.

Skeptics Remain Blind to the Influence of Biases

Skeptics claim they are merely staying loyal to the old "Occam's Razor" rule, created in the 14th century and followed by most scientists today, which states that the correct explanation of any phenomenon should be the one that relies on the fewest number of assumptions. The problem is that skeptics have twisted this rule when comes to trying to find an explanation for psychic phenomena. They argue that if an experience cannot be explained by physical phenomena, then it simply doesn't exist. Psychic explanations, they say, require too many assumptions.

Skeptics fail to see that they are simply succumbing to several psychological biases. They rely on their favorite explanation and fail to test anything else (the Congruence Bias). By accusing psychics of falling for the illusion of control, psychological bias (which arises when we think we can influence the outcome of a situation when in fact we cannot), skeptics have simply missed the boat. They have not even entertained the psychic premise seriously for a single moment. They never test it and they simply reject it out of hand because they already "knew" it was impossible!

One skeptic epitomizes this bias. Magician James Randi is a well-known debunker and skeptic-extraordinaire whose main claim to fame was allegedly to debunk Israeli psychic spoon-bender Uri Geller in the 1970s. Randi looks a little bit like Santa Claus with his fluffy white beard and mustache, round-rimmed spectacles, and bald head. But don't be deceived by his kindly outward appearance, because James Randi is a fearsome predator of mystics, paranormal investigators, energy healers, and psychics. To his credit, he has exposed some rather high-profile frauds. However, the problem is that he seems to believe that *all* such people are frauds.

For many years, his organization, the James Randi Educational Foundation (JREF), has offered a million-dollar reward to any person who can prove the existence of psychic phenomena. The problem is that the terms and conditions of such proof are completely controlled by him. Randi assumes that the lack of interest by psychics in taking him up on his generous offer proves they are frauds. To the contrary, in my opinion, there is simply no point in running through his rat maze for a piece of cheese that would only have been awarded if you had been a different animal at the starting gate! Consequently, there are very few psychics who have ever decided to take him up on his offer, and the few who tried failed miserably. Randi interprets this as more proof-positive that psychic phenomena does not exist.

Despite the fact that Randi does not understand psychic phenomena or how it functions, he has made a gross assumption that he is capable of *measuring* it. He uses scientific measurements that one would normally apply to phenomena in the physical world. As his Website shows, he will design the preliminary test, judged by his colleagues, and if the applicant is still successful at that point, the applicant will then go on to be tested by Randi's own protocols, conditions, and judges. This assumption is the height of arrogance! He is not equipped to judge psychic phenomena, and, worse still, he fails to recognize his own internal ignorance or biases.

The Confirmation Bias, otherwise known as the Tolstoy Syndrome, is heavily implicated in our inability to accept psychic phenomena as true, real, or accurate. Some of the most educated and intelligent scientists alive steadfastly refuse to accept or investigate such information because it so profoundly interferes with their pre-existing belief systems.

As the great Russian author Leo Tolstoy (1828–1910) once stated so succinctly:

"The most difficult subjects can be explained to the most slow-witted man if he has not formed any idea of them already; but the simplest thing cannot be made clear to the most intelligent man if he is firmly persuaded that he knows already, without a shadow of a doubt, what is laid before him." (*The Kingdom of God is Within You*)

The patterns we create in order to condense the wealth of information in our experience of reality, profoundly influence the patterns that we will see in the future. Our total universe is reduced by our expectations and beliefs.

The Law of Probabilities Contains Biases

The most common argument used by skeptics to disprove psychic phenomena is their argument that it is just a reflection of pure chance. Skeptics love to argue the law of probabilities. All things will randomly happen at some time or another; it's just a basic law of the universe. Whether these things happen to coincide with some psychic event or are caused by some psychic involvement is thus entirely irrelevant, they argue. True enough, we should be careful about engaging in wishful thinking about having an effect on events in the universe. However, one thing most skeptics don't seem to realize is that even their beloved law of probabilities is riddled with hidden psychological assumptions and biases! So, how can they be so sure that they are relying on the ultimate, unbiased authority?

In his book *Why Flip a Coin? The Art and Science of Good Decisions,* physicist H.W. Lewis describes various theories of probability and game theory when applied to gambling, stock market investments, war strategy, electoral and voting strategies, and dating. He discusses the famous Monty Hall Paradox, loosely based on the television game show *Let's Make a Deal* and the show's first host, Monty Hall. In this famous puzzle, a contestant is offered the choice of picking one of three curtains behind which is a free car. The contestant picks curtain one. The host then offers to reveal what is behind one of the two remaining curtains. The host reveals there is a goat behind curtain three, and tells the contestant he may now choose between either curtain one or two.

Here is the dilemma: Does he have better statistical odds of winning if he sticks with curtain one or switches to curtain two?

The answer is surprisingly counterintuitive. The contestant has dramatically better odds of winning if he switches to curtain two. The reason for this is that originally each curtain had a one-third chance of being correct. Once curtain three is eliminated, curtain two acquires a two-thirds chance of being correct—*not* a 50-50 probability with curtain one! The whole puzzle hinges on one basic assumption: The host's decision to reveal curtain three was not random—it was done to open a losing curtain without the car. If the host's strategy was never to open the curtain that had the car behind it, then the informational value has changed. Otherwise, the odds between the two remaining curtains one and two would have been 50-50.

The purpose of this entire story was to drive home my point that even the most seemingly logical rules of probability still contain assumptions and biases.

The bad news for skeptics is that, like any of the other human patterning mechanisms I have already discussed (sensory, cognitive, memory, or linguistic) even certain thinking processes, such as logic, contain all sorts of hidden assumptions. Logic does not determine reality, nor is it the king of clarity. The brain has already decided, in advance and without much conscious awareness, certain facts should count as important and others should not. These assumptions are based on past experience and, consequently, this arrives in our conscious awareness already *contaminated* by

Exercise

our brain's patterning prejudices and psychological biases. Skeptics are as guilty as the rest of us of being subjective with our facts.

Shuffle an ordinary deck of cards and turn them over. Guess whether the card is black or red before you turn it over. Try to feel the difference between red and black colors. Anything above 26 out of 52 cards is better than chance, and the more times you repeat the test, the lower the odds of success.

CHAPTER

Lesson #11:

The Psychic Senses Aren't Psychotic

Up to this point, I have demonstrated why psychic ability is a natural sensing ability that we all share. I have also tried to show how it is unlearned and dominated by more powerful patterning influences in the brain until it simply disappears off the radar of consciousness. This explains the bizarre fact that skeptics and believers *literally* do not share the same reality—and so when they argue who is right or wrong about psychic phenomena, they are both correct!

I will now switch my focus to understanding what psychic sensing feels like to the person who experiences it. I will try to convey the subjective experience of psychic sensing.

My Early Experiences as a Psychic Detective

My first foray into the psychic world came through my training as a psychic detective. One day, I was watching TV and saw a well-known psychic detective named Nancy Orlen Weber being interviewed. She seemed to have a good head on her shoulders and was very down to earth. Nancy was also a registered nurse and had worked for many years in a psychiatric hospital in a tough area of the Bronx. She has an honorary New Jersey State Police badge as a result of the good work she has done as a psychic detective. She seemed simultaneously incredibly compassionate, very bright, and street wise. It turned out she lived only five minutes away from me, and so I became apprenticed to her as a psychic detective.

Nancy also held a small class to teach psychic detective work on Thursday evenings at her home. This group became her advanced class after several years, and consisted of a core group of six women (myself included)from diverse backgrounds: One worked in a law firm, another was a director of computer technology, one was a Newark public school teacher, another was a concert pianist with the New Jersey Symphony Orchestra, and one was a corporate motivational speaker and airplane pilot.

We worked on numerous cases with police departments and law enforcement officials from several different states. However, we worked primarily with the families of victims, who seek answers when the police have run out of leads.

You may be asking yourself how anyone can get information out of thin air, or perhaps you are thinking this is all somewhat delusional or magical thinking when in fact we are doing nothing more than making good guesses. The best way to explain this to you is by giving a specific example of how psychic information arrives in the brain. It is extremely subtle, is often ignored, and took years of training—for all of us—to learn how not to discount and disregard our impressions as being nothing but foolish guessing or fantasies.

One particular evening, Nancy handed out a white, folded piece of paper to her circle of students. She told us to pass it around, not to open it or look at it, but simply to sense its vibrations. Then she told us to write down our impressions on a piece of paper. This is what we later came to call a blind read. We usually did a blind read before looking at any evidence in case.

I held the piece of folded paper in between my hands and tried to sense any vibrations emanating from it. I didn't feel any vibrations at all. Most people stop at this point. The average non-psychic person gives up because they don't feel what they *think* they are supposed to feel—namely, a pronounced physical vibration in their hands. Rather than let this lack of sensation dominate my conclusions, I decided to just follow my imagination and simply watched the images appear on my internal mental screen.

I found myself near a sloping hill in a lightly wooded area. The ground was covered with a thin layer of snow. There was nothing particularly fascinating about this scenery, so I examined the area in closer detail. There were lots of young trees and saplings. They were not crowded, but were spaced out a few feet away from one another.

I wrote all this down on my piece of paper. *Sloping hill; ground covered with a thin layer of snow; lots of young trees; young forest.*

I asked myself: "What am I doing here? Why is this important?"

My logical brain tried to answer the question, but I wouldn't allow it. The average non-psychic person will try to think his or her way out of this problem and find an answer that makes sense. I trusted myself sufficiently to simply sit back and wait for the answer to come to me instead of me trying to find the answer. Answers, in the psychic realm, often come in the form of images or paradoxes. You must trust implicitly that the brain is capable of clear thinking, even in the murky depths of your subconscious mind—and this is very difficult to believe!

I went back to my pseudo-sensory experience and my involuntary parade of images. I felt it was the scene of a homicide. Not a totally unreasonable guess because we generally investigated crimes or missing persons or animals. But whose? I sensed the presence of a young girl. I saw a blue scarf on the ground. So, I wrote down: *Homicide; young girl involved; blue scarf on ground.* My logical brain, which I had moved out of the driver's seat and sent to the passenger seat in the back of my brain, was still hard at work, but functioning now with less conscious awareness. It was telling me to look for evidence and bring it back to the real world. This backseat logic enabled me to set my intention like a flashlight searching in the dark so I could mentally scan the area for evidence while sensing the world of nonsensical images at the same time.

Out of nowhere, my mind conjured an image of a very large eyeball. I didn't know what to make of it becuase it didn't seem literal or real in the same sense as the rest of my wintery imagery. It simply stared at me.

I concluded it must be symbolic—but of what?

I asked myself this question and my mind answered back: "a witness." I interpreted this to mean that there had been a witness present at the scene of this homicide.

After I developed this thought and wrote it down, I was able to go back to my snowy scene. But now I realized, as I looked down at the snow-covered ground, that there were large drops of bright scarlet blood on the white, pristine snow. Worse still, my mind had conjured up a rather gruesome scene and there were clearly body parts—a face, hands, and upper body—partially exposed and sticking up from underneath the white snow. I immediately looked away in my mind. I did not want to see what I knew was there. I wrote down this information and decided I did not want to investigate further.

Remember: I got all of this from simply holding a folded piece of paper.

When we had all finished writing our impressions, Nancy had us go around the room, one by one, and read what we had written down on our papers. Everyone seemed to have radically different ideas and images. One person felt this was an event located in a tropical place such as Florida. Another felt a missing person. Another got images of an eagle. Another got a wooded landscape involving a road and a bridge. Another actually also got an image of a large eye, like me, but interpreted it differently as an evil eye.

Rather than dismiss these as irrelevant and inaccurate, Nancy explained, using both literal and symbolic interpretations, how all of these things were *actually* or *potentially* involved. I used to view this kind of evaluation as sloppy thinking, but I have since grown to appreciate that it is very important when beginning this type of work not to discount anything. Discounting and dismissing are the hallmarks of a logical brain and actually stifle intuitive data. A key to becoming psychic is learning how to trust your brain's ability to hone in on the correct answer without your conscious input. It seems too easy. It seems almost cheap! We have been taught that only conscientious thinking produces solid answers.

Nancy then revealed that the piece of paper was related to an active homicide case she was working on with police. It involved the apparent kidnapping and homicide of a man whose body had been dumped from a road at the top of a hill down a snowy slope in a lightly wooded area. Nancy did not tell us how the man had died. As it turned out, police suspected that the killer had an accomplice with him at the time he dumped the body.

Now, I gave you the complete collection of my impressions. Some were dead-on *accurate* (the homicide, description of the crime scene, and body partially exposed from under the snow), others were as yet *unverifiable* (they had not found a blue scarf), and others—at least in my estimation—were just plain *wrong*, such as my image of a "young girl" (although Nancy suggested I may have tuned in to the victim's young daughter). For anyone stuck on the law of probabilities, I would challenge them to hold a blank piece of paper and come up with half the accurate information that I did! Clearly, this is an example of a situation involving a universe of infinite variables.

Furthermore, Nancy pointed out that I had used the word *young* several times in my written impressions. I had used it to describe trees, the forest, and a girl. The sense of youngness pervaded my descriptions. Nancy smiled enigmatically.

She asked the person sitting next to her to unfold the piece of paper and to read it. There was a single word written on the paper in Nancy's handwriting: *Young.* But here's the thing: It wasn't a word. It was a name.

Nancy explained this was the name of the person that police suspected had acted as accomplice (or witness or eyeball) to the killer. Apparently, the police suspected that the killer had enlisted the help of this person when he disposed of the body and tossed it off the side of the road down the steep incline in the wooded area. They suspected that the accomplice's name was Young. Of course, my logical brain never once suspected that my overuse of the word young might actually refer to a person's name. But the sound of the word obviously filtered into my subconscious mind and reasserted itself enough times to make itself known. It is quite common in the psychic realm that you can come up with accurate facts and yet have no clue what they mean. This is extremely frustrating for anyone who likes to control what they think!

At the end of the session, everyone got up to leave and was putting on their coats. I pulled Nancy aside and said, "Can I ask you a question?"

"Sure."

"Well, I was just wondering if the victim died of a head wound to the left temple?"

I was too timid to actually use the word gunshot, but that's what I believed. I did not want to embarrass myself in front of the whole group by asking the question publicly.

"Oh yes," said Nancy very breezily as if my question was totally ordinary. "That was the first thing I got when I started working on this case. The victim died of a gunshot to that side of his head. But the police think he was shot someplace else and then brought to the place where they dumped the body."

How did I know (guess) this strange fact? While sitting and writing down my impressions, I became aware of the slightest little puff of air on my left temple. It was like someone whispering the letter P on that side of my head. It was barely strong enough as an impression to even register in my mind. It was just one shade away from being nothing but a thought. But having learned that I must be much more vigilant and observant, I track even the most subtle of feelings. It didn't make sense that a light, delicate puff of air would equate in my mind with a gunshot wound or with the case at all. My logical mind would have imagined that a psychic impression of a gunshot wound would be experienced by me as something sharp or painful. How else would you know it was a gunshot? That's the question. But something in my mind correlated this soft feeling with an illogical conclusion.

My point here is that our senses are infinitely subtle, and our minds do not capture enough of the truly subtle (or extra-spectral) sensory feelings to be able to understand them in the normal way. We have many, many misconceptions about our senses. We think we understand what we feel, but in truth, we really don't.

Psychic Information Comes Through the Psychic Senses

Traditionally, psychic ability has been generally broken down into five major sensory categories: *clairvoyance* (clear seeing), *clairaudience* (clear hearing), *clairsentience* (clear feeling or touching), *clairgustation* (clear tasting), and *clairolfaction* (clear smelling). Some people also include *clairintuition* (clear knowing) based on an indefinable, non-sensory feeling of certitude and knowledge without a source. They resemble—but are not identical to—our traditional five senses. The psychic senses may, or may not, utilize our real sensory organs, our eyes, ears, skin, nose, and mouth. It depends upon the intensity of the experience.

It is my belief that the psychic senses are not true sensory mechanisms but are actually a device used by our brain to communicate information to ourselves. What does that mean? Basically, the brain will select a particular sensory *format* to image (or create a mental representation) information it gets from both sensory and non-sensory sources in the body. Sometimes this format is visual, or it may come as auditory, olfactory, kinesthetic, or gustatory imaging in the mind.

Imagine each of your five real senses speaks a certain language. The eyes speak the language of visual, the ears speak the language of auditory, and so on. The *same* thought, idea, event, or object can be translated into many different sensory languages. Sometimes a thought will translate into visual images and other times into auditory sounds—but the meaning always remains the same. If you remember the chapter about language, you will appreciate that different information can be accessed depending upon the language you are speaking. I can say certain things in French or German that I simply cannot say in English.

The same goes for the psychic senses. I can get certain data more efficiently, say, in a visual format than in an olfactory format. Seeing shapes and colors will yield different information about an object than its smell—and yet both are referring to the same object. The psychic senses seem like shadow senses because while they don't exactly operate through the senses or sensory organs, they still speak a certain *sensory language* to our brain.

Sometimes these psychic sensory translations are really strong—as though we were a native-born speaker of that particular sensory language. When that happens, the psychic experience seems very *real* to us. It *mimics* the sensation of having our traditional senses experiencing an event. An example of this would be if we sensed the smell of lilacs, but no lilacs are in the room. The lilac smell is an olfactory language clue becuase we already understand the language of smell thanks to our nose. Our brain knows that this particular fragrance is linked to a particular purple flower called lilac. This smell language will then be properly interpreted by our brain, once we confirm there are no flowers in the room and clearly no physical source for our physical nose to make us think of our great aunt who used to wear lilac perfume. These experiences seem real to us and yet there is no physical source for the event.

Once you understand the psychic senses are only a *language* of the brain, then you can begin to accept the fluctuating relationship between the psychic senses and reality. Skeptics can then begin to understand and accept why psychics are not always dead-on accurate with their information. It requires a high level of interpretation (what appears green to one psychic may appear purple to another), unlike our regular five senses, which speak a consistent brain "language."

By allowing our logical brain to be temporarily turned off, we override our automatic patterning habits. We permit ourselves to tune in and experience subtle imagery and sensations that come from the psychic senses, which we would ordinarily discard. We enable ourselves to sense (see, hear, touch, taste, smell, know) new, unexpected, and seemingly illogical patterns in our world using this new language.

Exercise

Have someone find an article about a crime or missing person. Ask him or her to ask you some key questions that were later answered by police or investigators. You can try to psychically tune in to any details of the case—where the crime occurred, who was involved, a description of the perpetrator, the outcome. Verify it against the facts.

Lesson #12:

Psychic Seeing Is Brain Imaging

Claivoyance is related to vision. But this does not mean that psychics see anything at all with their eyes. Clairvoyance refers to the way information arrives in a person's brain. People who are clairvoyant receive information in a visual format. That is why they are sometimes called seers or visionaries.

Certain shamans, sages, and medicine men from more primitive cultures have long claimed to be clairvoyant.

According to Michael Harner, founder and director of the Foundation for Shamanic Studies, co-chairperson of the Anthropology Section of the New York Academy of Sciences, and author of *The Way of the Shaman,* shamans can literally see in the darkness. This kind of seeing, experienced by many shamans from diverse cultures of Indians and Eskimos from Mexico, western North America, the Canadian Arctic, the Upper Amazon, and Samiland (Lapland), is slightly different from either seeing with one's eyes or imagining with one's mind. The Iglulik Eskimo shamans, for instance, call this ability *qaumanEq.* It refers to an ability to see in the dark, both *literally* and *figuratively.* These shamans can "even with closed eyes, see through darkness and perceive things and coming events which are hidden from others; thus they look into the future and into the secrets of others" (p. 22).

I have spoken with spiritual mediums who also claim to have this ability to see in the pitch dark.

Our brain can somehow gather visual characteristics about something without the actual use or function of the retina in the eye. But what exactly does this feel like? The best way for me to describe it is by comparing it to the pit viper's ability to image its prey by tracking infrared thermal radiation with its pit organ, located between the nostril and eyes. This is not seeing with the eyes, but a kind of *sensing plus brain imaging*. This is why I am adamant that our imagination (the place where the brain images its sensory impressions) is not strictly fantasy-oriented. Our imagination is located at the crossroad of sensing and thinking—which is traditionally called perception. I will discuss this in a later chapter.

I was very surprised to learn in the course of my research that most famous mediums who give people messages from their dead relatives often don't really see the spirits at all! Despite this, they use language that *implies* they are really seeing something that is invisible to the rest of us. This unfortunate misuse of the English language causes us to think they are either magical or just plain nuts, and this, in turn, promotes justifiable skepticism.

Is Clairvoyance a Form of Hallucination?

Still I wondered about the difference, if any, between when a psychic sees something that is not real to anyone else and when a mentally ill person sees something?

The brain, more than the eyes, is responsible for creating these deceptive visions we call hallucinations. Visual hallucinations can be caused not only by organic brain diseases, such as schizophrenia and psychosis, but by lesions in the occipital lobe (responsible for the processing of vision) of the brain. They can also be caused by temporal lobe seizures, as during an epileptic fit. Other common forms of hallucinations are hypnogogic and occur just prior to falling asleep or waking up. Late- stage alcoholics can experience hallucinations with delirious tremors when withdrawing from alcohol. People with Parkinson's disease or Lewy Body Dementia can experience hallucinations. Approximately 30 million

Americans suffer from migraine headaches (me included), of which a large number experience migraines with an "aura," which is a state of experiencing bright shimmering lights, zigzags, wavy lines, hallucinations of familiar, scenes or vision loss. Charles Bonnet Syndrome is a condition where mentally healthy people with worsening eyesight, usually due to macular degeneration or glaucoma, begin to experience very complex and vivid hallucinations. Hallucinations may also occur in conjunction with the rare condition of peduncular hallucinosis, which can occur in connection with heart ailments and focal epilepsy.

We all tend to associate the word *hallucination* with mentally ill people. However, research has shown that hallucinations are actually a commonly reported phenomenon and occur uniformly in populations all around the world. According to some reports, *nearly half of the world's population* (39 percent) *has hallucinations!* That is an astoundingly high number. It also tends to indicate that hallucinations are part of the human condition and not purely a symptom of insanity.

If clairvoyance isn't a type of hallucination, then is it some kind of mental illusion or delusion? In the medical literature, hallucinations are distinguished from illusions. Illusions are defined as a "misperception of an external stimulus." In other words, with an illusion you get an *actual stimulus,* and with a hallucination you don't have any stimulus. With an illusion you *misperceive* the nature of the stimulus, and with a hallucination you *imagine* a stimulus where one doesn't exist.

Ultimately, I am not sure these are real distinctions. In the realm of the supernatural, it is entirely feasible that psychic sensory experiences—which would have to be presumed to be hallucinations under this definition because there is an absence of a recognizable physical stimulus—may be nothing more than a *different way of perceiving* a real external stimulus or one that is so subtle it cannot be detected by most other people.

Clairvoyance may just be a different way that the brain patterns its information. Any degree of perception, commonplace or psychic, is an illusion under the traditional definition.

Remote Viewing for the Military

You will recall that earlier I discussed the CIA's psychic spy, or remote viewing program that was established by Ingo Swann. Remote viewing is just a fancy term for clairvoyance performed under controlled conditions. Contrary to the rather occult-sounding term *clairvoyance, remote viewing* sounds very pragmatic, scientific, and more respectable. Many of the trainees in the remote viewing program became quite skilled at accurately identifying distant unseen and unknown locations simply by being given a pair of numbers or coordinates. Sometimes they were even able to see into the future.

One of the most famous examples of remote viewing occurred when the Department of Defense's secret remote viewing program was briefly allowed out of the closet and a presentation of the viewers' skills was made to four U.S. senators. In the spring of 1990, four remote viewers were asked to give a demonstration of their trained psychic ability to Warren Rudman (R-NH), William Cohen (R-NH), former astronaut John Glenn (D-OH), and Daniel Inouye (D-HI).

Remote viewer Gabrielle Pettingell began to describe an arid, desert landscape with a prominent factory or industrial complex in its midst. She described vile smells and the sensation of danger and chemicals. Her colleague and monitor during the session, fellow remote viewer Paul Smith, was petrified that she was way off target and couldn't imagine that the senators would want to test the remote viewers on something as commonplace as this type of target. The remote viewers generally worked on much more complex targets.

Senator Cohen held out a piece of paper upon which he had written the target. It was Colonel Qaddafi's secret chemical weapons factory in Rabta, Libya. In Smith's words, Pettingell had "nailed it" (Smith, Paul, p. 470).

Why does this kind of seeing seem so hit or miss? Why can't it be consistent like regular eyesight?

I do not believe it has to do so much with *guessing* (which is a type of intellectual conceptualizing) as it has to do with the actual quality of the mental imaging. These visions tend to arrive in piecemeal fashion. These images are often so vague in their shapes, contours, colors, and relationships that they lend themselves to a variety of different interpretations. They are a kind of mental pareidolia. It is like looking at the shadows in the moon and trying to decipher an image. People from one culture may see a man in the moon whereas those from another culture may see a dragon or a buffalo instead. The interpretations are different, but the facts are the same. The shapes of the shadows are inherently meaningless but the brain, using all its past knowledge of patterns, attempts to create meaning for the shapes. That is what clairvoyants and remote viewers do with the shapes that float around their mental screen. In my mind, this more likely accounts for failures to accurately identify targets in remote viewing and other types of clairvoyance.

Did Gabrielle Pettingell actually see the Libyan chemical weapons factory in question in the same way we might see something with our eyes?

I sincerely doubt it.

Nor do I believe she envisioned the factory with the clear mental precision of, let's say, a recent memory. It is much more likely she experienced only the salient aspects of the factory, visually and with the other four senses, focusing only on the boldest or most unusual details that stuck out in her mind. The best way to describe this kind of psychic experience is to compare it to a very old, faded memory or a vivid dream where only certain emotionally charged features stick out in your mind and all the other details slip away into a nondescript and unimportant background. According to the literature on the subject, remote viewing images most often arrive in a piecemeal fashion, like someone who has only several key pieces in a giant jigsaw puzzle and is trying to figure out where to place them in relation to one another without the benefit of the overall picture.

Clairvoyance is quite different from mental telepathy. Although both types of psychic abilities often share a visual aspect to the information, telepathy involves tapping into someone else's mind whereas clairvoyance does not.

In a sense, clairvoyance simply eliminates the middleman.

Pettingell's remote viewing exercise was most likely a case of clairvoyance. If Pettingell had read Senator Cohen's mind, in all likelihood, she would have accessed only the quality and quantity of information already experienced by the senator. She might have seen words of things the senator was reading or heard sounds of the name of the plant, the country, or Colonel Qaddafi—the words that were written on the piece of paper—but not the visual details of the plant itself—unless, of course, Senator Cohen had actually visited the plant or seen photographs of it.

On May 15, 1987, senior military remote viewer Paul Smith was tasked with a job, which he describes in his book *Reading the Enemy's Mind: Inside Star Gate America's Psychic Espionage Program*. Upon being given his co-ordinate numbers by his monitor, he began to describe what emerged in his mind as a series of images. He saw a warship with a sleeping crew, and then a bright flash of light, sound, and two cylindrical-shaped items dropped and left on the ship from a distance. The cylindrical objects were sent from a hot, desert area near the water's edge by a nationality of people different from those on the ship. Those on shore appeared in tan military uniforms with black belts with bits of red and green. Smith described a nearby city in an area that looked, in his words, like the Third World or like Greece with fewer trees (p. 350). It occurred to him that they might be speaking Arabic, but dismissed this thought as an unwanted logical intrusion into his clairvoyant vision because he speaks Arabic. He also felt there was a sense of ambiguous animosity toward the vessel and as if something was happening "accidentally on purpose." Then Smith described the awful sounds of the shivering, clanging, and screeching of metal as the ship shook. He felt the vessel was then transformed and was crumpled or bent. His monitor, Ed Dames, was apparently unimpressed with this information and no feedback was ever delivered. Smith assumed he was completely off-target.

Smith did not think anything more about it until he received an excited call the following Monday morning from an operations officer who asked him if he had seen headlines in the *Washington Post*. Smith opened up the newspaper and read the headlines: "Iraqi Missile Sets U.S. Frigate Ablaze, Causing Casualties" (p. 351). The warship U.S.S. *Stark* had been mistakenly hit by a missile fired from an Iraqi fighter-bomber while patrolling the Persian Gulf. The exploding cylinder he had seen in his vision turned out to be an Iraqi Exocet missile fired from more than 15 miles away from the ship and resulted in the deaths of 37 American sailors. The Iraqi plane then returned to its airfield just off the coast of the Gulf. The details of Smith's vision were strikingly accurate, right down to the color of the Iraqi uniforms and the "error" made by Iraq, which was, at that time, a friend and ally of the United States.

The strange and unusual thing about this remote viewing session was that it described an event that *did not happen until 50 hours later*. This was an unusual case of precognition or clairvoyance—a glimpse into the future—as opposed to remote viewing an event in real time but distant space. In fact, the target was not a usual target but rather what was called open search tasking developed by another remote viewer, Ed Dames, to describe basically "the most important thing for us to know right now." Naturally, he assumed that the session was a failure because it did not seem to relate to anything intended or known at the time. This actually points out another example of how real and accurate data was mistakenly disregarded because there was simply no way to verify an event that hadn't yet happened. If, however, the viewing data had been taken seriously enough to be considered potentially accurate like other types of intelligence, it might have been useful in helping U.S. forces go on a higher alert to prevent an attack on a ship in the Middle East.

These stories illustrate not only the ability for our visual imagination (psychic seeing) to accurately locate details in distant locations and times, but also bring home the importance of understanding the need for *patience* in verifying psychic visions. Cross-confirmation of psychically obtained information often takes time. Our regular physical senses are unable to confirm because they cannot pick up this kind of distant data.

How Can Clairvoyants See the Future?

To me, this stretchiness of time and space reminds of the feeling of sitting in an airplane. Suddenly you are big when you look out the window at the ground below and everything else—that you know is actually bigger than you in reality—is now little. The dimensions of everything else, *except you*, seem to change. This, in turn, tends to suggest that time zones come to the viewer within his or her own space/time position and are experienced by the viewer as being in the present tense. This idea that all time zones can be accessed from one's particular physical location in space/time suggests one of two things to me: either 1) all time exists concurrently, not linearly, or 2) our experience of our present-tense self exists simultaneously in all time zones. *In other words, either time is everywhere around us or we are everywhere in time!* Take your pick! Our conscious awareness of where we are would seem to be the only limiting factor to our experience of the whole enchilada.

The element of time, as explained by Barbara Ann Brennen in her book *Hands of Light: A Guide to Healing Through the Human Energy Field,* is quite differently experienced for clairvoyants. Ms. Brennen, who has a degree in atmospheric physics, is a practicing healer, psychotherapist, and former research scientist for NASA at the Goddard Space Flight Center. She has studied with American and Native American healers. In her book, she explains the phenomena of time as it relates to awareness:

The Native American culture, which didn't have clocks to create linear time, divided time into two aspects: the now and all other time. The Australian aborigines also have two kinds of time: the passing time and the Great Time. What occurs in the Great Time has sequence, but it cannot be dated.

Lawrence Le Shan, from his experience testing clairvoyants, has defined two times: the regular linear time and Clairvoyant Time. Clairvoyant Time is the quality of time experienced by clairvoyants when they are using their gifts. It is similar to the Great Time. What occurs has sequence but can only be seen from the point of view of being or experiencing that sequential flow. As soon as the clairvoyant actively tries to interfere with the sequence of events she is witnessing, she is immediately thrown back into linear time and will no longer be witnessing events outside the normal here-and-now framework.

The aborigine's Great Time may reflect the sense of simultaneity of all time as captured in the quantum physicists' notion of superposition (quantum particles can exist simultaneously in more than one physical location). The concept of different time dimensions may reflect different levels of awareness or states of consciousness regarding time. But the important point here is that they exist. Moreover, they affect the quality of the information that one can access about the environment. Clairvoyance, as we have seen, involves the interplay of time and sensory knowledge. *Clairvoyance is often just like ordinary vision but in extraordinary space/time.*

Our sense of time may be nothing but an internal brain wave.

Famed neurologist Dr. Rodolfo Llinás, one of the founding fathers of the field of neuroscience, has actually suggested our sense of time is intimately related to our biological organism. I had occasion to interview Dr. Llinás at New York University Medical Center, where he is chairman of the Department of Physiology and Neuroscience. He and I argued heatedly for nearly four hours about the existence of psychic phenomena and supernatural events.

With his Einstein-like shock of pure white hair and piercing blue eyes, and dressed in his white doctor's lab coat, Dr. Llinás was fiercely intellectual. He was like a gladiator who was ready to mortally wound his opponent upon finding the tiniest chink in his armor. He clearly would hold no prisoners in any argument. He was absolutely convinced that we are nothing without our physical body. All impressions and experiences arise out of and through the body. Spirit is an illusion generated by conscious awareness, which, in turn, only survives thanks to the cellular organization of certain physical matter. In other words, the sum of the human being is no larger than its parts. Cognition, or conscious awareness, is itself an illusion. We are fooled into thinking we experience things because our physical body coordinates sensory events and makes them seem as though they are connected together.

Dr. Llinás has proposed that certain cohesive electrical waves that occur naturally in the brain act as *unifiers* of all of our sensory inputs—the glue of consciousness. These brain waves fuse together sensory events and create a feeling of sequence, relationship, and organization. Our sensory inputs then become linked together, not by external sequence, but rather by our own private internal timer.

> Global temporal mapping generates cognition. The binding of sensory information into a single cognitive state is implemented through the temporal coherence of inputs from specific and nonspecific thalamic nuclei at the cortical level. This coincidence detection is the basis of temporal binding. (*I of the Vortex: From Neurons to Self,* p. 124)

This kind of global temporal mapping and creation of the sense of self is thought to be enabled by the 40-Hz. coherent waves that envelop the entire brain on a regular basis.

Under Dr. Llinás's theory, our lifetime of experiences—our self-narrative—are thus bound together sequentially like a paginated book. *These waves are thought to bind the neural events together so we are able to experience the various sensory inputs from the body as simultaneous and thus meaningful events.* The structure and function of the brain becomes a significant player in our experience of time. Without a sense of time, sensory inputs become jumbled up into senseless episodes and we lose a sense of self-identity as defined by our past, present, and future.

Now this got me to thinking: If time itself is nothing more than a relationship between sensory events in the body bound together by electrical forces in the brain, then it also stands to reason that time may exist very differently "out there" in the universe. Perhaps time isn't real at all. What if it doesn't exist and is just a brain-manufactured construct? Perhaps time is like color. Color isn't a property of the universe. Color is an illusion. Our world is colorless—like some of our enigmatic, colorless dreams. We know that color is nothing more than our brain's perception and interpretation of electromagnetic energies. Frequencies are colorless. The entire temporal organization of the universe may be vastly different from what we, as individual biological organisms, experience it to be. Maybe time does not travel, as we experience it, on a singular, consecutive, chronological line.

Who knows! Perhaps the aborigines were correct after all and the universe exists within a single, unified Great Time where all things exist simultaneously—a kind of mega-present time. That certainly would begin to explain how psychics, seers, and clairvoyants can access information in the past, present, or future—because it exists already.

Why can clairvoyants and psychics see into the "future" and others cannot?

Let's assume Dr. Llinás is right about how we experience time as a regular, tsunami-like brain wave that merges our senses together into consecutive "moments." What if our psychic sensory experiences never get fused together with these 40-Hz coherent brain waves because they are just too subtle to become welded into a unified concept of the present time along with our other physical five senses? Why would this happen? I would suggest to you that this may happen because our psychic sensory information rarely exists in our conscious mind. This kind of information flies below the radar of conscious experience. As a result, our psychic senses may not get chained to the biological rhythm of the human body and might be able to remain independent from our experience of time. This would explain how clairvoyants can accurately see into time zones that are invisible to the rest of us until our five senses experience them.

Exercise

Sit opposite someone and simply look at this person. Try to imagine what he or she looks like inside his or her body. Examine his or her skeletal, muscular, and nervous systems. Look at the major organs. Identify any health issues he or she may have by looking for anything that appears unusual in these systems. Ask for verification.

Lesson #13:

Psychic Hearing Is a Louder Mental Voice

Clairaudience refers to the ability to hear psychic sounds. This is the corollary to hearing with our ears and auditory system. Psychics hear many types of sounds. These sounds are generally experienced not as actual sound waves coming through their ears, but as something more akin to a mental thought. Of course, psychic sounds are experienced on a sliding scale and spectrum ranging from real-sounding to completely imaginary inside the mind.

Thus, it is a bit of a misnomer to say that a psychic is always actually hearing a voice of a spirit or a loud sound. It would be far more accurate to say that the psychic is simply receiving unidentifiable sensory data that has been translated by his or her brain as an *auditory* piece of information. This is not the same experience as hearing in the normal sense of the word. The brain plays a far more significant role in psychic hearing and sensing. Sometimes the brain turns up the volume on these experiences and they begin to resemble actual hearing.

The Strange Voices of Churchill, Washington, and Joan of Arc

Most people hear voices, more often inside their heads, and sometimes outside, but don't pay much attention to them because we believe they are generated by our own minds. There are some very interesting stories that have been recorded about externalized voices heard by some of the world's greatest leaders. These voices often gave them prophetic information about the future, and, to their credit, these leaders actually listened to the advice given by the voices.

In the fall of 1941, England's most famous prime minister, Sir Winston Churchill (1874–1965), ventured out during the German siege on London during World War II to visit, as was often his habit, the antiaircraft batteries during nighttime attacks. On this particular occasion, after having watched the gunners at their post for a while, Churchill decided to get back in his car and continue on, possibly to visit some more gun crews before dawn. An aide had already opened the car door on the side where Churchill normally sat, but Churchill ignored it, walked around to the other side of the car, opened the door, and got in.

Only a few moments later, as the car drove through the dark streets where all lights were extinguished by government order, a bomb went off close to the car. The car was literally lifted off the ground by the force of the explosion, onto two wheels, almost overturning, but fell back on all four wheels and then continued safely on to Churchill's next destination.

Churchill reportedly said later, "It must have been my beef on that side that pulled it down."

He meant that his weight on the other side of the car must have acted as a counterweight and stopped the car from flipping over. When asked by his wife, Lady Clementine, why he had not chosen to sit in his normal seat that evening and had deliberately chosen the other side of the car, at first Churchill said he didn't know why.

Upon further reflection, he said, "Of course I know. Something said 'Stop!' before I reached the car door held open for me. It then appeared to me that I was told I was meant to open the door on the other side and get in and sit there—and that's what I did."

To my knowledge, no one has ever suggested that Churchill was either psychic or delusional. So, then how do you explain his strange disembodied voice? The answer lies in the confirmation of what the voice told him. His voice accurately predicted the danger of the bomb and that was immediately cross-confirmed by his other physical senses the moment the bomb blew up. That made his voice a form of clairaudience. *The voice gave accurate information that was theoretically unknowable at the time.* The voice could not have been an inner voice or a psychological dissociation in the normal sense of the word, because the information given was not based on information yet known to Churchill.

President George Washington (1732–1799) reportedly also had some interesting mystical experiences about the future of the United States when he retreated to Valley Forge in the harsh winter of 1777. He repeatedly (perhaps up to four times) heard the voice of an angel say "Son of the Republic, look and learn." Was this the advice that tipped the balance of the Revolutionary War against the British in his favor? Unfortunately, we can't verify the relationship between his voice and its confirmation, but history reveals Washington as the clear winner in the war.

Joan of Arc (1412–1431), the 15th-century visionary female warrior, was another prominent person in history who not only heard voices, but used the information they gave her to guide her in her real life. Joan helped restore the uncrowned King Charles VII of France to the throne by leading his troops into battle and re-conquering French territory that had been taken by the English and their allies, the rival French Burgundian troops, during the Hundred Years' War.

What is so unusual about Joan's case is that we actually have a very detailed record of how and when she heard these voices.

After her capture and imprisonment by the Burgundian troops during a skirmish at Compiegne on May 23, 1430, Joan was turned over to the English and put on public trial. The transcripts are from the public and private so-called Condemnation Trial that took place in 1431 and consisted of six public examinations and nine private examinations during which Joan took the witness stand in her own defense because she had been denied legal counsel. The transcripts of these interrogations between Joan and the Assessors are quite fascinating because they reveal the attempts by Joan's interrogators to flush out all the facts relating to her ability to hear celestial voices, which she claimed to have guided her to meet with the King of France and convince him to allow her, a naïve young farm girl and daughter of a village tax collector, to lead his armies into battle.

The Assessors wanted to know whose voices spoke to her; if she saw their faces; what distance was she standing from a particular angel; if the angel's crown had a good odor; how tall the Angel was; how she could be sure it was the language of the angels; if the Voices counseled her in all acts of warfare; if the Voices told her about her future; if they designed her coat of arms on her standard; how old Saint Catherine and Saint Margaret were; what their clothing looked like; if they hated the English; if they had anything between their hair and their crowns; if Joan kissed them, if so, where, and if she felt warmth from their bodies; how she recognized the face of Saint Michael; if he was naked or clothed; if he had hair; if they came only when she called upon them or by themselves; if they appeared with light; what they told her about the outcome of her trial; if she actually saw angels with her eyes; if anyone else, such as the King, heard the Voices; if they physically touched her; and so on.

In the third public examination, held on February 24, 1431, the Assessors seemed even more anxious to determine the cause of Joan's voices in a kind of amateur, psychoanalytic way. Joan continued to hear her voices even while she was imprisoned during her trial.

How long is it since you have had food and drink?

Since yesterday afternoon.

How long is it since you heard your Voices?

I heard them yesterday and today.

At what hour yesterday did you hear them?

Yesterday I heard them three times—once in the morning, once at Vespers, and again when the Ave Maria rang in the evening. I have even heard them oftener than that.

What were you doing yesterday morning when the Voice came to you?

I was asleep: the Voice awoke me.

Was it by touching you on the arm?

It awoke me without touching me.

Was it in your room?

Not so far as I know, but in the castle.

Did you thank it? And did you go on your knees?

I did thank it. I was sitting on the bed; I joined my hands; I implored its help. The Voice said to me: "Answer boldly." I asked advice as to how I should answer, begging it to entreat for this the counsel of the Lord. The Voice said to me: "Answer boldly; God will help thee." Before I had prayed it to give me counsel, it said to me several words I could not readily understand. After I was awake, it said to me: "Answer boldly."

From this testimony, we can begin to understand a great deal about the subjective and objective nature of the Voices. The Voices were probably not a result of food deprivation because Joan was apparently eating her meals during her imprisonment. We know today, for example, that bad nutrition can result in low levels of certain vitamins. A deficiency in vitamins B1, B3, and B12 can cause auditory hallucinations, including tinnitus or ringing in the ears, as well as other neurological disorders. Joan's Voices coincided with the three major prayer times during the day, which suggests a possible psychological motive for her to create her own interior voices. We also know she did not experience any sense of physical touch from her spirits with whom she spoke. Interestingly, Joan heard the Voices in her sleep, when waking up, and while she was wide awake. They had a spatial location quite distant from Joan. They weren't inside her head or even in the same room with her because she heard them coming from elsewhere inside the castle. The Voices repeated their instructions several times (this makes one think more of the symptoms of mental illness) and were occasionally incomprehensible.

Ultimately, what can we say about her Voices? Did Joan of Arc suffer from some sort of organic brain disease or mental illness? It is possible. Her Voices might have been schizophrenic auditory hallucinations or the result of temporal lobe seizures. The fact that her Voices came from a location outside her head; were repetitive, sometimes incomprehensible, male and female, and pleasant; and gave unusual commands, would all be consistent with modern studies of the subjective experiences of schizophrenics.

Was she delusional? This is also possible. Her psychological profile indicates Joan was a deeply pious and religious person. The fact she claimed her Voices were those of angels and saints would suggest she might have been seeking some kind of spiritual wish-fulfillment. However, Joan's background doesn't suggest any particularly odd desire to achieve fame or recognition, act or dress like a man, or that she might have had a death wish by fighting the English. Therefore, it seems unlikely that the urging by her Voices to find the King of France and convince him to let her lead his troops into battle was the verbalization of some kind of subconscious psychological desire.

Regardless of the physiological or psychiatric origin of the Voices, were they psychic? Yes, this is also possible. The voices gave impossibly accurate information that was later confirmed. A person can be both psychic *and* psychotic.

Hearing Voices That Offer Life-Saving Advice

By my definition of psychic, I am suggesting that the act of hearing things that cannot be heard or experienced by others is actually rather common in all people, not just those with brain dysfunction. It is only *unless and until* these auditory "hallucinations" can be later verified by some other means that the act of sensing becomes truly psychic. It is the ability to sense real events or objects that are normally *distant in terms of space or time* that makes sensing psychic. As you can easily see, this creates a very thin (or even non-existent) line between the predictions made with normal sensing and the extraordinary predictions made by psychic sensing.

Let me give you some other good examples of what I mean by psychic hearing.

Remote viewer Ingo Swann had several vivid auditory experiences that he recounted in his writings that qualify as psychic under my definition. The most striking experience occurred while Ingo was stationed with the U.S. army in Korea right after the Korean War. At that time, Ingo's military duties involved helping U.S. officials in various aspects of protocol during monthly discussions between U.S. and North and South Korean officials held in Kaesong, a town located in the demilitarized zone. The meetings were held in one of the pre-fabricated buildings constructed along this zone, and soldiers on both sides of the zone were instructed to engage in a total cease-fire while meetings were being held. There was always the fear of assassination during these meetings and consequently everyone was given assigned seating and instructed not to stand up under any circumstances unless duly authorized.

Swann described his experience while attending one of these tense meetings.

I had been in my assigned chair at the end of the second row of "observers" for about five minutes after the meeting-confrontation had begun. Only the principals at the table were permitted to speak and then only in accord with items on the agenda, and according to their rank. I was very surprised, therefore, when I heard someone behind me say: "Get up, get up now." This was not just a whisper. I heard it as a high-volume command.

I stood up, and in doing so realized that there was no one behind me at all. The eyes of everyone in the room turned toward me. All conversation stopped, and hands reached for guns.

At that moment there was, in quick succession, a pop, and a thung. A bullet ripped through the prefab wall and hit the back of the chair where I had been sitting, striking right where my heart would have been if I had remained seated.

The North Koreans stood up and silently walked out. Most of the rest of us retired to the club-bar at Kaesong, tossed a few down, and then took some photos of the hole in the wall. These were later confiscated by investigative authorities, and the whole incident was hushed up. I was, of course, asked why I had stood up. I decided to be very honest: "A voice told me to do so, and I am goddamned glad I did." There was no official reprimand, since no one wanted to pursue this aspect of the case. (*Your Nostradamus Factor*)

This can only be viewed as an example of a type of psychic premonition that manifested itself as a voice.

Swann's account is interesting because he answers many key questions one might have about the subjective nature of the auditory experience. He experienced it as a voice, speaking at loud volume, from a location behind him (not inside his head). The voice spoke in understandable, clears English words. The voice could not have had any logical connection to the reality of the situation because there was no one seated behind him. The voice was so convincing in its realness that it convinced Ingo to stand up, contrary to strict military orders to remain seated.

Up to this point, there is nothing about Swann's voice that distinguishes it from the voices heard by schizophrenics. However, Swann's mental state was tested and analyzed many times because he was a subject in parapsychological and psychological research studies. He is not psychotic and has never had any reported incidents of mental illness. This means, almost by definition, that Swann would have understood the voice to have been his imagination. However, this was not the case. He interpreted the voice as being *real,* and took an unusual and drastic action to stand up.

There is one critical distinction. Neither psychotic voices nor imaginary voices bear any relationship to reality. They are unable to accurately predict anything. Psychotic voices, by definition, are *unrelated to reality* or exterior circumstances; they are often nonsensical, irrelevant, or paranoid. Similarly, voices from our imagination have no link to reality because, at least according to common understanding, they are mind-generated, not sensory-generated. Psychic voices can be confirmed with reality—like Swann's voice. Once again, this kind of information appears at the blurry crossroad of sensing and thinking. It qualifies as a form of psychic hearing.

We don't really understand why the brain chooses to "image" certain information in a particular given sensory format, such as visual or auditory. But if you think about it, in the cases cited by Ingo Swann and Sir Winston Churchill, an auditory command such as *get up* or *stop* was the swiftest and most effective means for the brain to communicate to itself that the individual was in immediate, impending danger. Suppose Swann had seen a psychic vision instead. Let's say he saw a visual image of a bullet flying through the air, or a swerving car. Chances are he would have reacted much slower and taken more time to reflect on their meaning. But the sharp words spoken by a voice caused him to take immediate action that saved his life.

Let's take a look at another example of a much more ambiguous kind of voice.

In 2003, a 27-year-old man, an experienced hiker and mountaineer named Aron Ralston, experienced a strange voice after he became trapped and nearly died in a crevice inside a canyon while hiking in Canyonlands National Park in Utah. He had failed to inform anyone of his whereabouts before taking a daytime hike into the canyon. When attempting to scramble over three large boulders wedged in the 3-foot-wide crevice, an 800-pound boulder fell on his arm, wedging it against the wall of the ravine and trapping him inside the narrow passageway.

In his book, *Between a Rock and a Hard Place*, and in various interviews, Ralston describes the ordeal of trying to free himself and save his own life during six traumatic days trapped in the canyon. At first, he had attempted to cut off his arm with the only tool he had with him: an inexpensive pocket knife he describes as being as blunt as a butter knife. Unable to cut off his own arm, Ralston prepared himself to die.

However, on the sixth day, as he described in an interview (with ABC Television), he had an unusual experience and heard a voice. He explained:

> In those...those few moments that I thrashed myself around... there was an epiphany that came to me. This, in my opinion, was a divine interaction. My spirituality engaging with God, that in a way...I heard, as if from an outside voice, but inside my head, that I could use this boulder to break the bones in my arm. And this voice just yelled out repeatedly, "That's it! That's it! Break the bones." And...I went about it. It took me just a few minutes to get my body into a position where I could...if you could imagine having a table vice with a two-by-four piece of lumber sticking out of it, and using that vice with leverage on the two-by-four to just...to torque it and break that piece of wood, that's exactly what I did. I bent my body around, contorting it, pushing up from underside the boulder, until I created enough force on that upper bone in my arm that it...it actually bent around its constriction...with the chock stone, and it snapped.

Ralston describes the voice as sounding as though it came from outside his head, like a real sound, but knowing or somehow understanding it was a voice from inside his head. The voice gave him the best advice of his life: It told him the precise mechanism by which he could release his arm and escape from the death trap. Was this simply his inner-voice rallying at the last possible moment to give him advice that he already knew, albeit unconsciously, but had avoided telling himself until the sixth day when it was obvious he was going to die unless he took some drastic action? Ralston doesn't think so. He seems to feel as though the voice was not his own, although it channeled through him. He expresses his belief that it was some sort of divine intervention or God's way of speaking directly to him. The voice gave him the idea of breaking his bones by using the torque and counterweight of his body against the solidly wedged arm.

What about organic changes in his brain brought about by dehydration, high mental stress, physical exhaustion, pain, extreme hunger, and fear, or any combination thereof? Could these elements have altered his state of mind to such an extent that he felt disembodied from himself and heard his own voice? Any reasonable person would have to accept this might have played a major role in his experience. He had been in his life-threatening predicament for six days, had etched the equivalent of his last will and testament into the rock in front of him, and had lost all hope of ever being found alive, because no one knew where he was and the crevice was too narrow to reveal his whereabouts by air. So Ralston's "voice" could just as easily have been deemed a hallucination as divine intervention (depending on your definition of what drives sensory perception). Either way, it is a form of self-to-self communication.

What is interesting, however, is the timing of the voice. This flash of insight could clearly have come to him at any time during his ordeal—but it did not. It came in the form of an exterior voice shouting at him long after his food and water had been used up and he had lost hope of ever coming out alive. Moreover, the voice supplied the *exact* answer to his freedom in the form of an insight that Ralston had simply not considered, in his conscious and rational mind, to be a real possibility. He took the next step of acting on this strange advice and successfully amputated his arm by severing the softer flesh between the broken bones with his previously useless dull penknife before making his way to freedom.

How Psychics and Mystics Experience Hearing Voices

Auditory psychics receive their information, not surprisingly, in an auditory format of sounds and words. Sometimes the voice comes from the exterior, but more often it is experienced as an internal or "imaginary" voice. This is why some psychic detectives are particularly good at identifying *names* (sound) as opposed to knowing what color clothing or cologne the perpetrator wore (sight, smell). They are receiving auditory information as their primary source. Generally, auditory psychics don't experience these as sounds outside their heads, although this is not always true.

If psychic detectives are asked to identify the perpetrator of a crime, they may hear certain letters or words in their mind. Letters are the phonetic building blocks of words and names. As such, they are much more like raw environmental sound. Often, sounds will evoke letters of the alphabet and letters will evoke names. For instance, psychics may hear staccato ticking sounds in their mind and associate them with a particular letter of the alphabet, such as T.

When they get some preliminary bits of auditory information, their thinking brain kicks in and engages in a higher level of interpretation of these sounds. For example, if the psychic hears the consonants T and M, this may be interpreted by the psychic to mean the perpetrator's name is Timmy, Tommy, or Tammy. Vowels are, not surprisingly, often more difficult to hear in this format than the clear, differentiated sounds of consonants.

You may recall from an earlier chapter how I described my own personal experience describing the spirit of an Indian woman's dead aunt. I told her I thought the woman's name was Mary, Marie, or Maria, and that her last name started with the letter S. I was getting auditory psychic sounds of the consonants M, R, and S (no vowel sounds). My brain then interpreted them into meaningful clusters to create actual names. Although I am primarily a visual psychic, I tend to get a lot of auditory information as well.

Many ghost hunters and teams of paranormal investigators now favor the use of certain spirit communication devices that randomly generate linguistic sounds and pieces of words. The Ovilus, for example, is an electronic device that creates auditory sounds in several ways. It operates in several different modes, including a Speech Mode that uses the environment to select words from its internal 512-word English-only dictionary, a Phonetic Mode that uses the environment to create sounds phonetically; and other modes that convert environment sounds into yes or no so the investigator can operate it as a dowsing tool.

There are also devices known as Ghost Boxes or Frank's Boxes that randomly skip around and land on different radio stations just long enough to pick up broken bits of chatter, noise, and conversation. Paranormal investigators claim these seemingly random words add up to meaningful communication from the spirit world. In essence, these devices are doing exactly the same thing as what auditory psychics do in their own minds: They hear phonemes mixed with raw environmental noise and then interpret them as words. Some investigators have had amazing luck with these machines and claim to be able to have intelligent conversations, or at least responses, from the spirit world and get unusual, accurate, and highly specific names or information in response to their questions.

Interestingly, the oracles at Delphi, Dodona, and Trophonius used to make their predictions about the future while speaking in tongues. They would utter nonsense words and sounds—rather like the psychics of today's world. These would be heard and understood by others as having a certain meaning. This kind of nonsense language is called *glossolalia*. Many other groups throughout history have believed that Spirit, however defined, speaks through humans in its own universal but unknowable language. For instance, the early spiritual Christian Roman Gnostics in the first few centuries AD memorialized in their writings certain seemingly nonsensical syllabic incantations such as *"ttttttttnnnnnnnnnnnddddddd."* Some historians believe these may be transliterations made of actual sounds of people speaking glossolalia.

The best-known speakers of glossolalia today are the Pentecostals who encourage their followers to speak in tongues during church service. The difference between the Pentecostal Church and other Charismatic Protestant sects is that the Pentecosts believe that a person can *only* be saved and baptized by the Holy Spirit if they speak in tongues. They base their belief on Acts 2:1–12 in the Bible, which describes the Day of Pentecost.

How "Normal" People Experience Hearing Voices

We all hear voices that don't exist. As much as we may try to deny this, it is a normal human experience. We don't think much about it because it is so normal and we certainly don't share this experience with others because we are afraid of being considered abnormal.

Think about it. How many people find it extremely difficult to meditate because they cannot calm down enough to turn off their loud and incessant brain chatter? *Brain chatter has a voice.*

Psychologists acknowledge that we all have an inner voice that speaks to us, sometimes while reading a book, thinking a thought, or actively engaged in some activity requiring concentration or emotional support, to the point that some people actually talk to themselves out loud. Some people actually carry on extended conversations with their interior mental voice. These people, though not considered to be technically ill, are deemed to be eccentric. So-called normal people are far more adept at keeping this inner dialogue discreetly to themselves. There is an unspoken taboo about revealing our inner voices to others.

This kind of interior voice is usually recognizable as what I will call a thought voice. It is not heard as much as it is experienced as a mental verbalization of a thought. It clearly belongs to us and no one else. This voice is most often experienced as our own voice, but sometimes seems to belong to other people, some known to us, such as family members, and others more impersonal, such as a film narrator. Although we can often identify the gender of the voice if we focus on it, very often it is too subtle or too deeply embedded as a thought, rather than a sound, to make it identifiable as either male or female.

Lots of people actually hear voices and talk in their sleep, and some are capable of carrying on lengthy and even logical conversations. They are responding to voices they hear in their dreams. The voices in our dreams belong to our cast of dream characters and range from male to female, adult to child, familiar to unfamiliar. The voices don't even have to speak our language! At age 9, I remember having a dream in French with subtitles in English written at the bottom of my visual screen (just in case I wasn't able to translate my mind's own language correctly). My brother, at age 7, a product of the new television generation, often had commercial breaks between his dreams! His dreams were apparently sponsored by a higher source!

It is not uncommon for people to hear someone calling their name when no one is there. The voice calling us creates enough sound in our mind to catch our attention, and yet it doesn't quite seem like a real voice. I believe these kinds of voices are like auditory pareidolia. Our brain constructs a logical meaning from neutral, ambiguous, raw sounds.

I often have the experience when I wake up in the middle of the night that I am listening one or several voices, male and/or female, droning on and on. They have the vocal inflections of newscasters on a cable news channel. I struggle to make out what they are saying. But it is the same sensation as having the words just on the tip of your tongue—you can't distinguish real words. Of course, when this happens, all of the television sets in the house are turned off. When I fully wake up, I realize I am listening to the sounds of raw silence and the voices eventually disappear. It is similar to the problem I have when trying to decipher or read text in a dream. I can see the actual words in a book, but they seem to dissolve or slip aside if

I look directly at them. Sometimes meaning arises all by itself without any understanding of the words. For example, once in a dream, I remember trying to read the text of a medical book that my grandfather had opened to a particular page. Although I wasn't able to read the words, I somehow instantly knew the text was discussing ophthalmology. My knowledge was beyond the words themselves.

My hunch is that when the right hemisphere of the brain is dominant, such as when we are sleeping, dreaming, or waking up, the linguistic faculties of the left hemisphere are turned off. This would explain why we struggle so hard to find meaning in written words. Of course, the flip side of this coin is that we can find meaning much faster in non-verbal environmental sounds. In my opinion, psychic auditory sensing is not mysterious at all. It is all about how the human brain seeks, finds, and develops meaning, then communicates that meaning to itself. Everything is an interpretation, and some interpretations are better than others.

How Schizophrenics Experience Hearing Voices

Are the voices heard by schizophrenics any different than the voices that all of us hear in our heads?

Most medical studies that have been done on schizophrenia do not focus on the subjective experience of schizophrenics, such as how they hear voices. Most tend to focus on objective criteria such as symptoms, evaluations of brain scans, and progression of the disease. I was, however, able to find a few studies that actually explore the subjective experiences of schizophrenics of their own hallucinations. These were quite useful in helping me understand the relationship between *thinking* and *hearing*. This, in turn, is valuable when you are trying to understand the difference between auditory psychics and schizophrenics.

Auditory hallucinations are the most common type of hallucination associated with schizophrenia. Researchers have estimated that 75 percent of all schizophrenics hear voices that are not really there. Schizophrenia is a mental disease characterized by delusions, disorganized speech and behavior, thought disorder, decrease in emotional range, apathy, and loss of cognitive abilities to focus attention and organize, all of which comes about as a result of organic deterioration of the brain. *This immediately distinguishes schizophrenics from psychics.* Research has shown schizophrenics often lose up to 25 percent of the gray matter in certain areas of the parietal and frontal lobes in their brains.

I was curious to know if schizophrenics hear voices with their ears (outside) or in their minds (inside). As already discussed, psychics are capable of hearing both ways, depending on the situation. Surprisingly, very few studies have ever been undertaken to investigate this rather important distinction.

One such study was conducted by Dr. David L. Copolov, professor of psychiatry at Monash University and former director of the Mental Health Research Institute of Victoria in Melbourne, Australia. His team found that 74 percent of the patients heard voices at least once each day. *A significant majority of these patients (80 percent) said they experienced the voices as real rather than imaginary.* The patients were divided by their perception of the origin of the voices. Thirty-four percent said the voices came from outside their heads; 28 percent said the voices were inside their heads; and 38 percent said the voices came from both inside and outside their heads. A large majority (70 percent) said the voices were almost always negative in tone, although some said they experienced the voices as supportive and positive. Some voices were experienced as a continual barrage of noise, whereas other voices were intermittent.

An even more detailed survey of schizophrenics and psychotics was conducted by Dr. Julie A. Holland (a physician specialized in psychopharmacology and psychiatry) and Kevin C. Riley, PhD, on 86 psychiatric patients, at a major metropolitan teaching hospital in Philadelphia, who were actively experiencing auditory hallucinations. The results of the survey are summarized in an article entitled "Characterizing Hallucinations: An Aid in the Differential Diagnosis of Malingering."

This study is interesting because the researchers attempted to categorize the patients' *subjective* sense of the auditory hallucinatory experiences. The survey also asked about the location of the voices: Were they inside or outside the mind, and, if outside, in what direction vis à vis the patient? A large number of the patients (38 percent) said the voices were stereophonic and heard in both ears, whereas 6 percent heard the voices only on the right side and only 4 percent heard them on the left side. The spatial orientation of the voice was apparently more difficult to approximate. Ten percent said the voice came from behind them, and an almost equal number (9 percent) said it came from in front of them.

If you think about it, the characterizations given by these patients of their voices don't seem that far off from *louder* versions of our own inner voices.

The schizophrenics' voices gave running narrative descriptions of the their lives, talked to them in insulting as well as pleasant ways, issued commands and orders, held conversations with the patient, and were experienced as gender-based voices, for the most part.

The close resemblance of psychotic voices to our own "normal" inner voice makes it very tempting to analyze these auditory hallucinations as nothing more than a louder conversation inside one's head. Why are schizophrenic's voices louder than the average internal voice? Perhaps they lack the ability to filter, dampen, or tune out the internal conversation.

The role of language is very important when you are discussing imaginary voices. Human speech is important for its content, not its sounds. Brain scan studies performed on schizophrenics with auditory hallucinations show that the language areas of their brains—known as Broca's and Wernicke's regions—become highly active. This is interesting because these language regions of the brain are located next to the auditory cortex of the brain, which processes hearing. *Speaking and listening are apparently not as distinct as we normally assume.* In schizophrenics who have auditory hallucinations, brain scan research has shown that the Broca's area (involved in the production of sounds of language) is actually more active than Wernicke's region (involved in language comprehension). This is somewhat counterintuitive. You would think that voices you listen to would come from the place where you *understand* language as opposed to the place where you make sounds! Still other studies suggest a different source for the psychotic voices. These suggest the arcuate fasciculus, the language processing tract connecting Broca's region to Wernicke's region, in schizophrenics, is abnormal.

Scientists have now discovered a way to temporarily stop schizophrenics from hearing voices! This research, in turn, provides one of the most tantalizing clues about the mystery of the location of schizophrenic voices.

Dr. Ralph Hoffman, a psychiatrist and professor at Yale University, conducted a study in which he found that auditory hallucinations could be temporarily eliminated by application of transcranial magnetic stimulation (TMS) ("Experts See Mind's Voices"). In these studies, an electromagnetic coil was placed over the Wernicke's region of the brain (implicated in language comprehension), that emitted a weak electromagnetic current. Dr. Hoffman has proposed that the loss of gray matter in schizophrenics' brains as a result of the disease, particularly in the superior temporal lobe containing Wernicke's region, may result in a bombardment of signals from Broca's region into Wernicke's region. Wernicke's region may then comprehend this loud data as external speech.

Even more interestingly, if we can understand schizophrenic voices as nothing but our internal voice (with the volume turned way up) then we can also begin to understand why schizophrenics can make good psychics, yet still be delusional. Psychic and psychotic states are not mutually exclusive. You can be both, just as you can be one or the other. But being psychic does not mean you are psychotic.

Certain raw sounds often lend themselves to a particular meaning or interpretation. Psychics often rely on their own personal interpretation of sounds to find meaning. Words do not only represent symbolic meaning; they are also a sensory experience. Sometimes sound and content express the same thing. The word *tack,* for example, which is defined as a "short, sharp-pointed nail" actually sounds hard and sharp! There is a unity of sound and meaning. Other words, however, are not unified in sound and meaning. For instance, the word *hammer* sounds soft and mushy even though the word itself refers to an iron-hard tool.

It seems to me that schizophrenics often cling to the feeling and sounds of words, such as when they engage in clanging, a psychological term referring to a type of speech that links words together by their rhyming or alliterative sounds, not by their meaning. An example of this comes from the fascinating blog of Pamela Wagner (*www.schizophrenia.com*), a brilliant student who was forced to drop out of her first year of medical school due to the onset of schizophrenia. In her blog, dated April 19, 2006, she wrote:

> Later again: now they've segued into singing or chanting, really: One, you're the One, you're the One, do your duty! One, you're the One, you're the One, do your duty! Duty! Duty! Do duty! Do Duty! Do do do do do Duty Duty Duty Dooty Dooty Dooty! Doooooooty d'ty d'ty d'ty d'ty d'ty d'ty d'ty d'ty...It has devolved into gibberish as they just play on that word and torment me.

[...]Okay, so my brain tells me, through some neurochemical glitch, that I am "hearing" voices that are talking to me, when in fact that is false, what the brain is telling me is not true. Though I do "hear" them, it is my brain that is conjuring the false sound of sounds, not my ears actually perceiving sounds...No sound waves actually stir the tiny hairs inside my inner ear or impinge on my ear drum. In fact (I suspect) my auditory cortex may not even be involved at all (though scientists may not yet know whether this is true or not). My brain creates the feeling/perception that I hear these voices and my mind creates the story (the DJ in the wall playing LPs) to explain the feeling to myself, to make my experience jibe with the world as I know it..."

Although Wagner clearly understands that her voices are not real, like other voices she can also hear, she desperately tries to find meaning in her clanging mental monologue by stringing together similar-sounding words. Schizophrenics cling to the feeling of the words because they cannot seem to think effectively and no longer find the meaning at all.

By contrast, psychics are able to find meaning by listening to raw sounds, then free-associating a proper meaning. The meaning arises, unaided, from the depths of the subconscious mind. Psychics have learned to trust this process. Most of us simply cannot believe there is a perfectly legitimate logic within us that exists without the benefit of formal thinking.

Exercise

Play a tape recording of someone's voice backward and see if you can distinguish any words or phrases that emerge from the "nonsense." See if these are significant to the speaker.

Lesson #14:

Psychic Touch Is Spirit Contact

Clairsentience refers to the sense of psychic touch. In the early days of my training as a psychic, I found it extremely difficult to imagine how this might work. I could understand how you might get pictures in your head or hear sounds in your mind, but how do you experience psychic touch? Normally, I see the psychic world in terms of ideas, emotions, and concepts. My world is mostly intellectual. However, I have several friends who are, unlike me, very grounded in the physical world of touch. Many are body workers, physical therapists, athletes, and massage therapists. They seem to "feel" information more intensely in their bodies in a very non-intellectual kind of way. They don't exactly think things in the same way they know things.

What exactly does psychic sense of touch feel like, I wondered? I had no idea because I had no experience with physical sensations that weren't real. How can you possibly explain psychic knowledge that doesn't come in the form of an idea, but from touch?

I wondered if there exists such a thing as a "touch hallucination." It seemed reasonable to me to assume that if you are going to explore the outer limits of touch, then you need to understand the psychological relationship of the mind to the skin.

Let me start by discussing the different ways that we can experience psychic touch. Most psychic touch stories are associated with ghosts. So, in this sense, touch is a form of spirit communication. It gives us knowledge about the spirit.

As a paranormal investigator, I have been affiliated over the years with several different paranormal teams—better known as ghost hunters. We visit well-known haunted buildings and locations, as well as being called into private residences where people are concerned about spirit activity. Half the time, the clients just want confirmation that they are not crazy. Sometimes they want the team to get rid of the ghosts—which is not always an easy proposition. At any rate, one bumps into a lot of very strange activity in this line of work.

As I mentioned in an earlier chapter, one way we experience spirits is as cold spots in the atmosphere. Cold air is commonly associated with the presence of spirits and it is believed the air gets cold because spirits draw energy from the surrounding atmosphere in order to manifest. I experienced this many times while on paranormal investigations. Cold air is not the only kind of psychic touching. Objects have been known to move and invisible ones can be felt. I have heard of many cases where, just like the Hollywood movies, spirits pull the covers off sleeping people or throw things through the air. But I have always been particularly intrigued by people who say they have been touched by a spirit. When I ask them what it feels like, most people are very clear about the sensation. It is usually a hand and they can feel its size, warmth, and texture just like a real hand— except it is invisible. I have spoken with other paranormal investigators who have had their faces and necks caressed, their bodies touched gently or jabbed sharply, sometimes pushed violently, their hair tugged, and—among the strangest cases—I have actually seen people's skin that appears to have been scratched, slapped until red, or bitten! My highest degree of skepticism always kicks in when I see this because it is just so difficult to believe this could be the result of spirit activity and not some scam. But people insist they did not do it to themselves and are often genuinely frightened.

I have also spoken with a few women who claim to have been fondled and even raped by a spirit in their bed!

One woman I spoke with, a level-headed investment banker, told me about how an elderly female spirit climbed into her bed with her one night while she was alone in her apartment! She said she could feel the mattress depress from the weight of the spirit and she could feel the old woman's body next to hers, but was too terrified to look at the woman. She claims she was not in a dream state or sleeping. Another woman I know told me she was "goosed" by a frisky male spirit who apparently is known for climbing into bed with good-looking blonde women at a historic battlefield hospital inn in Gettysburg, Pennsylvania. She, too, could feel the mattress depress as he climbed into bed with her, and she could feel that his hand was rather large.

Lest you think only women are having ghostly sex encounters, I also know one man, an electrician, who claimed someone climbed into bed with him one night while sleeping over at a friend's house, and spooned with him. When he rolled over to look at her, no one was there. I was told another story about a housekeeper at a haunted castle in Wales who went to the basement to collect fresh laundry and was scared out of her wits when she heard a man's voice whisper something lewd into one ear and touch her shoulder with his hand. There was no one in the basement except her. Since that time, apparently no housekeepers will venture into the basement alone.

Everything I have discussed so far represents touching sensations as a result of some spirit contact. But there are other ways in which psychic information can be obtained directly through the body. Dowsers claim to feel certain geomagnetic energies that run across ley lines in the earth, and their dowsing sticks or pendulums seem to confirm their sensations. Psychic detectives can often feel hot or sticky sensations when feeling a map to try to locate a missing person, lost animal, or oil reserves. Usually the person's hand will feel drawn to a particular location or get stuck there. One famous psychic detective with whom I spoke, Annette Martin, told me her hand will begin to perspire when it hits its mark on a map.

Similarly, energy healers feel parts of a patient's body that are sick, damaged, or painful with the palms of their hands. I have taught myself, over a period of many years, how to feel sickness or injuries simply by running my hands in the air about 4 to 5 inches above a person's body. I surprise myself over and over again by the accuracy with which I can feel a sensation—often magnetic, electrical, thick, hot, bumpy, tweaking, or any number of other extremely subtle variations that indicate the location of the injury.

Some people, called empaths, are so highly sensitive they can get a contact headache just by walking into a room where someone else with a headache is standing. They are like an open channel to receive physical sensations from other people. Many of these people do not know how to shut off this channel and it can become problematic for them.

It took me many years to understand the proper way to experience psychic touch. But I now better understand how to feel and interpret physical sensations. The sense of touch is actually comprised of many different senses. The somatosenses are not just limited to the skin and can occur on the inside of the body. They collectively include 1) *cutaneous* (skin on the surface of the body), 2) *kinesthesic* (movement of the physical body in space), and 3) *visceral* (internal sense of feeling that comes from within the body itself, such as stomach aches or heart tension). These generate a number of different physical sensations, including a sense of touch on exterior body, a sense of our internal body, a sense of pain, a sense of pressure, a sense of balance, a sense of our body in physical space, and a sense of temperature. Thus, when I am speaking about clairsentience as a sense of psychic touch, I am really including all of these various physical senses in my definition.

A Story of a Missing Man

Let me give you another example of the psychic sense of touch that involved a sensation on the *inside* of my body, in my lungs. This story involved several psychic senses, including clairsentience, clairvoyance, and clairintuition.

One day a friend of mine telephoned me because she knew I was training as a psychic detective. She told me the following story and asked if I could help. An employee at her company, a young man who worked in the warehouse, had a brother who had been missing for five days. The brother had recently gotten into a dispute with his fiancée and had moved back in with his mother. One morning, he said goodbye to his mother and went to the rural part of northwestern New Jersey not far from where they lived. He drove to a friend's house and borrowed a rifle to go hunting. This was not unusual, because the brother often visited this friend and went hunting on his large, wooded property. The only problem was that no one had heard from him for five days and everyone was very worried about him.

My friend had a hunch he had been injured or incapacitated in the woods, and then unable to get help. Maybe he tumbled into a ravine, got attacked by a wild animal, or had a heart attack. Alternatively, maybe because of his fight with his fiancée he decided to skip town and start a new life somewhere else. She believed he was still alive and wanted my help in locating him.

As I spoke with her on the phone, I asked a number of questions. I learned he had contacted a number of good friends that day and spoke with them all briefly. The brother did not seem upset, nor did he do anything that might have seemed unusual. He was carrying a cell phone, but since the day he disappeared he had not responded to any calls made to that number. He was a skilled hunter. He had never disappeared like that before. I wasn't very familiar with the region of New Jersey where he had last been seen, but I knew it was rural, wooded, and not densely populated.

Imagine for a moment that this is all the information you are given. Now try to come up with an answer to the questions: Where is he, and is he dead or alive? The logical mind can conjure several equally plausible scenarios based on rational thought progressions. Certainly, my logical mind was immediately disturbed that this guy was last seen with a gun in his hands and that he had recently broken up with his fiancée. That did not bode well for him. However, on the brighter side, he was a regular recreational hunter, behaved normally that day, had always been close with his brother who did not suspect anything, had not shown any signs of severe depression, and had spoken with a number of his friends who didn't suspect anything was wrong with him. So, the logical mind was at a standoff. The logical mind could only present a number of rational alternatives as to his whereabouts, but no definitive answer based on the evidence. Although my logical mind was hamstrung, my psychic mind was to free come up with its own answer.

Then I began to notice a very strange and subtle thing start to happen to me as I spoke with my friend on the telephone. Ever so slightly, my breathing seemed to change. At first I thought maybe it was the result of my being so nervous at trying to psychically solve a case—especially when the stakes were so real. I seemed to be slightly hyperventilating. I actually stopped for a moment and asked myself why my breathing seemed so labored. Could just talking about a case like this make me *that* nervous? Usually when I get nervous, I tend to hold my breath, not breathe harder! So this seemed an abnormal response to me.

Then I noticed that my breathing took on an additional, ever-so-subtle dimension. It almost felt like I was gasping for air; like I was trying to suck it all in on the inhale as if I just couldn't get enough oxygen. I started to have difficulty speaking because I felt out of breath. I had never felt anything like that before. Was that another kinesthetic experience? It crossed my mind at that point that I might have "linked" with this guy's spirit and was re-experiencing his last gulps of breath before dying. Dying, huh? Perhaps that was a clue.

I shut my eyes and tried to watch my mind's screen to see if any imagery would emerge. Almost immediately I got a strikingly clear mental image. It was as if I was floating about 30 or 40 feet up in the air looking down on the ground—sort of like one of those film camera cranes they use on movie sets to get the aerial shot above the action. I was looking down on a pale blue car, that was parked on a flat surface that roughly approximated the shape of Texas.

I did not need to see directly inside the car: I "knew" immediately that the brother was inside. He had shot himself with the rifle. I also knew somehow that there was no way I wanted to float down and get a better look inside the car. I knew the interior was covered with spattered blood and brains everywhere. There was blood all over the window on the driver's side of the car. In all of these instances, this funny kind of knowledge was a strange certainty that my fantasy imagery had settled and concluded itself in my mind. The imagery was strong and resisting being changed or traded for other fantasy imagery. It was not knowledge in the ordinary sense of the word, of being able to support a conclusion with evidence or a rational thought process.

Based on the quick image that passed before me on my mind's screen—it couldn't have lasted more than a total of a couple of seconds—I told my friend that I was very sorry, but I believed the brother had shot himself to death several days earlier inside his car. It is one thing to have this as a quirky little fantasy image in your head, and quite another to actually share this image and your understanding of what it means with someone who is deeply emotionally affected by the situation. You pray you are not simply enflaming an already-bad situation by giving your completely unfounded opinion. You realize that what you say will have real consequences—and that is very frightening. I felt bad even making this suggestion knowing how upset she was already.

Having determined in my mind that the man was dead, I felt morally obligated to try to help my friend locate the body. After all, if I was going to be at all useful in this matter, I couldn't very well stop at the pronouncement of his death! I then continued to pose more questions to myself: Where was the body? What clues could I offer that would help the family or the police find the body? The only clue I had to go on based on my mental image was the fact that I had seen the car sitting on a flat surface in the shape of Texas. What the heck was that supposed to mean, anyway? I had a sneaking suspicion that the shape of Texas was symbolic and not literal, but it wasn't entirely obvious to me. That was why I did not immediately assume his body would be physically located in the state of Texas or that he had decided to leave New Jersey on a trek toward Texas.

I told my friend I would call her back. As soon as I hung up with her, I got on the Internet and started looking for anything in Warren and Sussex counties, near the location of the hunting buddy's property, that might be shaped sort of like Texas. I scoured various maps of the area and local tourist attractions to see if anything would ring a mental bell with me. I looked at parks, cemeteries, zoned areas—anything that might resemble the state of Texas. I was hoping maybe I could try to do something I had read that psychic detectives can do—namely, place their fingers over a map and feel the hot spot associated with the location of the body. Never having attempted this before, I wasn't sure that it would even work using an Internet map, especially given all the electromagnetic interference given off by the computer screen. I didn't really pick up anything at all. At one point, I saw a large state park in Warren County that bore some vague resemblance to Texas so I decided to go with it as a possible lead.

I called my friend back and suggested that the brother might have driven his car to this particular state park (particularly because there is a highway running right through it), taken a small road into the wooded area where it would not be seen, and then shot himself in the car. It felt a little lame, but I figured it was better than nothing. She thanked me for my efforts and we hung up.

About four weeks later, I received an e-mail from my friend. She wrote:

I wanted to give you an update on our warehouse guy's missing brother. Sadly, you were right. He killed himself in his car.... They finally found him in the parking lot at the apartment building where his mom lives. Apparently it's a huge lot, he parked in a far-away corner, between two trucks that must not have been moved too often, and shot himself. Exactly what you sensed. We got all this info in bits and pieces and our guy only just came back to work.

Apparently, he killed himself almost immediately after getting that gun and it just took them so long to find him. Guess no one thought to look so close to home. There's just not too much to say. I feel really dreadful....

As soon as I received this e-mail, I felt like an electric drill had just buzzed its way through my head and entire body. It was kind of too scary for words. I felt witchy, even to myself! Naturally, I felt terrible for my friend and her employee who had lost his brother. But in a selfish sort of way, I felt proud that I had at least had the courage to give my opinion, even though it was very frightening to do so. The fact that I had been wrong about both the color of the car (it was white, not pale blue) and the location of the car didn't disturb me. But what did bother me was that I had no explanation for the Texas shape that had featured so prominently in my mind.

Weeks later, I happened to recount this story to another friend. I explained that I had never been able to account for the bizarre Texas shape I had gotten and that seemed to be irrelevant to anything related to the case. She asked me, "Where did this man's mother live?" I had learned *after* receiving my friend's e-mail that the parking lot behind the mother's house was located in Morris County, New Jersey. My friend smiled and said, "Have you ever looked at the shape of Morris County?"

Why didn't I think of that? Sure enough, it just never dawned on me because I was so mentally focused on Warren and Sussex counties. The shape of Morris County, located in central northern New Jersey, is a dead-ringer for the state of Texas!

Body Delusions and Hallucinations

I want to discuss the difference between psychic touch and "normal" touch sensations. It is difficult for most of us to imagine that our sense of touch can be wrong. We tend to believe in this physical sensation as an absolute indicator of reality—but it isn't! The goal here is to try to understand whether psychic touch is similar or distinguishable from other forms of "delusional" or hallucinogenic touch sensations.

First, I will give you a bit of background about how we "feel" things in our body. The skin is the largest of all body organs. It weighs from 6 to 10 pounds. There are three major layers of skin: The *epidermis* is the paper-thin outer layer; the *dermis* is the middle layer filled with blood vessels, protein, collagen, and elastin; and the *subcutis* that is the deepest layer and contains fat and muscle. The middle layer, the dermis, is loaded with roughly 20 different types of nerve endings that send information to the brain about the physical environment coming into contact with the skin. *Pain receptors* (including itch and tickle) are the most common and relay data about temperature, vibration, texture, hair deflection, and pressure. *Mechanoreceptors* measure pressure or deformation of the skin. *Thermoreceptors* measure hot and cold temperatures using a system of nerve receptors with different degrees of myelin, a protective sheath of electrically insulating phospholipid material that surrounds the neural axons of the receptors. *Chemoreceptors* convert the effects of chemicals on the skin into electrical impulses that are then sent to the brain.

The density of the population of these sensory receptions in any given area of skin is unequal and will determine our degree of sensitivity and discrimination between different sensations. There are approximately 50 touch receptors for every square centimeter and about 5 million sensory cells in the entire body. The least sensitive part of the body is the middle back, whereas the most sensitive areas are the face, lips, tongue, neck, hands, fingertips, and feet. The fingertips have 100 times more receptors per square centimeter than the center of the back!

The brain is intimately linked with our perception of our sense of touch. Consequently, the skin, like all other sensory organs, is indeed subject to all kinds of possible hallucinations and illusions like our other senses.

The classic touch acuity experiment, called the Two Point Threshold Test, perfectly demonstrates the discrepancy between actual physical sensation and reality. This simple test shows us that when the skin is simultaneously touched in two places at a certain close proximity, it will feel like a single touch. This is the brain's misinterpretation of reality. It is an illusion of touch, but not technically a hallucination. Rather, it is a misperception of the brain based on its limited physiological resources and the number of receptors in the skin. In fact, the brain attempts to fill in the gaps—just as it does for optical illusions—to account for the missing sensory data. It makes a snap judgment, a kind of educated guess, about the type of touch being physically delivered to the skin. What we experience as real is not really real!

One of the most common types of skin hallucinations is called *formication*. This refers to the unpleasant sensation of having ants or small insects crawling on or underneath the skin. Another example is *parasthesia*, a medical term that refers to a burning or prickling sensation most often appearing in the hands, feet, legs, or arms, but that can occur anywhere in the body. It can be experienced as burning, prickling, numbness, crawling, or itching sensations, and is often referred to as the "pins and needles" feeling after a limb has had its blood supply cut off for a while. In all these instances, there are no actual pins and needles poking our skin or any other real physical stimulus, such as ants. These sensations don't quite rise to the level of actual hallucinations because there is a "real" reason for the sensation, but it almost rises to the level of an "illusion" or "imaginary" experience because there is nothing actually touching or piercing the skin. Once again, the brain has attached its own meaning (pins and needles or ants) to a physical sensation.

Another type of physical sense of touch illusion can be found in our experience of pain. Referred pain occurs when one experiences pain in a different location of the body from the actual site of the injury. Clearly, this would not fall under our classic definition of a "real" experience because the pain is felt in a location without a corresponding actual physical stimulus in the same location. Referred pain is real pain without a logical source. It is a mild form of a tactile illusion and is a remarkably common human experience. Examples of referred pain would be when a person suffers a myocardial infarction (heart attack) but instead of feeling chest pain, only experiences pain along the left arm.

Phantom Limb Pain and Virtual Limb Sensation

Another example of a touch delusion is the condition known as phantom limb pain. This is a condition where a person who has lost a limb continues to experience real, sometimes excruciatingly painful, sensations such as burning or crushing feelings in the limb that no longer exists. In fact, 50 to 80 percent of all amputees experience phantom limb pain. Scientists do not presently understand the cause of phantom limb pain, although it has been suggested that it may be due in part of damaged nerve endings at the location of the amputation.

Researchers have demonstrated that phantom limb pain can be alleviated by tricking the brain. One study performed in 1996 by neuroscientist Dr. V.S. Ramachandran, professor and director of the Center for Brain and Cognition at the University of California, San Diego, had patients place their amputated limb into a mirror box. The mirror was positioned in such a way that it did not reflect the amputated stump, but rather the image of the patient's other, fully intact, limb. The patients were able to see their amputated limb as if it were fully reconstituted. This had an interesting effect on their brain. They obtained immediate pain relief—merely by tricking the brain into thinking the body was complete, and could control and move its amputated limb! This has caused some researchers to suggest that the brain may be the real culprit in this type of pain. It has been suggested that the brain suffers some adverse reaction generating real pain at having an incomplete body image. All of this demonstrates that, to a great extent, real body awareness resides ironically not in the body, but in the brain—the place of *thinking,* not feeling!

Not only can we experience hallucinations and illusions with the sense of touch—we can also experience the illusion of *virtual touch* (touchless touch).

In February 2007, researchers at the Neural Engineering Center for Artificial Limbs at the Rehabilitation Institute of Chicago announced an innovative new method of nerve regrowth that incredibly allows a patient with a prosthetic arm to actually feel its movements and touch sensations! The first patient was a 24-year-old woman who had lost her arm in a motorcycle accident. The new method, called targeted muscled reinnervation (TMR), works by sending signals from the prosthesis to the nerves that used to go to the arm. The nerves are relocated into the muscle and skin in the patient's chest in areas that are no longer biomechanically functional. So, for example, if the patient thinks to herself "close my hand," the myoelectric signal moves from the brain, through the spinal cord, out to the hand nerve, but because the hand no longer exists, a tiny piece of muscle in the chest contracts and can send signals to move the joints in the prosthetic arm.

Dr. Susan J. Lederman, a psychophysicist researcher and professor in the department of psychology and school of computing at Queen's University, Kingston, Canada, is a leading researcher in the field of subjective haptic perception. This intriguing field exists at the crossroad of psychology, neurology, and the basic physiology of movement. Dr. Lederman's goal has been to incorporate the *subjective experience* of touch into our total understanding of the mechanics of touch.

In studies conducted in 1998, Dr. Lederman was able to demonstrate that our mental expectations will actually change our physical body sensations. Think about that: *Our expectations change our reality!*

She created a study in which golfers and non-golfers were asked to hold different golf balls, real golf balls and practice golf balls (which are lighter in weight than the real ones), and asked both groups to use their hands to judge the comparative weights of the balls. The golfers already knew that practice golf balls are lighter and therefore had a preconceived judgment about their weight. The golfers concluded the balls had different weights. By contrast, the non-golfers were ignorant of the weight differences and therefore did not have any preconceptions. They judged the practice golf balls to have the same exact weight as the regular golf balls. Our sense of touch is very much a product of our mind!

Hopefully, Dr. Lederman's golf ball illusion experiment may have reminded you of parapsychologist Gertrude Schmeidler's sheep-goat study, which I mentioned in the first chapter of this book. Schmeidler clinically demonstrated that non-skeptics (people with no preconceptions about psychic phenomena) are able to experience psychic phenomena far more easily than skeptics. Just like the non-golfers, non-skeptics do not color their judgments of physical sensations with their belief systems.

Psychological Origins of Disease and Cures

Can we make painless situations painful without a physical stimulus? The answer is absolutely yes!

We all know that the immune system of the body can be compromised by our state of mind, especially if we are under chronic stress. Viral or bacterial disease that might easily be defeated by a strong immune system can flourish in a body with a weakened immune system. So we know that our state of mind has a "real" relationship to the state of our body. In fact, any quick review of the medical field of immunology reveals that the line between mind and body is virtually indistinguishable.

For instance, autoimmune diseases, such as rheumatoid arthritis, certain types of lupus, certain disorders of the thyroid (Grave's Disease and Hashimoto's Disease), multiple sclerosis, Crohn's Disease, and scleroderma, reveal just how profoundly one's state of mind can affect one's state of body. Autoimmune disease is defined as the inability of the body to recognize its own constituent parts on a subcellular level and a failure to recognize "self." As a result, the body launches a full-scale attack on its own tissues and organs. Clearly, the mind's thoughts and emotions are linked to the body's physical reactions, so what one merely *imagines* in one's mind is often very real indeed! Our body will respond to perceived danger the same way it will respond to real danger.

The counterpart to an imagined illness is an imagined cure. One such example of an imagined cure is the famous "placebo effect," which amounts to an objective (measurable or observable) or subjective (entirely self-evaluated) improvement in health that is not attributable to treatment. A placebo is usually a sugar or starch pill or some other completely benign compound with absolutely no known healing power and is pharmacologically inert.

Interestingly, the word *placebo* derives from Latin, meaning "I shall please." Kind of an odd reference, I thought. The word originally used to refer to a funeral crasher! This was a stranger who would show up unexpectedly at a funeral, falsely claiming to have been a friend or acquaintance of the deceased, in order to get free food and drink. The pretender would have to recite Psalm 114:9 in the Roman Catholic Office of the Dead prayer ritual and, along with the other grievers, announce: "placebo Domino in regione vivorum," meaning "I shall please the Lord in the land of the living."

In a strange way, a placebo is like the funeral crasher. The placebo pretends to be a helpful medicine and purports to be old friends with the human body. Instead it is really an imposter—but an incredibly good one. So good, in fact, that it has acquired a reputation for healing! The famed placebo effect, despite having been very well-documented over the years, is still little understood. What is the mechanism for natural self-healing? Spontaneous healing (like the term *placebo effect*) just describes an *outcome,* but doesn't explain why it happens.

Emotional Pain and Empathetic Pain

Another way our body can experience physical pain without an actual physical stimulus is through emotional pain. Emotional pain can actually be experienced as real physical pain. Researchers have long known that depression and physical pain share many of the same nerve pathways leading to the brain. Moreover, other seemingly purely psychological emotions also activate the anterior cingulate region of the brain known as the pain center because it lights up on brain scans when a person experiences physical pain. Strangely, something as simple as a social snub can cause this pain region of the brain to become activated.

In 2003, researchers at the University of California in Los Angeles conducted an experiment whereby volunteers were hooked up to a brain scan and asked to play a computer game that involved catching a virtual ball on a computer screen and, by pressing buttons on the game machine, to send it to one of two other players who were allegedly also hooked up to brain scans at other remote locations. The volunteers were told the outcome of the game was unimportant and that the sole purpose was to check the connections between the machines of the other players. In fact, there were no other players involved and they were only playing against a computer.

At a certain point, the computer was directed to stop throwing the ball to the volunteer. The other two players appeared to be playing by themselves and actively excluding the volunteer. During the session, the brain scans showed that the pain center became extremely activated, especially in the brains of those volunteers who came out of the session not only miffed, but outraged by the nasty behavior of the other two players. The brain registers emotional pain in the same way it registers physical pain.

What about a slightly different kind of emotional pain—one that is not the direct result of one's own emotions, but belongs to someone else? This is empathic pain, the kind of emotional or physical pain one suffers when putting themselves in the shoes of someone else. In light of the scientific evidence showing the link between physical and emotional pain, a psychic empath's ability to emotionally connect with another person and then literally feel the other person's pain as if it were his own, is not such a far stretch from reality! Our experience of pain can be activated simply by looking at or imagining a painful situation. Because our physical sensations are so intimately connected with our thoughts, it is impossible to say whether this kind of psychic sensing is delusional or actual. Once again, the only way to know is by cross-confirming the data with our other senses.

Exercise

Place your hands with palms facing each other about 2 inches apart and imagine you can feel the density of the energy between them. Create an increasingly large ball of energy as you put more space between your hands. It should feel like two magnets of the same polarity pushing each other apart.

Lesson #15:

Psychic Taste and Smell Defy Laws of Science

I chose to combine clairgustation (psychic sense of taste) with clairolfaction (psychic sense of smell) for a couple of reasons.

First of all, the real senses of smell and taste are intimately related to each other. It is impossible to taste something if you cannot smell it.

Second, I really don't have much to say about psychic tasting. I have no personal experience with it. As far as I know, I have never intuited something merely by the taste in my mouth. Certainly, the expression that a person or event left you with a "bad taste in your mouth" does suggest that this is well within the human experience.

However, it is important to point out that, just as with all the other real senses, our sense of taste is also subject to hallucinations. These taste hallucinations are referred to as *phantageusia* in medical literature. They are a real phenomenon (usually caused by exposure to toxic chemicals, epilepsy, dry mouth, prescription drugs, hormones, smoking, brain disorders, and mineral deficiencies). A taste hallucination is almost always an unpleasant taste, such as the taste of metal. I don't have any personal knowledge of stories about psychic taste, and it is probably the least common of all of the psychic senses.

Much more common than psychic taste are psychic smells.

I wondered to myself: Would I be able to recognize a psychic smell if I experienced it? How would I know? How would it differ from a regular smell? Stories about smells are always difficult to believe because smells are, by definition, invisible, intangible, and fleeting, and people might be tempted to confuse them with faint real smells. Clairolfaction refers to the psychic sense of smell, which, according to most psychics, is far less common than most of the other psychic senses. As far as I knew, I had never experienced this before. As I soon discovered, psychic smells come in all varieties. Some of the most common psychic smells identified by people are flowers, manure, rotten flesh, perfume or aftershave cologne, food, burning wood, ashes, tobacco smoke, and sickness.

Strange Psychic Smells: Marijuana Smoke to Rotten Flesh

A neighbor with whom I was friendly told me a story about a strange smell she couldn't explain. It happened after her childhood home went on the market for sale. She was curious to see what the house looked like on the inside, just for old time's sake. The real estate broker opened the side door of the empty house with a broker's key, and the two went inside. As soon as they walked inside, they both heard guitar music and smelled marijuana smoke. The sound and the smell were distinctly coming from the third floor. This was particularly odd because the house had been locked and vacant for a long time and there was no one else inside.

My neighbor immediately correlated these experiences with her deceased brother. Her teenage brother had died decades earlier in a motorcycle accident while her family had been living in this house. His room had been on the third floor. And yes, he had played guitar and smoked pot. The experience was so bizarre, especially in light of the fact that the house was vacated and locked, that both my friend and the broker abruptly left in a hurry.

Anyone tempted to say that this was a psychological delusion suffered by my friend who had certain expectations upon entering her old home would be at a loss to explain why the broker—who had no such psychological expectations—also heard and smelled the same things. Moreover, there was a logical connection between the perceived ghost and the sound of the guitar, the smell of marijuana, and the fact that it came from the third floor.

Other psychic smells apparently appear and reappear with great regularity despite the lack of a source. There is a place in Georgia known as Tunnel Hill, which has become famous for what is known as the death smell. Many particularly brutal and bloody Civil War battles were fought in the fields surrounding the old, abandoned tunnel. Every year, military reenactments are performed for the public at this spot. The area has long been reputed to be haunted, and there have been many reports of sightings of ghostly figures in military uniforms from the Civil War period, ghostly campfires and strange lights, hideous shrieks, marching dead Confederate soldiers, and so on. One of the military re-enactors, a local man named Ken Sumner, started out as an avid skeptic, but after seven years of experiencing supernatural phenomena at this site, he has changed his tune. One of the most common ghostly experiences at Tunnel Hill is a strong ghostly smell. According to Sumner:

> It's like a death stench, the smell of rotted human flesh. On the first occasion I was affronted with it, only [I] smelled it. None of the other men did, even though they were only a few feet away from me. Since that time, many others have smelled it. Sometimes as many as five or six at a time smell it.
>
> *(www.brownsguides.com/blog/weird-georgia-a-tunnel-to-hell/)*

Strangely, each time the death smell presents itself, some people on location experience it, but others do not. The fact that sometimes several people smell the odor and other times only one person smells it would suggest this is not a hallucination, but rather some kind of shared phenomenon. When groups of people experience an unreal experience, it is often called mass hysteria—a psychologically generated phenomenon, but not a real experience. But what about when different groups of people independently experience the same smell—then what? Then it becomes inexplicably real!

Jung's Psychological Explanation for a Ghostly Death Smell

I was amused to learn that even famed Swiss psychologist Carl Jung had actually experienced a psychic smell and then bravely attempted to analyze it. Jung's psychic olfactory experience was that of a smell of rotting flesh in a haunted house outside of London. He attempted to explain it away in psychological terms later, in highly intellectualized terms such as hypnoid states and autonomous complexes of the human psyche, but it is clear that he had a healthy respect for an experience that grabbed him unexpectedly with the full force of all of his bodily sensations.

In 1920, Jung was invited to lecture in London and a colleague of his arranged for him to stay at a summer weekend rental cottage in Buckinghamshire at a "ridiculously low price." In his account, he meticulously described the interior layout of the house—the rooms, placement of furniture, location of fireplaces, and so on. The first night, he went to bed at 11 o'clock. However, instead of falling into a deep sleep as he was accustomed to doing, he remained half-awake in a sort of torpor (a state of suspended activity), unable to move. Despite the fact that two windows were open and blew in the "flowery scents of high summer," he identified an "indefinable, nasty smell" in the room along with a strange stuffiness in the air.

> The next night, he casually mentioned to his host that he had not slept well, and so his colleague suggested he drink a bottle of beer before going to bed. Jung followed this advice and went to bed. The air in his room was fresh for about a half hour, but soon turned "stale and fuggy, and finally somehow repulsive." (*Psychology and the Occult*, p. 147)

He said: "[t]he only thing that came into my mind was that there was something sickly about it" (p. 147).

Each weekend that Jung spent at the cottage, his nighttime experiences intensified, much to his chagrin. He began to hear furniture creaking and rustling sounds in the corners of the room, and the repulsive smell returned along with his sense of torpor. He sensed a strange restlessness in the air and actually got up to close the windows, at which point he saw that the night was still and there was no wind at all.

As I read his account, I smiled as I imagined Jung, the great psychologist, becoming increasingly disturbed by things he could not explain in psychological terms. I could picture Jung as he downed more bedtime beers with growing anxiety and prowled around the property with his candle, looking for ghosts.

The fifth weekend was the culminating ghostly experience:

The fifth weekend was so unbearable that I asked my host to give me another room. This is what happened: it was a beautiful moonlight night, with no wind; in the room there were rustlings, creakings, and bangings; from outside, blows rained on the walls. I had a feeling there was something near me, and opened my eyes. There, beside me on the pillow, I saw the head of an old woman, and the right eye, wide open, glared at me. The left half of the face was missing below the eye. The sight of it was so sudden and unexpected that I leapt out of bed with one bound, lit the candle, and spent the rest of the night in an armchair. The next day I moved into the adjoining room, where I slept splendidly and was no longer disturbed during this or the following weekend. (pp. 149–150)

This experience convinced Jung that he had experienced something unearthly. He later learned from the two women who cleaned the house that it was well-known to be haunted by a ghost, which was why Jung got such a cheap rental price!

In later analysis of the situation, Jung searched in his own mind to make a connection between the putrid odor in the room and the smell of a cancerous patient. He constantly checked the degree of air blowing in the room through the open windows. In short, Jung gave us, through his account of seeing a ghost, the opportunity to challenge his physical sensations. Thus, Jung laid out in great detail both the physical and psychological factors that could have influenced his judgment or receptivity of the experience. Unfortunately, most people fail to do this—especially people with a desire to believe in an afterlife—when describing an encounter with a ghost.

Although he later discounted many of his sensations as being mere "hypnoid states" or hallucinations, Jung's explanation of the psychic smell is most interesting. He concludes the odors he smelled may actually have reflected some connection with the people who had previously lived in that room. Jung goes on to suggest that these smells may have been sublimated into our mental sense of intuition.

It is also conceivable that intuition in man has taken the place of the world of smells that were lost to him with the degeneration of the olfactory organ. The effect of intuition on man is indeed very similar to the instant fascination which smells have for animals. I myself have had a number of experiences in which "psychic smells," or olfactory hallucinations, turned out to be subliminal intuitions which I was able to verify afterwards. (*Psychology and the Occult,* p. 152)

Jung was right on the money when he cautioned that "parapsychology would do well to take account of the modern psychology of the unconscious" (p.152). Even Jung's mentor, the father of psychoanalysis, Sigmund Freud, who is mostly remembered as a staunch critic of supernatural phenomena, softened toward the idea of paranormal activity very late in his career. Freud actually wrote a mild defense in favor of keeping an open mind toward telepathic and other thought-transference phenomena (see Pratt, J.G., et al):

No doubt you would prefer that I should hold fast to a moderate theism, and turn relentlessly against anything occult. But I am not concerned to seek any one's favor, and I must suggest to you that you should think more kindly of the objective possibility of thought-transference and therefore also of telepathy.

Furthermore, at the age of 65, Freud seems to have had a similar revelation as Jung's. In a letter to American researcher Herewood Carrington, Freud makes the somewhat startling confession: "If I had to start my life over again I would rather be a parapsychologist than a psychoanalyst" (Holzer).

It is ironic, to say the least, that both Jung and Freud, toward the end of their tremendously successful medical careers in psychiatry, both began to accept psychic phenomena as something meriting their attention and serious study.

Smell Hallucinations

I learned that a number of recognized smell disorders do actually exist. These include a reduction in one's sense of smell, called *hyposmia*, and a total loss of smell, called *anosmia*, which occurs in roughly 1–2 percent of the total American population, the majority of whom are over the age of 65, when sense of smell naturally decreases. Other types of smell disorders can occur when a person's perception of an odor becomes distorted, as when a normally pleasant smell is experienced as unpleasant, or when a person perceives a smell that isn't present at all.

However, generally speaking, smell disorders only occur in people who have experienced trauma or injury; most often head injuries and upper respiratory illnesses are implicated. Other causes for smell disturbances are polyps in the nasal cavities, sinus infections, hormonal disturbances, dental problems, cancer radiation treatments, and exposure to certain chemicals, such as insecticides and solvents.

In fact, smell hallucinations do exist! Temporary olfactory hallucinations can occur coupled with sensation of *déjà vu* during uncinate seizures, which are a form of temporal lobe epilepsy. The uncus, which is part of the smell-brain, known as the rhinencephalon, is located within the limbic system of the brain. The limbic system includes the amygdala, known for regulating our emotions, and the hippocampus, known for preserving memories. The closeness in proximity of the olfactory bulb to these structures regulating emotions results in a close linkage between smells and the emotions they evoke. This beeline to the much older and more primitive structure of the brain (the limbic system) is unique to the sense of smell.

I contacted the Monell Chemical Senses Center in Philadelphia, an independent research organization devoted to the senses of smell and taste, and asked scientists there who were specialized in smell disorders whether anyone had ever documented a case of mass smell hallucinations (multiple people claiming to smell the same thing). I was told they had never run across such a thing. This leads me to my next story. If it wasn't a real smell or a mass smell hallucination, then what the heck was it?

Psychic Smell in My Psychic Detective Class

On May 3, 2006, I finally had my opportunity to find out whether a psychic smell actually smells differently than a regular smell. I went to my psychic detective workshop at Nancy Orlen Weber's house. We had been talking and working on cases for nearly three hours, when Nancy decided to give us some new assignments of psychic detective cases. She went into the back office to make photocopies of whatever information she happened to have on the case (usually an e-mail from a distraught relative or a missing person's police flier), and then handed each of us a copy. We were instructed by her to hold the paper face down without looking at it. She told us to focus on the folded sheet of paper in our hands, and then write down our impressions on a separate piece of paper.

This particular night we all seemed to be in rare form. For some reason, all of us had a curious case of the giggles. It had started early on in the evening. There were five of us, all women, sitting in the living room.

As she held the paper in her hands, Christina said with a serious voice, "It's definitely giving off a lot of heat" (referring to the psychic vibes of the piece of paper).

I said (being the token skeptic in the group) with an equally serious tone, "Well, it's fresh off the photocopy machine!"

We all got a good laugh. We were all giddy. Nancy left us and started walking around tidying things while we focused our attention on the paper and our psychic readings.

Suddenly, I smelled a very bad smell. I wrinkled my nose and made a face as I looked across the room (roughly 14 feet away) at Janine and the other two women sitting next to her. Janine asked why I had wrinkled my nose (apparently she was not smelling what I smelled). I looked at the only woman sitting near me (who wishes to remain anonymous), and she seemed to have caught a whiff of the same odor. I joked (in extremely poor taste) that perhaps she had experienced a bout of flatulence.

She responded with indignity, "I did not! And whatever that is, it *stinks!*"

Within a few moments, the other three women on the other side of the room suddenly began to smell the same odor that she and I smelled. All three began wrinkling up their noses and complaining about the stench. In my mind, I was sure that when Nancy had briefly opened the front door behind me only minutes before, that air must have suddenly entered the room from outside. I assumed immediately it must have been a dead animal somewhere on her front stone porch. This didn't seem very logical, however, because when I had entered her house three hours earlier by walking up the long walkway to her porch and through the same front door, I had not smelled anything at all. It takes longer than three hours (especially in the cool of the evening) for flesh to decay to the point where it strongly reeks. In fact, earlier in the evening, I had commented how lovely it was to drive up the road to her house because the fragrant smell of lilacs and flowering trees filled the air. I, like my mother, have an acute sense of smell.

However, when I turned my head around to find the presumed source of the smell from the door I assumed had a screen on it, I saw that the solid glass and metal-framed exterior door remained tightly closed. This meant the smell was not wafting inside from the outdoors. Even stranger, the smell was becoming stronger—like an odor that was infusing itself throughout the room. It did not appear to have a source location from which it was traveling. At first, I had wondered vaguely if it might have been one of Nancy's two cats that had made a particularly pungent deposit outside of their kitty litter box (which is not located anywhere near the living room), but it was clearly *not* that kind of smell. It was not any type of a sewage smell; it was a rotting, dead flesh smell. It is a smell that occurs when small rodents die in between the walls of a house and the room stinks for days on end. It is very distinctive.

I wondered if perhaps one of the cats had dragged a trophy mouse into the house and had left it somewhere in my vicinity—perhaps under my chair. But that theory didn't really make any sense, either. We had been in the house, in the same room, for three hours and there hadn't even been a hint of this smell before. In fact, Nancy's house never smelled bad. Normally, the air was rather thick with the sweet, pungent smells of her essential oils. Not only that, but the intensity of this smell had magnified 10-fold over the course of only a minute and seemed to be spreading across the room without losing its intensity from where I was sitting. As anyone knows, this is unnatural for a smell. Normally, there is a directional source and a slow dissipation based upon its movement through a larger volume of space. This smell was not being blown across the room and was not moving along with its spread. Instead it seemed to be growing larger and stronger.

The women on the other side of the room verbalized what the woman sitting next to me and I already knew: It was the stench of death. When we all realized that we were experiencing the same stench of death together and, because as psychics we have learned to associate simultaneous but logically unconnected events, it became instantly clear to all of us that it was related to the case we were working on. We all simultaneously realized that the smell was way too powerful, overwhelming, and without a logical source to be of this world. It was a spiritual message or a spirit presence. In the course of my year and half of attending those workshops, nothing even remotely similar had ever happened. The case we were working on had been assigned to me.

When Nancy came back in the room, as if she instantly understood the situation and without saying a word about the smell, she asked the group, "Do you all need something to take care of this? Some protection? White light? Essential oils? White Angelica?"

The immediate, loud, unanimous, and urgent response of all the women present in the room was "Yes!"

So, she left the room and came back with a bottle of one of the essential oils called White Angelica that she uses to elevate one's spiritual level. We all smeared on little drops of the sweet-smelling oil, "cleansed our psyches," and then resumed the task at hand. As quickly as it had appeared, the smell suddenly vanished.

Another indicator that was not logical was that the essential oil sweet smell could not, in any realistic sense, have covered up or overpowered the stench that fast. They were equally powerful smells: one good, one bad. The stench, had it behaved like a normal smell, would have spent some moments intermingling with the sweet smell—there would have been some brief overlap of smells—before disappearing. But there wasn't. A powerful stench generally sticks around and takes longer to dissipate than a lighter smell. This heavy stench, however, disappeared instantly from all corners of the room! And it did not return for the remainder of the evening—not even a tiny trace smell. That was also truly remarkable.

What was even more interesting was that when I later asked Nancy whether she had in fact smelled this odor even though she had not been in the room with us until we were all overpowered by it, she told me that she had smelled it while she was in the kitchen! It would have been absolutely impossible for a normal smell to have migrated from where I sat by the front door, across the living room (roughly 20 feet), around the corner into the dining area connected to the far end of the living room, and then a sharp right into the kitchen. To achieve this result, the smell would have had to have been virtually pumped up through the walls of every room simultaneously.

The presence of this mysterious odor soon became obvious to all of us sitting in the room when Nancy finally instructed us to turn over the piece of paper we had been holding and doing a reading on. We saw that it was a missing person's bio distributed by the New Jersey State police and the Office of the Attorney General. It showed a photograph of a young man named John Fiocco Jr., a 19-year-old student at the College of New Jersey in Ewing, New Jersey, who was last seen about a month and a half prior at the college. During each stage of the investigation, this case had been reported on local television. The victim had mysteriously disappeared from his college campus without a trace.

Roughly three weeks later, there was a follow-up report on the news. This time, the reporter indicated that police had done an extensive search of the surrounding college campus and had located suspicious blood and bloodied items in a dumpster near his dormitory.

A couple of weeks later, the boy's DNA was identified on the blood found in the dumpster. I learned (the day *after* the experience at Nancy's house) that his body was then reportedly found in a Buck's County, Pennsylvania, landfill where the school dumpster was unloaded. The strange "coincidence" between our psychic reading of this case and the stench of rotten, dead flesh was striking. There was no way any of us could have imagined or anticipated that we were working on the case of a man whose body had been rotting in a landfill because none of us had looked at the printed side of the paper. Nor had this ever happened on any of the other missing person or homicide cases we had worked on. The fact that the stench did not behave as a normal smell, in terms of lack of source, multidirectional and simultaneous movement and expansion, and sudden dissipation also suggested it was not a smell in the normal sense of the word.

In the case of our death stench, six of us smelled it or, assuming it was some unlikely form of hallucination, collectively shared this mental experience. I tend not to believe it was a hallucination because, although as psychic detectives we frequently work with death in the spiritual realm and thus might be expected to have anticipated another death situation (and therefore a death smell), we had never before experienced any group or individual olfactory sensations in connection with any other cases. Moreover, the stench created a strong, almost visceral and physical reaction in many of the women. It certainly did not seem like an imaginary sensation. We had no obvious reason to be collectively hallucinating—theoretically, at least, we would all have to be having simultaneous seizures or olfactory degenerative disorder!

Of course, this kind of psychic smell has never—to my knowledge—been replicated under laboratory conditions. So, for all intents and purposes, it does not exist in the world of science. The problem is, if you don't know how to re-create whatever caused the initial sensory event, then you cannot verify it again under carefully controlled scientific conditions. If I smell the citrusy scent of orange in the air, I know that I can reproduce that olfactory sensation again and again, as long as I slice open another orange. The fruit supplies the "cause" for my sensory event. The problem is that you can't force a ghost to appear on command. Furthermore, we don't yet understand the mechanism in the brain that causes us to interpret sensory data as a psychic *smell* versus a psychic vision, sense of touch, or a sound. We don't know why the brain images data in one sensory format or another.

Given this dearth of information on the subject of psychic smell, I figured the next best thing would be to ask all the other women in my class to share their experience of this smell. That way I could compare our impressions of how it appeared and traveled throughout the house. The results are quite interesting, just as much for how they differ as for they are similar!

I was quite interested to learn that Christina, who was sitting on the other side of the living room closer to the kitchen and further away from the front door, experienced the smell as having a place of origin in the kitchen. My own sense had been that the smell clearly originated near the door behind me! Christina's logical mind first began by wondering if it wasn't something rotten in the refrigerator that Nancy might have opened. Then she quickly equated the stench with a memory of the smell of her aunt's decomposing body at her wake. Christina explained it as follows:

> So cool about the smell last night...this was the first time I've ever smelled something so strong and putrid in a "mediumship" environment. I first got a subtle whiff soon after Nancy went to the kitchen. In fact, my logical thoughts were that something might have been spoiled from the refrigerator (remember she went in to get us some munchies). But then, the more I smelled it, the sicker I felt. My stomach became nauseous. I was getting psychic impressions of body parts, mainly in the upper body—head, ears, chin—being sliced open, rotting and something that had been sitting there for days. Then, I literally felt as if an invisible vapor of death/stench circled around my body, behind my back, under

my legs. It was everywhere in the room. I felt like it was hovering above our heads. Also, I felt as if the more we acknowledged the stench, the stronger it became. It felt like an energy that wanted to grab our attention.

Now that I've had some time to process it, I know it was the smell of death. This is gruesome but here is how I recognize it... when my aunt Irma passed away from pancreatic cancer in Mexico, the body was prepared for a short viewing but the insides were not flushed. Because of the heat and rate of decomposition, later in the day the fluids started to gurgle out of the nostrils and side of mouth. At the same time, I could smell the stench of the decomposing body. I will *never* forget that smell. It's been 10 years and I can still visualize the whole thing.

Clearly, what can also be determined from Christina's statement is that the smell was highly recognizable and had a definite memory category for her as the stench of death. Thus, it becomes more difficult for the skeptical mind to argue that it might have been a smell that was putrid but otherwise unidentifiable.

Ellen, who was sitting on the far side of the room near the kitchen next to Christina and Janine, had a similar processing of the growing smell in the room. However, unlike Christina, it was Ellen's impression that the smell originated from the other end of the room near the front door where the other woman and I were seated. She wrote:

Here it is, from my notes: I first caught whiff of the smell when Nancy started passing around the papers with the guy's picture. At first, I thought the storm door had opened and something outside came wafting in, but that wasn't it. Then I thought I was imagining it. It smelled like something rotting—it reminded me of a time the cat brought home some poor hapless creature she had killed and I put it in a Ziploc bag in the garbage can, thinking the Ziploc would contain the smell until trash day. I was wrong! It was a bad smell at first, then became a horrific stench, but just for a moment. I stopped smelling it so strongly when we all began laughing, and it completely dissipated when someone (I don't recall who) opened the bottle of White Angelica.

Janine, who was seated next to Ellen, experienced the smell as follows:

OK—Here's my smell tell: I also thought that the smell was something outside. I initially looked at the window to see if it was open, then to the door—both of course were not. I got the smell of trash, but then much worse—the smell of something dead and rotting.... The smell entered and moved about the room. It didn't just fill the room and then get faint or fade away. It changed from just bad garbage to the smell of something definitely dead and it continued to move about the room, getting stronger for some and lighter for others, then stronger again. I believe he [the victim] was there on Thursday.

The woman who was seated near me by the front door, indicated that she was also immediately certain that it was the smell of death, although she admitted she had never smelled death before. Her sense was that the smell encircled all of us immediately (no source location). She makes the interesting comment that it seemed connected with certain negative emotions. She wrote:

Here are my thoughts. Everyone was really not focusing on the subject at hand. I was kind of mad about that because I felt that it was important and we should be giving it to our attention. All at once there was a smell in the room out of nowhere...it circled us. I knew what it was a once. Death. It had a mixture of common bad smells, yet there was a bit of it [that was] uncommon[.] I knew that smell from somewhere, but not because I have ever really smelled anything dead. It was a rotting smell and mixed with fear and hate. The funny thing here is that I can remove myself from the smell... it didn't go home with me and it isn't with me now, but I can recall it and pick it up again.

Even more strangely, from her location in the kitchen (not in the living room with the rest of us), Nancy had originally thought perhaps the smell had emanated from the basement where her husband was working. She soon discounted that idea in favor of a more spiritual interpretation of the smell. She interpreted the smell as death also—and of a spiritual message from the dead boy. She wrote:

Okay—smell—I believe [the victim] was giving us the only message he was capable of giving—a smell that hints at either what happened—the event and where it took place and/or where his body is now. I feel it is more about where the body was left. I think he watched while out of body. Why can't he give other pieces??? Sight—perhaps like psychic sight—he did not see the whole event and was unconscious—truly without recall—and the thing that "woke" his senses up while unconscious—was the smell because... smell is the last sense to leave us when dying. Smell is the most potent physical sense—the olfactory bulb is the biggest neural info center for the brain and perhaps as is in the physical world, in the world of spirit, the most potent awakener there.

I think it's pretty clear from this story that all six of us could not have been hallucinating a smell at the same time. Furthermore, the smell was powerful and identifiable for all of us, just like a real smell. But it could not have been a real smell because it did not behave like one. This leaves only one remaining possibility: It was a psychic sense of smell. This explanation works with regard to the case we were actually working on at the time involving a body in a landfill dump because it correlates with the type of putrid smell we experienced.

This got me thinking about the relationship between thoughts and smells. If I now tried to explain the difference between a psychic smell and an ordinary smell, I would have to explain it this way: Surprisingly, a psychic smell is just as seemingly real in the quality of its odor as a real smell. However, it is different from a real smell because 1) it has no logical source and 2) it does not behave (arrive, travel, or dissipate) like a normal smell. A psychic smell seems to defy normal rules of chemistry and physics. This type of experience of a smell is, like all other types of psychic phenomena, difficult to explain to other people who are not present for the actual experience.

Exercise

Sit back to back with someone. Have him or her taste something (salt, sugar, cinnamon, cocoa, chili powder) and try to imagine the taste in his or her mouth. Do the same with smells. Get feedback.

Lesson #16:

Psychics and Autistic Savants Have Instant Knowing

There is one psychic sense that does not correspond to our five senses of sight, sound, touch, smell, and taste. This is known as *clairintuition* and refers to psychic knowledge that arrives very mysteriously without any known sensory vehicle.

Clairintuition arrives as a sudden *feeling of certitude* about something without having any underlying factual knowledge or sense of how we know. So, for example, we might suddenly just know someone is going to call us on the telephone. We don't psychically see an image of this person in our mind or hear his or her voice; we just know it's him or her. Whatever our brain has done to process this kind of psychically obtained information, it has not only chosen to bypass all the various languages of the different senses, but it has also bypassed all our regular intellectual, logical, and linguistic channels. We end up having no clue how we know something, and we certainly cannot explain it to anyone else. Clairintuition is really the final frontier for understanding psychic ability.

Obviously, it is pointless to compare this kind of psychic ability with mental illness or sensory hallucinations, as I have done in previous chapters with other kinds of psychic senses, because no senses are implicated. However, it occurred to me that clairintuition—or immediate knowledge without a source—in some ways resembles another kind of mental disorder known as savantism in which people are able to access extraordinary information without thinking.

Autistic savants are people who suffer from a very particular form of autism. They comprise only 10 percent of all autistics. Until 1978, these people were called idiot savants, a term coined in 1887 by Dr. J. Langdon Down, who aptly noted their extraordinary memory was often associated with a great defect in reasoning power. Autistic savants usually have a very low IQ and the functioning ability of a mentally challenged person. They are known for their incredible naiveté because of their tendency to take everything so literally. They simply don't understand cunning or deceptive behavior. The flip side of this is that they generally have no concept of social tact, politeness, or empathetic concern that creates a need for kindness. Tactfulness is actually a mild form of deception—done in the name of not hurting someone else's feelings.

However, they generally have one extraordinary—seemingly super-human—skill. In his book *An Anthropologist on Mars*, Dr. Oliver Sacks describes a number of different ways in which Savant Syndrome can manifest itself as different skills. These include the so-called human calculators who can instantly perform huge and seemingly impossible mathematical calculations, others who can understand complex watch mechanisms and disassemble and swiftly reassemble watches with no prior training. Some savants have extraordinary musical ability and can reproduce a piece of complex music such as a symphony perfectly, note for note, after hearing it only one time. Other savants can make miniature models of ships and machines. Some savants are capable of extraordinary feats of athletic skills or acrobatics without any training. There was the famous case of a young autistic girl named Nadia who, at the age of 3, was able to sketch horses with a skill in terms of contour, perspective, shading, and design that seemed to rival those of Leonardo Da Vinci when he was in his prime! Savants generally have only one skill, but it is always extraordinary, as if they took their entire brain power and channeled it wholesale into a single, focused endeavor.

I figured it might be worth taking a closer look at the similarities between clairintuition and autistic savantism in order to understand the thinking or sensing mechanism that results in such extraordinary ability in both cases.

My Weird 11s

In May 2006, I began to experience something strange. It started very slowly and I didn't even notice at first. But by July, it was too damn obvious to ignore. My brain had, for reasons unknown to me, begun to focus on the number 11. I had no clue why. It seemed as though everywhere I looked the number 11 would appear—on alarm clocks, billboards, magazines, television, computers, cameras, and so on. Pretty soon, every time I randomly looked up at a clock it would invariably be 11 minutes past the hour. This would happen up to seven or eight times a day! This had never happened to me before and I was curious to understand if it had any significance. The normal reaction would be to dismiss this experience as merely coincidental and insignificant.

Obviously, I am aware that once you see something, the brain will begin to subconsciously seek it out. Was it possible I had become sensitized to recognize the number 11 and disregard other numbers? It did not feel like that. The 11s seemed to pop into my physical reality when I was least expecting them. It felt random and out of my personal control. It happened so frequently that I began to wonder if there wasn't some psychic or prophetic significance to it.

The only strong psychological association I had with the number 11 was 9/11, or September 11th, 2001, the date when the terrorists crashed two airplanes into the World Trade Center in New York. I had been living and working in Manhattan at the time and was, like every other New Yorker, traumatized by the event. I began to wonder if the persistent appearance of 11s wasn't some bizarre premonition about the upcoming anniversary of this disaster. I began to feel nervous as the month of September approached. But September 11th came and went without incident. I breathed a sigh of relief and figured my 11s fixation would go away. But it didn't. I continued to see the number 11 everywhere I went. What the hell was this?

On October 11th, a small private airplane piloted by 34-year-old Cory Lidle, a pitcher for the New York Yankees, crashed headlong into the 31st floor of a 50-story luxury apartment building on East 72nd Street on New York's Upper East Side. The impact of the crash damaged 10 stories and set much of the apartment building on fire. Lidle and his flight instructor were both killed. Fortunately, no one in the apartment building was harmed, although the damage to the building was extensive. Of course, in every New

Yorker's mind, it was like an instant flashback to the fear and panic of September 11th. Everyone assumed it was another terrorist attack. People went screaming and running for cover away from the flames and burning debris. It turned out to be a bizarre accident due to pilot error.

This crash seemed as though it might solve the significance of my 11s. It occurred on the 11th of the month. Eleven of the 160 firemen who battled the blaze were injured. So, all in all, I figured this must have been what my recurring 11s premonition was all about.

So, I breathed another sigh of relief.

But the 11s kept coming, and they were coming faster and more frequently than ever! I was actually starting to feel a bit frantic and slightly nuts. I was so disturbed I started telling a few close friends and my husband about this weird phenomenon. I was seeing an 11 almost every time I looked up at a clock or television, and it had nothing to do with having a rough idea of the time. It was totally random. Nervously, I gave myself a new deadline. I figured once November 11th (or 11/11) passed, this whole thing would go away. But it didn't. Every day I would randomly glance at a clock, no matter what day, day or night, and it would be 11 minutes past the hour. This would happen, on average, maybe seven times a day.

One night, I woke up out of a deep sleep. I was strangely concerned that the clock would be on the 11 in its increasingly creepy way. So, I decided to outsmart myself. I waited a few minutes before opening my eyes and then looked at the clock. I figured this would throw off my innate sense of timing (assuming it actually existed). To my shock, when I opened my eyes and looked at the clock, it read 4:11 a.m. This only fueled my desire to outsmart myself. I decided to test myself to see if I could fall back asleep and then wake up at the next 11 occurrence.

When I next opened my eyes it was 4:43 a.m. I felt vindicated. At last, I had proven to myself that my little preoccupation was ridiculous— obviously I was incapable of psychically sensing when 11 would happen. I went back to sleep without any intention of testing myself again. But when I awoke and looked over at the clock, it was 5:11. I fell back asleep and when I next dared to open my eyes and look at the clock, it was almost as if someone was playing some terrible and mischievous game with me: It was 5:43. It felt like a tease—as if someone were saying to me: "You are way out of your league—don't even try to tamper with this again!" It seemed like some kind of a cosmic joke.

This phenomenon dragged on for months, then years. I began to look into numerology to see what the number 11 meant. I had never been interested in numerology or astrology. I had no idea what particular numbers meant, although I was vaguely aware that each number meant something different. As it turned out, according to numerologists, the number 11 is considered a "master number." The number 11 is associated with divine revelation and the side-by-side 1s in number 11 symbolize a channel from higher dimensions.

In March 2007, I decided to have a psychic reading done as a birthday present to myself. After only a few minutes, the psychic on the phone proceeded to ask me if I had ever had my astrological chart done. I answered no.

"What about numerology? Have you ever had that done?"

Again, I replied no.

"Well, that's interesting," she said, "Because I am getting a very strong number associated with you. It is *11-11*."

I nearly fell out of my seat with surprise when she said this, and I started laughing. There is no way she ever could have known about my little preoccupation with the number. She went on to tell me that in numerology this represents the number most associated with the highest spiritual source. "Spirits from the highest level of the spirit world are using this as a confirmation that they are communicating with you and helping you to write your book. This is confirmation you are on the right path." (I had told her in advance I was working on a book, but did not tell her the topic).

This raised a new issue for me: Was my 11-phenomenon merely an uncannily accurate sense of time, or was it actually a confirmation of a spirit communication? Was this an attempt by the spiritual world to grab my attention? Was I psychically hearing a communication from the great beyond for the first time in these very unconventional terms? Was this kind of savant-like ability to sense time actually a window into a totally different experience of the universe?

Knowing Without Knowing

I believe autistic savants clearly demonstrate the ability to be clairintuitive, but we rarely give them credit for it. Instead, we are far more likely to perceive them as having some phenomenal, but still rather pedestrian, skill, such as counting or computing things mathematically—and we don't normally regard this kind of skill as a form of intuition. Intuition is normally linked with a kind of deep wisdom or ability to perceive *meaning*. Autistic savants are notoriously *unintuitive* in this regard. However, I believe we underrate their intuitive ability to feel their world in a highly sensory way that permits them to obtain extraordinary information. This is unavoidable for most autistics due to their defect in reasoning power—in Dr. Down's words. Psychics, however, are often accused of being flaky or irrational—which also implies some defect in their reasoning power. This coincidence suggests that rational thinking may inhibit extraordinary thinking abilities.

Take the case of the two identical twin autistic calendar savants, John and Michael, for example. The twins managed to catch the attention of famed neurologist Dr. Oliver Sacks, who paid them a visit in 1966. Despite their very low IQs of only 60, both twins were able to calculate dates and days 40,000 years in the past or in the future with instantaneous ease.

As Dr. Sacks pointed out, their memory for numerical digits was simply incredible. They could calculate numbers with hundreds of digits with no apparent problem. But outside of their tiny fiefdom of calendar calculations, they failed abysmally—even in the field of mathematics. They were incapable of performing even simple calculations involving addition, subtraction, multiplication, or division. They just couldn't seem to grasp the concept of mathematical operations. They had no intuitive sense of logic or pragmatism.

At some point during his interview with the twins, a box of matches fell on the floor, scattering matches everywhere. The twins both immediately cried out "111!" There was no way in the world that they could have actually counted the matches that quickly.

When Dr. Sacks slowly and painstakingly sat down and counted the exact number of matches on the floor, he discovered there were 111. How can that be? How could anybody calculate that rapidly? When Dr. Sacks asked them this question, they responded that they did not count—they saw. Of course, they were not seeing in the ordinary sense of the word. This kind of seeing lies somewhere between seeing with one's eyes and seeing with one's mind—which is exactly what psychics do. It is a limbo between what we call reality and the imagination. The twins explained that they didn't count; they simply saw the number 111. Like Daniel Tammet, they were not thinking in mathematical terms like the rest of us do. They were *feeling* a holistic sense of a number in a very intuitive way. How does one *feel* numbers? For starters, one must not *think* about them.

This event caused Dr. Sacks to spend some time seriously reflecting upon what process they could be using to arrive at the correct answer. He wanted to understand what this sense or visual image of "111-ness" or "triple 37-ness" was. He struggled mightily with this problem, speculating that the twins had an inner landscape, a kind of "immense mnemonic tapestry" in which "everything could be seen, either isolated or in relation."

At some other point, Dr. Sacks speculated that perhaps the twins could "see" some enormous number vine, with all its number-leaves, number-tendrils, and number-fruit. He also thought perhaps numbers became familiar and known to the twins, kind of like old friends who know everything about each other. This, he postulated, might account for their instant recognition of numbers and particularly their love of prime numbers.

This sense of immediate, holistic recognition of an entity—a number—was compared by Dr. Sacks to the phenomenon of facial recognition. Normally, the brain recognizes the face of someone in a holistic instant, and not by a method of aggregation—that is, recognizing the bits and pieces and then totaling them up together to arrive at an aggregated sum like an exercise in arithmetic.

Ultimately, Dr. Sacks seemed to prefer an explanation for the twins' calculator ability given to him by a colleague who suggested that the twins were not using conventional methods of arithmetic operations, but rather a form of modular arithmetic. "If such methods, such visualizations, are regarded as algorithms, they are algorithms of a peculiar sort—organized, not algebraically, but spatially, as trees, spirals, architectures, 'thought-scapes'—configurations in a formal yet quasi-sensory mental space" (*The Man Who Mistook...* p. 211).

Dr. Sacks's description of a "quasi-sensory mental space" is right on the money. This is the place where *sensory* experience meets *cognitive* experience. They become virtually indistinguishable from one another.

Psychics are almost as inarticulate as autistic savants when trying to explain how they knew something. They will tell you, "I don't know. I just *knew* it!" It sounds awfully lame. This non-explanation for extraordinary thinking ability is very frustrating indeed for anyone who genuinely wants to understand the mechanism for how this works! Moreover, psychics seem to arrive at their conclusions in very much the holistic fashion as the twins when making their calendar calculations. The answer appears suddenly, in its totality, and almost with the quality of a sensory—as opposed to a cognitive—experience. Psychics also tend to use the language of the senses (*I feel, I see, I hear*) when trying to describe their experience. A psychic's sensory experience appears to operate on a strictly mental level, with stimuli arriving at and affecting only the person's mind, not sensory organs.

Feeling an essence of a number, space, time, color, or event evokes sensations or pictures. Pictures or shapes can be recalled more easily and contain huge amounts of information. As I have already mentioned before, shapes are merely snapshots of entire trends of movement. They are information-rich. The less we attempt to make logical connections, the better our ability to recall.

However, unlike savants, most of us are saddled with a lifelong burden of making meaningful relationships between things. This gives us an edge on being able to engage in abstract thought, but it also means that we are at a disadvantage in the sense that we cannot see the world in terms of unique and unrelated objects. Everything in our "normal" world is colored with a certain amount of relativity.

I was curious to know whether Dr. Sacks had ever investigated psychic phenomena as part of his research into weird and unusual neurological conditions. After all, if you really believe psychics are delusional; shouldn't they be medically analyzed like other crazy people? So, I wrote to him to find out.

In November 2001, I received a lovely letter from Dr. Sacks. He is probably the last human being on earth to write his letters on an old-fashioned typewriter. I had the intuitive sense from looking at his letter that he uses the "hunt and peck" method of typing. He wrote to me: "I confess I have never given much thought to 'psychic' phenomena—partly because I cannot imagine, at least with some of them, what sort of physical basis they might have whereas, say, I can at least imagine a neural basis for aesthetic or mystical feeling."

Dr. Sacks, one of my personal heroes, clearly has an understanding of the depth of the human spirit and the ways in which neurological wiring integrates itself and infiltrates our individual talents, gifts, sensations, and even our most fundamental sense of chronological self. If all he is looking for is some shred of a neural basis for psychic sensing, I believe that day has arrived.

A Sense of Time

I was very surprised to learn that many autistic savants have an almost inhuman ability to precisely tell time.

In his book *Phantoms in the Brain*, Dr. V.S. Ramachandran wrote about the different ways in which Savant Syndrome can manifest itself. He describes a young boy who knows the time whether he is asleep or awake!

> Other savants have incredibly specific talents. One boy can tell you the time of day, to the exact second, without referring to any timepiece. He can do this even in his sleep, sometimes mumbling the exact time while dreaming. The "clock" inside his head is as accurate as any Rolex. (p. 193)

I was interested in this account for the obvious reason that this autistic savant boy seemed to share my ability to tune into time on a highly accurate and subconscious level. Of course, his ability was far more advanced than mine, and mine only seemed to work on the 11s. Many of us, myself included, have the ability to wake ourselves up the next morning at a precise time without the benefit of an alarm clock. I can often wake myself up at the exact minute and hour I selected the previous night.

So, this uncanny ability to know and feel time is clearly some kind of a general human skill, although some people are better at it than others.

I wondered if my ability to tap into time intervals was similar to this autistic skill. And if I were enhancing some sensing ability, perhaps that was also opening the door into some kind of psychic perception. Possibly I was increasing my sensory awareness of my mind's language to itself—a kind of self-to-self or spirit-to-self dialogue. The number 11, with all its attendant significance, seemed to be a wake-up call to my own spirit. Or, perhaps I was suddenly becoming tuned in to some recurring event within myself, such as the 40-Hz. coherent electrical wave that engulfs the brain at regular intervals, or some other natural rhythm of the body. In any event, this uncanny ability to know time in a clairintuitive way tends to confirm my belief that the there exists a sense of time and it can be useful (like all of our other senses) for prediction when we stop thinking about it.

Then I read about another savant—a 50-year-old woman named Ellen. She was unusual, for starters, because there are very few autistic savants who are women. Men are 10 times more likely to suffer from autism than women. Dr. Darold A. Treffert, a leading researcher in the field of Savant Syndrome and clinical professor of psychiatry at the University of Wisconsin Medical School in Madison, wrote an article about Ellen that appeared on the Website of the Foundation for the Study of Savant Syndrome (hosted by Wisconsin Medical Society).

According to Dr. Treffert, this time-keeping ability is actually rather *common* among savants. At precisely the moment when her favorite news program is about to air, Ellen will stop whatever she was doing and turn on the television set, and the announcer will start the show as if on cue! This is reminiscent of the movie *Rain Man* in which the fictional autistic Raymond Babbit (based on the real-life autistic Kim Peek) would have to drop everything he was doing at exactly 4:00 p.m. every day in order to watch his favorite television show, *The People's Court,* with Judge Wapner. One of the most famous lines from the movie is Raymond's insistent and increasingly urgent chant "ten minutes to Wapner."

> Ellen's highly developed sense of timekeeping became evident at about age 8. To help Ellen overcome a fear of the telephone that she seemed to have at that age, her mother coaxed her one day to listen to the automatic time recording, or the "time lady" available in those days. Ellen listened for about ten minutes and returned to her room where she mimicked what she had heard on the phone. She correctly understood the sequence of seconds, and when she came to "one fifty-nine and fifty-nine seconds" Ellen announced, "The time is two o'clock." The mystery is that, during the ten minutes she had listened, there was no change from one hour to the next, and no explanation as to how Ellen knew to change the hour at the 59-minute, 59-second point. She had obviously never seen a clock, and neither the concept of time elapsing nor the workings of a clock have ever been explained to her.

It occurred to me that time seems to take on a very special importance for many autistic savants. We measure time with a sequence of numerical units. Otherwise, time would simply be an infinite state of being-ness in the present without boundaries. Many savants are obsessive about sequence and order.

As English autistic savant Daniel Tammet wrote in his extraordinary book, *Born on a Blue Day*, "Numbers are my first language, one I often think and feel in" (p. 7). Note he uses the word *feel* in addition to *think*. How do you feel a number? Normally, we don't feel numbers—or, at least, we think we don't.

Elsewhere he wrote, "When I count, the numbers form pictures and patterns in my mind that are consistent and reassuring to me. Then I can relax and interact with whatever situation I'm in" (p. 7). He would spend hours during his childhood playing games with huge numbers and inventing new math games. Whenever he was upset, particularly when his daily routine was disturbed, he would begin to count and the process of counting would calm him down. Sequence—which creates order, structure, and a sense of future that can be anticipated—is the cornerstone of much savant thinking. Certainly music, an area in which many savants excel, is dependent upon a sequential order with mathematically defined rhythms and vibrational frequencies. Music can be counted just like numbers or time.

Interestingly, savants may also count space.

Dr. Ramachandran described another savant in his book who had an amazing sense of physical space. She was able to "estimate the exact width of an object seen from twenty feet away. You or I would give a ballpark figure. She would say, 'That rock is exactly two feet, eleven and three-quarter inches wide.' And she'd be right" (p. 193). It seems likely that this ability to gauge precise measurements of space is that of an autistic savant who pays very special attention to the numeric or sequential attributes of the space around her.

Autistic savants appear to be tapped into a superhighway of knowledge that involves feeling numerical measurements in a very kinesthetic way. It has nothing to do with counting or calculating in the normal sense of the word. I wondered whether my strange sense of 11s was also related to a way of feeling time instead of thinking about it.

Thinking in Sounds

Perfect pitch (also sometimes called "absolute pitch") is the ability to discern the difference between the rate and frequency of the tones on a scale of auditory vibrations. A person with perfect pitch will be able to distinguish between pitches with only 6 percent difference in frequency. Perfect pitch recognizes each note for itself, as unique, and does not require another note for purposes of comparing the musical interval in one's mind. In fact, people with the unusual genetic disorder known as Williams-Beuren Syndrome (a condition similar to autism) and autistics both have significantly higher rates of perfect pitch than the average population. Why is that?

I believe perfect pitch is simply a way of sensing sound in a literal way. People who have *relative pitch*, which is fairly common among musicians, particularly those who play by ear, create a relationship between two notes in order to calculate the musical distance between them. They need a set point of reference before finding the second note. In other words, a person with relative pitch will only be able to identify the musical note F after he or she hums the note C as a reference point and then counts up the scale to find F. Relative pitch can easily be developed by ear training and is considered a skill, not a gift.

Relational thinking leads to abstract thought.

The point is that people with relative pitch are actually thinking differently about sound than people with perfect pitch. A musical interval between two notes is like a poetic metaphor ("The sky was glowing like a copper pan"). It creates a relationship between two different images. Relative pitch is hearing a comparison between two things, like a poetic metaphor. Autistics are unable to appreciate metaphors and comparisons. Remember how Temple Grandin was unable to think about a "dog" but had to research her vast memory banks for all unique dogs she had ever seen? She had no ability to compare them in her mind. Most of us experience our senses figuratively, not literally, like most autistic savants or psychics.

In 1901, a German physician named Dr. Otto Abraham (1872–1926), one of the founders of the field of ethnomusicology at the Psychological Institute of Berlin, theorized that most people are actually born with musical perfect pitch! However, very few people are able to hold on to this ability. Why? For exactly the same reason we cannot retain our inborn psychic, linguistic, or synesthetic abilities: We start to *think* too much!

Dr. Abraham's theory has recently gained acceptance among many developmental psychologists as a way to explain why so few people in our population have perfect pitch. His theory is called the Unlearning Theory. His theory basically proposes that we are all born with absolute pitch, just like other animals, such as wolves and songbirds, but that we slowly lose this ability over time. The primary culprit for "unlearning" perfect pitch is attributed to the acquisition of cognitive styles that involve *relational processing*. Remember that: We lose a natural sensory gift because we teach ourselves certain intellectual relationships between sounds. The cognitive process (thinking) causes us not to hear. We cease to experience sensory phenomena with our *sensing-mind*, and instead replace it with our *thinking-mind*.

Recent studies have shown that perfect pitch can be effectively taught as a skill to children between the ages of 2 and 4, but the same programs are ineffective after the age of 5. This suggests perfect pitch may be an innate ability that we lose over time. This childhood window of time for unlearning perfect pitch also correlates with those ages when it is believed we also unlearn our linguistic and synesthetic abilities. It has also been suggested by most psychics (although not scientifically verified) that we are all born psychic but lose that ability in early childhood through a similar process of unlearning.

Remember: Psychics think in sounds.

Thinking in Pictures

There have been a number of recent developments in the field of neuroscience that are beginning to shed light on exactly why autistics think differently than the rest of us. They don't think; they simply see.

An article that appeared on September 10, 2006, in *Brain*, an on-line neurology journal, detailed a study performed by researchers from the Center for Cognitive Brain Imaging at Carnegie Mellon University and the departments of psychiatry and neurology at the University of Pittsburgh School of Medicine. *The results suggest that literal thinking means not thinking in words.*

The study showed some very interesting results from fMRI brain scans comparing the way an autistic brain lights up while reading a passage out of a book versus a normal person. When reading a text loaded with visual imagery, a normal person's brain will show activity not only in the language center of the brain, but also the occipital region toward the back of the brain, which processes visual imagery. A normal person will also show a great deal of interaction and interconnectivity between these cortical regions while reading a text. An autistic person will see the images described by the words—even in sentences containing very little visual imagery—while a non-autistic person will think about the words. Autistics have low connectivity between these brain regions.

Autistic savant Temple Grandin explains in her book, aptly entitled *Thinking in Pictures,* that it came as something of a shock to her when she learned that other people thought in words, not pictures. As she explains:

> It wasn't until I went to college that I realized some people are completely verbal and think only in words. I first suspected this when I read an article in a science magazine about the development of tool use in prehistoric humans. Some renowned scientists speculated that humans had to develop language before they could develop tools. I thought this was ridiculous, and this article gave me the first inkling that my thought processes were truly different from those of many other people. When I invent things, I do not use language. Some other people think in vividly detailed pictures, but most think in a combination of words and vague generalized pictures. (p. 27)

Grandin, a designer of livestock handling facilities and a professor of animal science at Colorado State University, invented a number of cattle-handling facilities, including stalls, dip-vats, pens, chutes, and loading ramps. She has designed an incredible one-third of all of the livestock handling facilities in the country. She claims that every one of her inventions and designs begins as a highly detailed picture image in her imagination. She is able to examine her creative image from any angle or perspective and still retain incredible detail. She describes this ability as having her own personal, internal, 3-D computer graphics system. Not only can she turn it in different directions, but she can also change out parts and "install" new fixtures on to her ideas with total ease. Grandin thus maintains a mental library of *photographic memories* of machines and parts.

This ability to mentally examine an object from any perspective in space is very similar to the process employed by psychics. Psychics, like autistics, see in pictures. This enables them to access extraordinary information because they are not bogged down by thinking.

Seeing, Instead of Thinking, Can Be Trained

During the course of my research and interviews with some of the most famous psychics in the world, I learned that most of them admitted to having a *photographic memory!* That is extremely significant. That means that psychics have a highly developed a method of memorizing that *does not involve thinking.* They are able to revisit information in their heads by seeing it again. Their brains are able to capture data without words. They are then able to use this wordless technique of thinking in order to capture (and remember) other types of information about their environment.

This psychic ability to think in pictures can be trained. You do not need to have some inborn photographic memory—although it certainly helps to have one. I realized that I, too, have a mild form of photographic memory, but it took me years of training before I reached the point where my flat, two-dimensional, mental still-life images finally began to move, become fluid, and interact with other images, and come alive.

Let me give you an example of two-dimensional seeing.

I once was getting a massage at a luxurious spa in the Mirage Hotel in Las Vegas. The massage therapist and I never exchanged a single word except to say hello, and of course I had never met her before in my life. At the very end of the session, I asked her if I could ask her a crazy question.

She said, "Sure."

"Well," I said, "While you were massaging me I got a very clear photographic image in my mind. I actually watched it develop like the old-fashioned Polaroid instant camera."

I explained to her that the photo image had developed from the top of the frame and slowly worked its way down. As it developed, I began to see sprigs of dark green, pointed, shiny leaves and then some small, round, red berries appear. I assumed I was looking at a picture of holly and for some reason, I associated it with her.

So I asked her, "Do you know anyone named Holly?"

I was sure my funny little image was pure nonsense, but had learned to force myself to double-check it with reality as part of an ongoing series of psychic experiments I was conducting on myself. I had no legitimate reason to think of the word *holly*. It was June in Las Vegas and a steamy 100 degrees outside. It was not Christmastime. Nor was the name Holly anywhere in my own personal lexicon of friends' names: I had never known anyone named Holly.

The massage therapist looked at me with a rather surprised expression. "Well, if you really want to know," she said, "Right before your appointment I was on the phone talking with my sister in Florida. She was telling me about her best friend who just got pregnant and we're all kind of upset about it. Her name is Holly. I was thinking about her while I was massaging you."

As time went on and I began to develop my psychic abilities, I was soon able to not just passively observe a single image, but I was able to move my line of sight around the image and examine it without losing it altogether. This involves a great deal of mental concentration and focus. This is a difficult exercise in the early stages of psychic development because these images are so delicate and tenuous that it is hard to remember them. They are usually visually unclear, imprecise, and often colorless to start. It requires a very good skill set to learn how to retrieve this kind of amorphous information in your brain. At this point, you need to learn how to integrate wordless judgments (often these are just feelings) about visual images into your understanding of this image itself. Often the wordless feeling will help you identify the object.

I remember very clearly the first time my psychic sensing morphed from two-dimensional imagery into a three-dimensional video format.

For me, this happened when trying to psychically tune in to a total stranger's medical history. I was able to accurately "diagnose" a woman's medical condition knowing absolutely nothing about her except that she was female and extremely ill. I wasn't even told her name, age, or location—absolutely nothing! In my mind, I saw a highly detailed image of two vertical, almond-shaped organs that were pulsating, were blood-red, and held in place by a network of sinews. I was able to view this image as if I were a movie camera on a crane swiveling smoothly around the object—rather like a computer-generated image. I was able to zoom in for a close-up to see a higher degree of detail and then zoom out at will. The strange organs seemed to be thyroid glands, although I had never seen any before and didn't know what they looked like. I felt she had thyroid cancer, although this seemed illogical because the woman was described as extremely ill and

I knew thyroid cancer has a successful cure rate. However, it turned out I was correct: She was suffering from thyroid cancer. I was also able to accurately describe her physical appearance.

This method of thinking in pictures, however, has its drawbacks. Autistic savant Daniel Tammet has described how such visual effects and mental associations can actually cause mental confusion.

> I often found my mind wandering, in part because I remember so much of what I see and read and a chance word or name in the middle of a conversation can cause a flood of associations in my mind like a domino effect. Today, when I hear the name Ian a mental picture of someone I know with this name comes spontaneously into my head, without me having to think about it at all. Then the picture jumps to one of the Mini he drives, which in turn causes me to picture various scenes from *The Italian Job*. The sequence of my thoughts is not always logical, but often comes together by a form of visual association. (p. 76)

For Tammet, the visual imagery locks in the meaning of different words and names. It is always very specific, and his logic is re-created from his associated visual picture groups, not groups clustered by associated meanings. This thinking process results in what appears to be a dysfunction of normal thought process and causes autistics to struggle with even the most basic concepts.

Psychics and other types of intensely creative people, such as artists and inventors, also frequently think in pictures, but are not disabled by them like most autistics. When you are working in the weird world of the paranormal, it is far easier to "think in pictures" when trying to access non-verbal phenomena. It is far more effective than trying to attach words to alien images, inexplicable sensations, or nonsensical thoughts that occur in altered states of mind. Thinking in pictures is the hallmark of creative thinking, psychic sensing, and eidetic memory (similar to photographic memory, though not limited to visual images). However, psychics do not suffer from brain dysfunction, which limits them to this method of thinking, and are able to transfer most of their thoughts back to the realm of the left hemisphere—something autistics cannot do.

Edgar Cayce, one of the greatest American psychics and certainly the most heavily documented psychic in history, obtained knowledge through pictures. In 1892, when he was just 15 years old, he was considered the best student in his class. His teacher was interested to know his study methods. Cayce's father told the teacher that all Cayce had to do was literally sleep on his books and the knowledge contained in those books would somehow seep into his brain in the form of pictures.

"I've been talking to your father. I remarked to him that you were my best student; that you always knew your lessons. He told me that you go to sleep to learn them. Others have mentioned the same thing. What is it? How do you do it?"

"I don't know really…I just seemed to know once that, if I put my head on a book and went to sleep, I'd know the lesson. Then I did it with other books, and it worked. I don't know what it is."

He was embarrassed, blushing.

"There's nothing odd about it," Mr. Thomb said. "Don't feel that you are different. There are many strange things in life that we know nothing about. How do you see your lessons, in pictures?"

"Yes, I see pictures of the pages" (Surgrue p. 49).

Similarly, the Croatian-born great genius and inventor Nikola Tesla (1856–1943), had a photographic memory and was capable of memorizing many complete books. An electrical engineer by training, Tesla invented the AC (alternating current) induction motor, which made the universal transmission and distribution of electricity possible. He worked for Thomas Edison, who advocated the inferior DC power transmission system. Much of Tesla's phenomenal research anticipated and paved the road for today's modern inventions, including worldwide wireless communications, fax machines, radar, radio-guided missiles and aircraft, auto ignition, telephone, alternating current power generation and transmission, radio, and television.

His autobiography, *My Inventions: The Autobiography of Nikola Tesla,* describes the manner in which many of his greatest thoughts came to him. During his childhood, he suffered from an affliction in which he would experience blinding flashes of light in front of his eyes and sometimes hallucinations. His visions were often linked to a word or idea he may have encountered, and just by hearing the word, he could involuntarily envision it in realistic detail. He would see the idea non-verbally and in very precise form. In this way, he was able to visualize his inventions very completely before he ever moved on to the construction stage.

The great physicist Albert Einstein made famous the concept of a thought experiment. This is another way of thinking in pictures. His most famous thought experiment involved imagining himself doing the impossible—riding on a beam of light waves—and gave him his greatest insight about physics, ultimately paving the way for his theory of relativity.

So, the point of all this so far, has been to demonstrate the similarities between autistic savants and psychics. Yes, they share a number of important ways of thinking about the world, and yet they are clearly not identical. *Literal thinking and literal sensing are a mixed blessing. They grant us access into new realms of sensing information, but are not easily communicated or transferred into logic.* Looking at the world literally and allowing yourself to experience your senses literally permits you see *more,* even if what you see doesn't make sense at all.

Induced Savantism in Regular People

If one member of a species manifests a special ability—in this case the human species—then it exists potentially in *all* members of that species.

Professor Allen Snyder, neuroscientist and director of the Centre for the Mind in Sydney, Australia, made the argument in 1999 that these seemingly superhuman autistic savant skills are biologically latent in all of us.

In 2002, he and his colleagues reported they had discovered a way to created what they called *induced savantism* in normal people by temporarily shutting down the left hemisphere of the brain (with its speech and short-term memory functions) using transcranial magnetic stimulation (TMS). In other words, Dr. Snyder had apparently figured out a way to unlock one's inner genius simply by tinkering with magnetic stimulation of the brain! His study showed that his subjects were able to vastly increase their artistic drawing and mathematical/counting skills within 15 minutes after magnetic stimulation of their brain, creating "instant savants" from normal people!

Amazingly, this inhibition of the electrical signals in the left hemisphere's neurons resembles the brain patterns of autistic savants. Most of us draw what we think something should look like rather than draw what we actually see. Thinking interferes with sensing. It is the same thing as learning a second language as an adult. We are not as adept as children because we are too busy translating foreign words into what we think they should sound like and we fail to listen.

He has theorized that the human brain develops through left-brained language and reasoning concepts. This style of thinking has the effect of suppressing the right-brain's ability to have access to details that comprise the larger, holistic picture. By inhibiting the left-brain (either by accidental means such as illness or brain trauma, or by deliberate means by using magnetic impulses to temporarily disable it), the right-brain's "genius" is able to flourish.

Dr. Snyder's conclusions are remarkable. His study demonstrated that when the left temporal lobe is shut down, the brain is capable of experiencing numbers in a holistic, literal, non-sequential fashion and the skills improve over time, suggesting this ability is trainable! Indeed his conclusions about the normalcy of savant gifts coincide with what I have argued is the operative factor in whether one is able to tune into or access one's innate psychic abilities or not—namely, we are handicapped by thinking too much. Our meaningful mental patterns end up becoming a sensory bias and this prevents us from experiencing the world literally and accurately.

A Psychic's Perception of an Autistic Savant

Most of you will probably remember Kim Peek, the real life superstar autistic savant and the inspiration for Dustin Hoffman's character in the movie *Rain Man*. Kim, who passed away in 2009 at the age of 59, was a mega-savant.

Unlike most savants who are only talented in one or two areas of expertise, he was skilled in 15 different fields—including literature, geography, mathematics, history, and sports. With his unusual photographic memory, he was able to memorize entire phone books, all kinds of sports trivia, and calendar calculations. He had 12,000 books in his personal library, all of which he had memorized word for word. Kim's brain was unusual in that he did not have a corpus callosum, which normally connects the left and right hemispheres of the brain. While reading a book, his left eye would read the left page and the right eye would read the right page simultaneously. For all of his superhuman abilities, Kim couldn't button his own shirt and couldn't walk up a flight of stairs until he was 16 years old. He gave the physical impression of being mentally disabled.

A friend of mine, who is an exceptionally gifted psychic, told me an interesting story about Kim Peek. She had gone to a restaurant late one night in Salt Lake City with a friend. They were seated at a small table next to the wall and near a window. Kim was having dinner a few tables away with his father. The two got up to leave but were stopped by a man seated at a nearby table with his wife, toddler daughter, and infant in a baby carriage. He was curious to see Kim's amazing brain in action and asked him a question about some complex calculation or obscure factual question.

Kim, who was standing only about 4 feet away from my friend at that point, began to think about answering the man's question. At that moment, his entire head lit up with brilliant light. My friend said it was as if some invisible cap had been removed from his head, revealing an extraordinary beacon, such as a lighthouse, of blinding yellow and white light! Simultaneous with this light from the top of his head, she experienced a booming and loud humming vibration that quickly encompassed the entire restaurant. It was so powerful it pounded every cell in her body and literally made the window panes next to her rattle! She had to stop eating her food and felt an impulse to run away. The intense vibration made her sick to her stomach. She noticed that even the man's toddler was holding her hands over her ears as if trying to block out this horrific noise. My friend looked over the table at her friend who seemed oblivious to this noise and was busy eating her pasta. My friend told her to stand up immediately. Her friend was confused, but obeyed. As soon as she stood up, she vomited uncontrollably all over the table! When I asked my friend why she had asked her friend to stand up, she said she knew her friend was suffering from the same sickening sensations as a result of the vibrations from Kim Peek's brain vibrations!

As soon as Kim delivered his answer to the man, the vibrations stopped and the light disappeared. So what did this mean, I asked my friend. She said Kim's mental energy was so strong and focused that he was tapping the furthest ethers of the universe for knowledge, and that his brain emitted an actual sound and light vibration. His lack of connective brain tissue between the two halves of his brain only served to intensify the electrical energy. Thoughts have energy—literally! Autistic savants and psychics share amazing powers of perception and thinking. They are both able to tap into the invisible world of vibrations to obtain extraordinary information.

Exercise

Ask a friend to try to share a dream with you on the same night. Write down you dream and compare. Also compare any thoughts you had right before going to sleep or upon awakening, and make note of the time. See if your friend had similar thoughts.

Lesson #17:

Psychics and Synesthetes Speak the Language of Senses

A certain group of people with a neurological condition known as synesthesia experience confusion of their senses so, for instance, a person may see musical sounds as splashes of color in the air, taste abstract shapes, feel the texture or landscape of certain letters of the alphabet or numbers, see colors in the days of the week, and so on. This is a form of what I call *multi-modal sensing*. Just as I showed in the previous chapter that we all theoretically share the amazing skills of autistic savants, I believe we also share synesthetic sensibilities that, when properly developed, begin to resemble psychic sensing. Synesthestes, like autistic savants, are very literal, but in a different way. They do not experience their senses like poetic metaphors—they are real and literal transpositions from one sense into another sense.

There are many different types of synesthesia, including *auditory color* (sounds such as voices, noises, and music have color); *lexical-gustatory* (words or letters have taste); *ordinal-linguistic personification (OLP;* sequences of letters, numbers, calendars have personalities); *number form* (numbers have shapes); and *grapheme color* (letters have color). Often this produces very weird sensations. For example, one synesthete, James Wannerton, experienced the taste of egg in his mouth every time he heard the letter "k" pronounced (regardless of whether it appeared as a "c" in accept, "ck" as in back, "x" as in fax, or "k" as in pork). His association of taste was with the phoneme (sound) not the grapheme (spelling).

Although synesthesic perceptions certainly bear a striking resemblance to the way in which a creative person constructs cross-modal sensory metaphors (*sharp* cheese, *soft* yellow color, *bitter* feelings, a *loud* pattern), it is not the same experience. The synesthete has no choice but to experience the overlapping senses. They are not hypothetical or metaphorical at all; they are *actual* and *literal*. They are not products of the imagination. It is the difference between "B.B. King played the blues on his guitar" and "B.B. King made blue splashes of color come out of his guitar." Research shows synesthesia is actually seven times more common among artists, novelists, and poets (creative types) than the rest of the general public. Examining how synesthetes sense the world is instructive in learning how to understand and develop psychic abilities.

What Color Is Monday?

Is it possible that the days of the week actually have a color? Or is that simply crazy talk? When I first read Daniel Tammet's book, *Born on a Blue Day*, I learned that synesthetes often see colors associated with each day of the week. This seemed pretty bizarre to me at the time. Tammet, an autistic savant and synesthete, was born on a Wednesday, which he experiences as being the color blue.

Now, supposedly, "normal" people know and understand that days do not have colors. Days of the week are merely abstract ideas and ideas don't have colors, right? I am not so sure.

One night as I was dozing off to sleep trying to imagine what color Monday might look like, and struggling with the colorless translucency of the intellectual concept, I suddenly realized that if I stopped actively *looking* for a color, and instead merely sensed its presence, the colors for all the days of the week suddenly popped out in unbelievable precision in my mind! In other words, I had to stop believing that colors are strictly products of the eye. For the first time in my life, I realized every day of the week indeed *already* had a very specific color association in my mind. They were: Sunday/white, Monday/navy blue, Tuesday/green, Wednesday/ mustard yellow, Thursday/deep purple, Friday/orange, and Saturday/aqua blue. It was almost as if it had been there all along—obvious as daylight—but without any conscious awareness of it until then.

I wasn't exactly seeing the colors as much as I seemed to be feeling the sense of the colors. Had I merely posed the question to myself slightly differently, as in "What does Monday *feel* like?" I would have been able to come up with my answer a lot faster. But when I had initially posed the question, I asked myself, "What does Monday *look* like?" By phrasing my question this way, I ended up trying to find a visual color in the way I understand visual colors normally function. By the time I finally gave myself permission to freely experience color in whatever way it presented itself—as a *sense* of a color rather than a *visual* color, then I was finally able to make very strong color associations. Failing to use the correct word with myself had completely blocked a sensory experience. This is the extraordinary power of semantics. It reminded me of Ingo Swann's stern warnings to me during my interview with him that my failure to phrase a question correctly would inevitably lead to the wrong answer in the field of psychic phenomena.

I was so intrigued with my little discovery, I decided to test it out on other people to see if they could just as easily imagine or invent colors for the days of the week even if they didn't exactly see them in the normal sense. I went to a friend's house for dinner one night, and as everyone was relaxing during dessert, I pulled out several small pieces of paper and gave everyone a pencil. I asked them to write down the days of the week in a column. Then I asked them to silently, and without thinking about it, write down the color of each day.

Of the eight people present, there was only one who was unable to do this. Our hostess, who suffered from severe fibromyalagia and was on heavy pain medication, said she couldn't see any colors associated with days. The rest of the answers were handed back to me fairly swiftly and anonymously. Here is what came back:

Monday—blue/red/blue/blue/orange/blue/gray/blue

Tuesday—green/green/black/green/green/yellow/aqua/gray

Wednesday—orange/yellow/orange/red/gray/red/blue/red

Thursday—purple/blue/brown/yellow/purple/brown/purple/blue

Friday—red/orange/green/orange/orange/green/green/yellow

Saturday—red/light blue/yellow/white/red/gold/yellow/green

Sunday—white/white/turquoise/red/white/blue/silver/blue

The results were strangely consistent. For Monday, 5 out of 8 were blue; for Tuesday, half were green; for Wednesday a majority (6 out of 8) were for a vibrant, warm color (yellow/orange/red); for Thursday, a majority (7 out of 8) were for a somber, cool color (purple/blue/brown); for Friday more vibrant colors surfaced again *and* 8 out of 8 (green/orange/yellow/red); Sunday was a clear majority (7 out of 8) in the white/silver/blue range. The only day that seemed all over the place was Saturday; there was no clear agreement on that day. Interestingly, I had the most difficult time assigning a color to Saturday as well. Were we all having a collective imaginary experience? And if so, why? Or were we perhaps tapping into some sub-sensory experience that actually exists?

I wondered what factors might have influenced my "subjects." They were certainly a varied group. In terms of gender, there were five men and three women. In terms of nationality, there was one French person, one English person, one Pakistani, and the rest were born and raised in the United States. They were all middle-aged, in their 40s and early 50s. One couple lived in Colorado and the others lived in New Jersey.

Of course, I reflected on the various intellectual or cultural meanings that certain days have acquired that might have influenced these subjects in their answers. We all know that different cultures have different color associations. The color red means good luck and happiness in China, whereas in America it is more often associated with romantic love, passion, and sex. The color white in India is associated with death, whereas here, black is the color associated with death. But apparently these cultural associations were not necessarily operating in my little experiment.

Aside from cultural associations, we also operate on a number of intellectual and personal associations. It did not surprise me, for instance, that the majority of my subjects chose white or silver for Sunday, because white is often considered a holy color. Nor was it a surprise that Monday would be predominantly blue because we are all familiar with the "Monday morning blues" of going back to work after the weekend. I thought I might see more black for Tuesday, particularly given its association with "Black Tuesday," referring to the stock market crash of 2001. But the overall consensus on the rest of the days was a mystery to me. What it suggested was that we may be dealing not simply with the intellectual meaning of colors, but some invisible sensing mechanism of colors.

Just as with psychic sensing, I have come to believe that it doesn't matter if we all share the same sensory experience. What matters is that we establish *our own internal code,* which we can then use to arrive at accurate conclusions about reality.

Are Synesthetes Hallucinating?

One of the great hallmarks of real sensory experience is that we all seem to share the same experience—that's how we know it is real. Even though the color red I see may not be the same shade of red that you see, we can both agree upon the fact that it is red. Not so for synesthetes. There is no general agreement among grapheme-color synesthetes as to what colors are associated with the letters of the alphabet. Though research shows the letter A is most commonly experienced by synesthetes as being a shade of red, it is by no means the only color they see. Some synesthetes see the letter A as green or blue. Likewise, musical synesthetes do not experience the same musical note as having the same color. The musical note D was visualized by jazz great Duke Ellington, pianist Brooks Kerr, and French pianist Helene Grimaud as dark blue, yet all their other note-color associations were very different.

Just as synesthetes don't agree across the board on their associations, psychics do not always agree on their psychic imagery or symbolism. One psychic may see something as yellow whereas another might see it as green. I would suggest to you that this kind of discrepancy is due to the fact that *everyone is using their own individual code to interpret* a real stimulus. As with synesthesia, this doesn't make psychic sensing any less real because it isn't a shared phenomenon. Every psychic adopts his or her own personal internal code of imagery associations.

On the other side of the coin, however, is the fact that synesthetes will generally perceive the same letter as having the same color for their entire lifetime. This tends to suggest their perceptions are real. All synesthetes maintain an internal sensory code, which they keep for a lifetime. This strange consistency makes it very difficult to label a synesthete's experience as mere hallucination. Nor can they be labeled delusions. Delusions, as you recall, are defined as a *misperception* of the true nature of a physical stimulus. Synesthetes are fully capable of accurately sensing something. Their problem—if you can call it that—is they experience a kind of sensory bonus, a sort of sense on top of a sense, that the rest of us don't share.

So, this wouldn't appear to qualify as a delusion in the strict sense of the word. Synesthetes, like psychics, experience reality quite accurately but get additional extrasensory information as well.

Just as schizophrenics can frequently tell the difference between real and psychotic visions or sounds, synesthetes know the difference between the real and synesthetic colors. Daniel Tammet actually described the experience of seeing two different colors for the same object as being irritating! "On the other hand, if the numbers don't match my experience of them—if, for example, a shop sign's price has '99 pence' in red or green (instead of blue)—then I find that uncomfortable and irritating" (p. 6).

Clearly, this indicates a synesthete sees two different (potentially conflicting) colors simultaneously. I imagine this must feel frustratingly similar to trying to read the names of the colors out loud when they are written in a different colored ink (the word *green* written in pink letters).

The Thin Line Between Thinking and Sensing

The more I studied synesthesia, the more I began to realize the relationship between ideas and meanings and the synesthetic experience. Interestingly, many of the cross-modal perceptions found in synesthesia have a semantic influence. The word *semantic* refers to meaning. Scientists have noticed that some lexical-gustatory synesthetes (people who taste words) are often influenced by the meanings associated with the words. So, for example, one synesthete experienced the word *blue* as having an inky taste. Because ink is often a dark blue color, the sensory perception is literally colored by its meaning-association.

Other synesthetes claim their color associations with letters and words will actually change depending on the contextual meaning of the words! As explained by a grapheme-color synesthete named Cassidy Curtis in an article entitled "Letter-Color Synesthesia" in 1998 (*www.otherthings.com*): "This may seem odd, but it gets stranger. What you see above are the colors of the letters taken in isolation. But when placed in the context of a *word*, a letter's color can change quite dramatically."

So, for example, if the letter H is normally blue, it may become silver when it appears in the word *shine*, which refers to a silvery light. What is so interesting about synesthesia is that it clearly illustrates how fragile our sensory-based reality is. Meaning can alter our senses—not just for people with synesthesia, but, as the color grue research showed, meaning can alter everyone's senses! Psychics, like synesthetes, seem to have a thinner boundary between meaning and sensing.

The Overlap of Psychic Sensory Experience

Most psychics understand that vibrations can be understood and interpreted by the human body in many different ways and with different senses. The mind collects neutral data about the universe, such as electromagnetic waves and chemicals, converts them to electrical impulses, and then presents them within the format of one of our physical senses. *Psychics know that the sensory format is interchangeable.* The same exterior vibrations can be imaged as sight, sound, touch, taste, or smell. This kind of interchangeability of sensory experience resembles poetic metaphor.

It may sound crazy, but if you can permit yourself to experience, say, a park bench as not just *looking* like a gray, wooden piece of furniture, but also *sounding* like the wheezing of an old man, *smelling* like a musty attic, or *tasting* like a cup of weak coffee, then you can take any one of these other sensory images and explore their character traits. These traits will give you additional information about the park bench that might not simply have been available if you had regarded it purely as a visual image. So, for example, the wheezing sound might tell you that the wood planks of the bench are compromised and in need of repair. The watered-down coffee image might suggest that the bench was a cheap reproduction of a more high-end model. The musty attic smell might tell you that no one has sat on the bench for a very long time. Cross-modal sensory traits carry loads of literal and symbolic information that isn't necessarily available in just one sensory receptor. And this is how psychics can access seemingly invisible data.

In the words of well-known and scientifically documented psychic healer Rosalyn Bruyere (trained as an engineer), in her book *Wheels of Light*, healing sickness in other human beings is founded on an appreciation of the electromagnetic field that surrounds the human body that creates a colorful glow, called the aura. The aura is experienced in a cross-modal sensory way.

Vibration, color, and *sound* are all interrelated, and all three represent a means of determining or monitoring the *frequency* of energy in the auric field. When a healer is channeling energy into a person, the healer will often feel a vibration within the muscles of his or her own body. Correspondingly, the client may also feel a similar vibration. This vibration is directly related to the color being channeled. Thus, the healer can kinesthetically sense (and thereby know without seeing) the color of energy being channeled into a client. Some healers are able to hear (clairaudiently) the sound of the color being channeled." (p. 63)

Ms. Bruyere's account clearly demonstrates the cross-modal sensory aspects of psychic phenomena. Psychics are capable of translating the information available in the electromagnetic spectrum across several different sensory organs. The experience doesn't necessarily rise to the level of really seeing a color or hearing a sound, but replicates the experience sufficiently in order to convey information to the brain. The varying frequencies of these vibrations thus carry vital data into the brain and we use our understanding of our five senses to translate the meanings of these frequencies.

In his book *The Seventh Sense*, former U.S. Intelligence Officer and military remote viewer Lyn Buchanan describes the process in which he began learning remote viewing techniques, which, as I have already explained, is a highly regimented form of clairvoyance using nothing but target coordinate numbers to mentally "access" the target location. After several weeks in the program, he began feeling sensory *confusion* that he had never felt before. Information that was supposed to appear in one sensory channel seemed to be getting all mixed up with other senses.

He cites as an example of this sensory confusion a day when he sat down for a practice training session of remote viewing. He sat in an empty office with only a desk, chair, piece of paper, and pencil. Seated opposite Buchanan was his monitor, who would give him a pair of coordinate numbers representing a location, in this case the altar of a cathedral. He then had to imagine the location of these two numbers and describe what he saw. The targets of these sessions were never revealed to the students until after the completion of their exercise for the sole purpose of allowing them to experience feedback on their wild "guessing." Without any information whatsoever in front of him other than a pair of number coordinates, Buchanan began writing down his mental observations of the place, such as "clothy texture, long, wide, overhanging, tastes purple, soft, clean, cloth-like." His monitor stopped him and questioned him about his observation that something at the location "tastes purple."

"What does purple taste like?" he asked. "Do you mean, like wine?"

"No," I answered, not really understanding his question, "It tastes purple."

"And what does purple taste like?" he continued.

I thought for a moment, still not understanding why he would ask such a simple and obvious question. "Well...you know... purple tastes purple." I spoke somewhat slowly, in order to say it as simply and clearly as I could. I still could not understand why he was asking me a question about such a simple thing. Maybe he had not really understood me. I thought I had been clear enough about it, but evidently I had not. (p. 97)

Clearly, Buchanan was tapping into an entirely different way of experiencing his normal sensory modes as he was making progress in his clairvoyant abilities. The target tasted purple, but the target wasn't necessarily purple in color. The purple taste was an essential quality that he could not explain in any other logical format. There are no real words to explain the taste of purple—other than by comparing it to purple-colored drinks such as wine or grape juice. We all *know* purple doesn't have a taste—or at least that's what we know with our logical mind, which *understands* that visual electromagnetic data has no chemical gustatory component to it. Once we toss logic out the door, our brain begins to demonstrate a substrate of knowledge that *understands* there is absolutely a very real, yet illogical, linkage between sight and taste sensations.

Most psychics are completely at ease translating their sensory experiences into the language of other senses. Psychic Edgar Cayce believed every visual color in the rainbow has an association with a particular audible frequency. In his book, entitled *Auras,* he describes the meanings of the different colors seen in the aura of a person. Red corresponds to *do*, the first note C on the musical scale; orange corresponds to *re*; yellow corresponds to *mi*; green corresponds to *fa*; blue corresponds to *so*; and indigo/violet corresponds to *la*. Thus, his rule seems to be that the smaller the visual electromagnetic frequencies, the higher the auditory vibration.

Big, slow-moving red waves are low sounds, and high, fast-moving blue frequencies are high-pitched. The wave forms correlate.

Psychics aren't the only human beings convinced there are vibrational equivalents in our different senses. Throughout the centuries, some of our greatest thinkers have attempted to make direct correlations between the different senses. This is often based on the assumption that there must be a common mathematical or numerical (think: vibrational) language linking the two together.

The great Greek mathematician and philosopher Pythagoras (580 BC–500 BC) was suddenly struck one day while passing blacksmiths at work by how beautifully the sounds of their tools striking the anvils sounded. To him it sounded like music! And knowing that musical sounds were the equivalent of audible numbers, Pythagoras set about trying to figure out how the striking of the anvils was creating a form of music. After interviewing the blacksmiths, he realized that the sizes of the different anvils were all in simple ratios to one another. One was half the size of the first, the next was two-thirds the size, and so on. In effect, the sizes represented musical harmonics. Think about that for a second: *Different shapes correlate with different sounds*. The shapes and sounds bore a mathematical relationship to one another.

Some of our greatest thinkers, such as physicist Sir Isaac Newton (1643–1727) and philosopher Johann Wolfgang von Goethe (1749–1832), have attempted to make direct correlations between the different senses. This is often based on the assumption that there must be a common mathematical or numerical (translate: vibrational) "language" linking the two together. My point here is that human beings seem to understand intuitively that our senses share vibrational equivalents. In other words, the world "out there" is experienced by us as different kinds of frequencies ,and these frequencies can be translated into the different languages of our senses. Imagine the additional information we would have at our fingertips if we could just crack the secret code!

Exercise

Take a complex, three-dimensional object (plastic figurine, egg timer, fishing reel, and so on). Describe it to a person who is wearing a blindfold. Describe the object using only simple adjectives as if you were a space alien unfamiliar with earthly objects and materials. See if the person can guess what it is.

Lesson #18:

The Imagination Is the Largest Sensory Organ

Dr. Oliver Sacks's words to me kept ringing in my mind. I realized he was probably speaking for the entire skeptical, non-believer camp when he told me he could not conceive of a theoretical or neurological basis for psychic ability to justify his interest in the field. It is simply not enough to recount your own personal anecdotes or fascinating true stories of the paranormal.

My solution has been to show you that psychic ability is a legitimate human skill by showing that it is not equivalent to psychosis, and it shares similarities with existing neurological conditions, such as Savant Syndrome and synesthesia. Psychic ability is not some weird mental aberration. At the bare minimum, I hope to provide scientists with a theoretical springboard from which to launch a serious study into the mechanics of psychic ability without worrying about the paranormal stigma.

This last chapter is devoted to an exploration of possible neurological explanations for psychic ability. I propose three aspects of the brain in which scientists are likely to uncover valuable information about psychic ability: the angular gyrus, the temporal lobes, and the imagination.

The Angular Gyrus

The angular gyrus is a good place to start hunting for the origin of psychic ability. It is a small structure located in the parietal lobe that governs spatial perceptions. The angular gyrus is situated just behind Wernicke's language comprehension region of the brain, and is considered to be an important *multimodal* associative area. That means the angular gyrus receives auditory, visual, and somatosensory inputs from all the different primary sensory regions (sight, sound, touch, smell, taste). It is like the central military command post, which receives incoming reports from the war fronts from all different parts of the sensory world and synthesizes them into a single, cohesive battle plan to determine *meaning*. Thus, the neurons of the angular gyrus process both the phonological and semantic aspects of language—the fusion of sounds and meanings. It appears to be the true intersection of thought and sensing.

In 2005, Dr. Ramachandran and his colleagues conducted an experiment, not on autistics, but people who similarly are incapable of understanding figurative language. They tested four right-handed patients with damage to the left angular gyrus. The patients were all fluent in English, lucid, and highly functional. However, they were unable to understand simple metaphorical statements (like autistics) such as "The grass is always greener on the other side of the fence" or "An empty vessel makes more noise." Dr. Ramachandran concluded the angular gyrus is involved in how we understand metaphors and learn how to create categories of similar objects.

The subjects in the study resembled autistics because they were unable to understand how a single category or statement can *symbolically* represent many other similar, but not identical, situations. They failed to comprehend relationships between verbal comparisons, metaphors, and similes. This boiled down to a fundamental problem of not understanding how to create categories of things.

In 2006, Harvard researchers discovered that the angular gyrus region of the brain also lights up in monkeys when they learn how to categorize visual items by looking at them on a computer. The researchers found that when the monkeys were forced to rearrange their visual categories of objects as part of the test, the angular gyrus was active.

Dr. Ramachandran has speculated that the inability of autistics and patients suffering from a damaged angular gyrus to understand metaphoric speech may be related to a defective mirror neuron system within the angular gyrus. Mirror neurons are what enable us to mimic behavior: monkey see, monkey do. When we watch a person lift a glass with his or her hands, our mirror neurons travel the same neural pathways in our brain as if we had lifted the glass ourselves. Mirror neurons have also been implicated in empathy—a trait often found in psychics and empaths.

How does this relate to psychic ability? I have made the argument that psychics think like autistic savants because they experience sensory data very literally. Psychics do not create mental categories and patterns like the rest of us. Because the angular gyrus is the place where the brain creates patterns, this is a good starting point to examine how and whether the angular gyrus of psychics operates differently.

Other researchers have found that the angular gyrus is somehow implicated in the way we sense out-of-body experiences and spiritual beings.

In 2006, Dr. Olaf Blanke, a neurologist at the École Polytechnique Fédérale de Lausanne in Switzerland, was conducting an evaluation of two women slated for brain surgery to alleviate their epileptic seizures. Dozens of electrodes were implanted in their brains to help identify and locate the areas of the brain causing the seizures. When the angular gyrus was stimulated with small currents of electricity, both women had seemingly paranormal experiences.

The first patient told researchers during the actual procedure that she felt as though she had left her physical body and was floating near the ceiling. As soon as the electrical stimulation stopped, she suddenly found herself back inside her body. When the stimulation of the angular gyrus resumed again, she felt as if she were back up near the ceiling looking down at her legs. When she closed her eyes, she felt as though she were doing sit-ups.

Her description closely resembles accounts of Near Death or out-of-body experiences. Near Death Experiences have been reported when patients who are clinically dead claim to have felt like they were looking down from the ceiling at their body. Often they are able to recount exact details of what the doctors and nurses said and did while the patient was technically "dead." In out-of-body situations, people will often describe a form of astral traveling or spirit travel where they are able to accurately describe things occurring in distant places beyond their physical location.

The other patient in Dr. Blanke's research study had a different experience when her angular gyrus was stimulated by electrodes. When the electrical current was turned on, she kept looking over to her right. She later told researchers she had felt the presence of an "other"—a kind of shadow figure or her doppelgänger, though strangely masculine—lying next to her. When she sat up, so did he. The researchers were confused because they did not understand at the time why the patient kept looking over to her right side as if there was someone next to her. When she was handed a card to read, she felt that he was trying to take it away from her or interfere with her reading it. The shadow figure immediately disappeared when the electrical stimulation stopped.

The Temporal Lobes

The temporal lobes of the brain, located on either side of the head near the ears, have also been pinpointed as an area that gives rise to paranormal types of experiences. Dr. Michael Persinger, Canadian cognitive neuroscientist and professor at Laurentian University in Sudbury, Ontario, has conducted numerous studies where he has been able to artificially induce religious experiences in people by stimulating their temporal lobes with a weak magnetic field. He is considered to be the founding father of the burgeoning field of neurotheology. The temporal lobes are known for processing auditory stimuli, language, attention, and memory. Dr. Persinger's subjects have reported seeing or experiencing seemingly supernatural beings such as God, angels, ghosts, or religious prophets while wearing his transcranial magnetic stimulation (TMS) device on their heads, affectionately known as the God Helmet.

An article in the October 2002 issue of *Saturday Night Magazine*, by Robert Hercz, discusses some of the mystical—and accompanying sensory —experiences people have had while wearing the God Helmet:

> Astonishing things have happened in this chamber. One woman believed her dead mother had materialized beside her. Another felt a presence so powerful and benign that she wept when it faded. British journalist Ian Cotton understood that he was, and always had been, a Tibetan monk. Psychologist Susan Blackmore, writing in *New Scientist*, said she felt something "get hold of my leg and pull it, distort it, and drag it up the wall... Totally out of the blue, but intensely and vividly, I suddenly felt anger... Later, it was

replaced by an equally sudden attack of fear." Over a thousand volunteers have worn the helmet, and 80 percent of them, Persinger says, experienced a "sensed presence—the feeling that someone's standing near you, the feelings there must be something greater, the feeling of infinite possibilities." (pp. 40–60)

It has long been known that people suffering from temporal lobe epilepsy experience moments of mystical revelation and ecstasy during epileptic fits. Thus, it is understandable that tinkering with the temporal lobes might generate similar experiences. Dr. Persinger theorizes that such visions or sensations are actually caused by harmless and temporary mini-seizures in the temporal lobe during transcranial magnetic stimulation. He has further suggested that the sense of a tangible "other" created by TMS may actually be the brain's awareness of its unconscious self.

In 2006, I visited Dr. Persinger in the small Canadian nickel mining town of Sudbury. In the popular book *Spook,* author Mary Roach described Dr. Persinger, Sudbury's biggest celebrity, as a strange, nocturnal man who reportedly "mows his lawn in a three-piece suit" (p. 217). When I met Dr. Persinger he was indeed wearing a sober, conservative, charcoal-black three-piece suit with an old-fashioned pocket watch. Without exaggeration, every minute of his day is allocated. The first time I called him for a phone interview I was told to call him on a Sunday at precisely 8:17 p.m. No kidding! His lab office was chaotic, and enormous piles of documents cluttered the floor and every desktop nearly up to the ceiling. I couldn't imagine how one could work in such an unwieldy environment. He was clearly eccentric, driven, and absolutely brilliant. I liked him immediately.

He invited me to test out his new invention dubbed the Octopus. This technology also uses TMS and is the successor technology to the God Helmet. The Octopus derives its name from the fact that it uses a similar kind of helmet equipped with a circumcerebral eight solenoid device (a device that encircles the head with eight objects emitting bursts of electricity around the head counterclockwise). Low-level electromagnetic currents are directed in sequence in a counter-clockwise motion around the temporal lobes around the wearer's head. I was only about the 11th person to have ever been tested using this new device. According to Dr. Persinger, the Octopus is a far more subtle and sophisticated device than the God Helmet. It explores the origins of memory and consciousness by artificially altering brain wave patterns.

After completing a battery of written psychological tests, I was invited to sit in a comfortable, overstuffed armchair in a tiny sound-proofed, dimly lit room with a shag rug resembling someone's basement recreation room. The room is known as the Experimental Cave. Dr. Persinger put a circular metal band around the top of my head that had all kinds of electrodes and wires coming out of it. My eyes were blindfolded. He then left me alone in the room and manned the controls from the computers situated on the other side of the wall. There were no noises and no distractions. It wasn't exactly total sensory deprivation, but something like it.

Although I did not have any religious or paranormal experiences, I did have some odd sensations about physical space. Although my eyes were covered with a dark cloth, I felt as though physical space had become highly dimensional. My thoughts and mental images seemed to position themselves in real space as things, not thoughts. My ideas assumed quasi-real forms as if they had three-dimensional shapes. Space felt thick like Jell-O. It was smooth and spongy, very three-dimensional, and spatially dominated. It was a very subtle experience but striking, just the same. Was I seeing something real for the first time or was this a delusion? Dr. Persinger, being the true scientist that he is, refuses to speculate. His refusal to rule out paranormal possibilities have put him at odds with many in the scientific establishment.

TMS may hold the key to understanding psychic ability. As I have already mentioned in this book, it has been used to achieve amazing results by numerous scientists.

> › Dr. Persinger uses TMS to induce visions and sensations of God, spirits, angels, and doppelgängers, and altered states of consciousness.

> › Dr. Snyder, as you will recall, uses TMS to induce savant-like skills, gifts, and talents in otherwise, normal individuals.

> › Scientists studying vision have used TMS to generate the appearance of sparkling lights or stars in one's vision, known as phosphenes.

> › Dr. Hoffman used TMS to temporarily turn off the internalized voices from talking in the minds of schizophrenic patients.

I am sure there are many more usages of which I am simply unaware.

This all suggests that TMS provides a sort of missing link between altered states of consciousness. These studies provide evidence that suggests we are much more than we *think* we are. We have skills, talents, perceptions, and insights that normally don't exist in our conscious awareness and are not under our conscious control. It stands to reason there must be some aspect of what we experience under this kind of artificial electromagnetic influence that stimulates brain activity—or suppresses it—to create "real" insights that are not normally available to us. The fact that these experiences can be induced by electromagnetic stimulation to the brain raises one fundamental question: Is this an artificially induced illusion (a form of temporary insanity) or does it merely release us from our normal thought-constraints, permitting us to experience what we normally suppress? Is it fake or is it real? Consciousness only knows itself through its own awareness. Most of us prefer to believe in what we already understand—namely, the version that corresponds to our conscious awareness. But I hope you now realize that what is real is only a matter of metaphors and patterns.

The Imagination

Unlike the angular gyrus and the temporal lobes, the imagination is not a specific region of the brain. We actually don't even know what it is! Very little scientific research has been conducted to date. Most dictionaries define the imagination as a cognitive process, a form of thinking. After years of psychic training, I now believe the imagination is actually our most important sensory organ, which transforms senses into thoughts. It is the point of entry for extra-spectral thoughts and other sensory data that isn't picked up by our "normal" sensory organs such as our eyes or ears. Contrary to popular opinion, I do not believe our imagination is simply a place in our minds where we think private, fictional thoughts.

In 2008, researchers at Vanderbilt University showed that our imagination can actually alter our real sensory perceptions ("'Mind's Eye' Influences Visual Perception")! The study subjects were first asked to *imagine* a pattern of vertical stripes in their minds. Then they were told to look at a pattern on paper that had green horizontal stripes and red vertical stripes. Strangely, after imagining vertical stripes, the subjects were unable to see the actual horizontal stripes in the paper pattern. They only saw the vertical stripes. The subjects did not report seeing the pattern they had not imagined in their mind.

These findings validate Gertrude Schmeidler's Goat-Sheep Effect that skeptics won't experience psychic phenomena because they can't "imagine" it. As Einstein once noted in 1926 during a physics lecture by Heisenberg: "Whether you can observe a thing or not depends on the theory which you use. It is the theory which decides what can be observed." (*Unification of Fundamental Forces*, by Abdus Salam (1990)).

Although we don't know exactly what the imagination is, scientists recently suggested it exists in three specific areas of the brain.

In its 2007 year-in-review issue for the top 10 most noteworthy scientific breakthroughs of the year, *Science* Magazine cited research done in January of that year by a team lead by Dr. Eleanor Maguire of the UCL Institute of Neurology regarding how the imagination functions. Her team discovered that people who suffered from amnesia due to damage to the hippocampus resulting in memory loss were unable to *imagine* future scenarios, such as taking a shopping trip or spending a day at the beach. Patients were unable to place themselves in such a situation by using their imaginations. They lacked the ability to assemble sensory details such as smells, sounds, and sights as if they couldn't quite put all the fragmented pieces into a holistic, spatially connected sequence.

The researchers postulated that the *hippocampus*, the part of the brain responsible for memory storage, may be responsible for our ability to create new experiences (imagine) because it somehow binds together the old ones into a unified context. They also suggested the *medial temporal lobes* may enable us to distinguish between true and false memories—a false memory would be a hypothetical or imaginary one. They also found the *pre-frontal cortex,* the region of the brain responsible for organization and planning, become activated when subjects are asked to imagine a hypothetical scenario. Presumably, this happens because this area of the brain enables us to artificially manipulate memories and thoughts.

Although this research may explain certain aspects of the imagination, it only explains what parts of the brain are involved when we make a *conscious* effort to imagine a scenario. This is what I call *goal-directed* imagination. The subjects were told in advance what to imagine—being on a beach or going shopping. It seems clear that any time the brain is tasked with goal-directed thinking, the hippocampal memories and pre-frontal decision-making thought processes will be implicated. These researchers discovered that the imagination is located in the thinking regions of the brain only because they have started out with the underlying erroneous assumption that *all* imaginary thoughts are goal-directed thoughts.

Unfortunately, these researchers never investigated the types of thoughts that arrive in the imagination via the subconscious mind. I call these thoughts *non-goal directed* imaginary thoughts or *sensing-thinking*. These are imaginary thoughts that cannot be tamed into submission by the rational mind. These are thoughts we haven't consciously tried to create. This is the realm of the imagination in which I am most interested. Psychics often use their imagination to access real data. How is that possible? I suggest to you that the answer to this lies in the fact that when you cannot rely on your brain to *think* a logical answer or scenario, then you must rely on it to *sense* the answer. The psychic imagination falls into this latter category of imagination. It is a highly passive experience in which you do not shape your thoughts; you merely watch them. You don't go to them; they come to you!

The reason why psychics can imagine things in their minds that end up as accurately predicted events in reality is because they are using their mind as a sensing instrument. *The imagination is a place where the brain images its perceptions.* And, as I have said, perceptions occur at the crossroad of thinking and sensing.

If you ever wondered (or feared) how psychics sometimes seem to have an uncanny ability to see inside you and to read your innermost thoughts, perhaps you should really be worried about something else. You have probably failed to realize that most of your deepest thoughts simply don't belong to you. They are not your personal, secret, private property. Your thoughts are not invisible; they are in a public fishbowl for all to see. Why? They are the products of your sensing abilities and record real phenomena.

With respect to your imagination, *you are less an inventor, than an interpreter, of images.*

Neuroscience of the Imagination

My theory of the imagination as a sensory organ can best be explained by comparing it to the assembly line in a car factory. There are four basic production centers of the brain that handle increasingly more complex sensations: 1) the primary sensory cortices, 2) the unimodal cortices, 3) the supramodal cortices, and 4) the prefrontal cortex.

First Stage: Raw Material Organization

When you build a car, you start out with the most basic raw materials such as tiny nuts, bolts, sheet metal, and other items that arrive at the factory and are unloaded from the truck dock. These parts are then organized and sorted into boxes. Then they are assembled into small components such as side-view mirrors, doors, seats, and windshield wipers. These small units are assembled together until they get larger and larger. Finally, other unrelated types of machines and big components, such as the car engine or electronics, are added in. When all units have been put together, the car is complete.

In my way of looking at things, the raw materials such as nuts and bolts are like raw sensory data. The fully finished car is like a cognitive thought. The real problem is in trying to decide: *At what point does sensory data become cognitive?* When does the sum of all the parts become a car? When do physical sensations become thoughts?

It is impossible to answer these questions—and that's exactly my point.

Thoughts are not separate from our sensory perceptions. They are completely integrated together at various levels of construction. You may recall that at the beginning of this book I explained intuition and psychic ability both exist on the same sliding scale of insights. These range from educated guesses, to gut feelings and hunches, to psychic sensing. Neurologically speaking, it is clear that our thinking and sensing mechanisms are fused together. They only differ by degrees of conscious awareness and access to our preverbal, subconscious thoughts.

The first stage of production is when the primary sensory data, in the form of tiny electrical impulses, reaches the perimeters of our body such as our skin, our retina, our nostrils, and so on. The sensory data is delivered to our doorstep just like the delivery of thousands of nuts, bolts, raw materials, and tiny parts to the factory. These parts need to be sorted and organized according to type in the *primary sensory cortices* of our brain.

Visual data goes to a place in the occipital lobe in the back of the head. Auditory data goes to an area in the temporal lobe on the sides of the head. Touch data goes to places in the parietal lobe at the top of the head.

Smell data goes to the olfactory bulb deep inside the brain. Taste data is carried to the part of the brain stem called the nucleus of the solitary tract.

Second Stage: Small Part Assembly

Once the raw data has been organized, the initial production phase begins.

In the second stage, to use my car factory analogy, certain specific groups of nuts, bolts, screws, and materials will be assembled to produce small components such as mirrors, handles, ashtrays, and so on. Similarly, the brain takes certain related bits of data from each primary sensory cortex and begins to make associations and comparisons among the data from the same cortex. In these so-called *unimodal* associative cortices, all the data from a single sensory organ is assembled together. Here, for example, the basic colors, shapes, and spatial orientation of objects may be grouped together in such a way that more complex judgments, such as movement or distance of objects, can be constructed. Depth perception, for instance, is nothing but a judgment made by the brain after evaluating small cues, such as the relative size of objects, color saturation or contrast, and so on.

Third Stage: Large Part Assembly

The third step requires teamwork from several different divisions of the brain and the products arrive at the larger production centers called *supramodal* centers. These centers assemble the synthesized information from all five sensory organs. It is here, for example, that complex visual images will be matched with sounds and smells. This is like the final assembly at the car factory where the largest car parts such as the engine, wheel assembly, transmission, steering mechanism, and axles are mounted and fitted together. The end result is a single finished event: a car or a thought. Likewise, in this location in the brain, patterns from different senses are contrasted, compared, and merged. The most sophisticated products from each of the five senses are integrated together to form a single idea, concept, or event.

Final Stage: Drive Away

In the final step, the *pre-frontal cortex*, the seat of planning and organizing in the human brain, takes over. This is analogous to the factory employee who drives the completed car off the assembly line and makes a decision about where to park it in the parking lot outside.

So, let's go back to my example from an earlier chapter of a sensory event called a rose. The brain assembles all the visual information about this flower (red, round-shaped, nearby location, motionless, green leaves) along with the tactile information (soft petals, sharp thorns, cold stem), the olfactory information (sweet, perfumed scent), the gustatory information (chlorophyll, bitter taste), and the auditory information (soft, rustling sound). All of these sensory packages are compiled into one event or object—in this case, a rose. When this happens, we are no longer overwhelmed with unrelated bits and pieces of raw sensory data, but we have created a very fundamental meaning to the convergence of all these events. We have the concurrence of data together so we can understand it. The concept of a rose has become a single thought. Our brain (like the car factory) has manufactured a finished product.

Hopefully, you have begun to notice something slightly strange about this whole process. As a physical sensation is processed up the complex hierarchy of associative centers, it begins to look, feel, and sound more and more like a thought, and less like a sensation!

Sensory impressions begin to resemble primitive thoughts.

The higher up it goes, the more the brain begins to interfere by applying its own logic to the raw sensory perception. As a result, as I have discussed in earlier chapters, the brain begins to make *autopilot decisions* about how we should perceive or assemble information about our world. We begin to see (or rather, *imagine*) color in our peripheral vision where none exists; we see the world right-side up instead of upside down; we unconsciously make assumptions about distance and location for sounds; our knowledge of language begins to actually influence what we perceive with our senses, like the hybrid perception of the color grue. The brain begins to hijack our thought process before we are even aware of it. The brain's subconscious tendency toward creating sensible patterns out of its environment is a form of thinking. It is also a form of unconscious and preverbal logic.

As these sensory impressions that look more and more like primitive thoughts are moved up the mental ladder and processed by the higher-level associative centers, they are reworked into even larger, more sophisticated *predictions*. Predictions are the brain's way of trying to imagine its environment for our human survival. Remember: All sensory perception is organized, even at its most basic level, to permit the human organism to make predictions about its environment, such as depth perception or echo location so we don't bump into things. Predictions are the ultimate "useful" tool for humans. *These sensory thought-predictions are the stuff of psychic data.*

Psychics are, in my opinion, able to access these mega-sensory impressions *before* they are routed on up to the next associative center, the prefrontal cortex, the conscious thinking brain. This is the difference between goal-directed and non-goal-directed thoughts. Psychics must "interpret" this sensory level of information before it gets contaminated by our preconceived, pre-patterned conscious thoughts. These aren't the same as guesses, which are pure goal-directed thoughts and products of the logical mind. Psychics are actually thinking differently from the rest of us and using their imaginations as a source of sensory information.

It is really no coincidence that they begin to resemble predictions such as prophecies, mind-reading, telepathy, and clairvoyance. The psychic imagination is made of mega-sensory impressions that have been accurately interpreted by the brain. *Psychic impressions are merely thoughts without a driver.*

Exercise

Imagine that you can see the future. Make predictions for tomorrow, for the next several months, or even years. You can predict the weather, the stock market, the behavior of your friends, whether you will find a parking spot—anything as long as it is verifiable with facts! Write them down and then match them up with real events. Track your progress and the accuracy of your predictions.

You may have noticed while reading this book that I have made very little attempt to explain the origin of psychic *phenomena*. This was intentional. I have stuck with the narrower and simpler task of trying to explain the origin of psychic *ability*. This assumes the data exists out there and can be accessed by the human brain. It's kind of like starting backward to prove a point.

This being said, I do not—for one second—discount the possibility that our minds and physical senses operate on some level of attunement with spiritual energy that can propagate inter-dimensional information from the far corners of the universe.

We as members of the human species may all have access to a much larger pool of information that exists among us and around us. I believe we all share a form of *Collective Consciousness* that is, at least in my definition, a shared awareness of activity by all other human beings from *all time periods*. This collective consciousness contains information that is larger than the individual consciousness of any one member of the species who is stuck in his or her little space/time location.

The very foundation of consciousness may boil down to little more than a collective awareness of the other parts of an entity. Human consciousness may be nothing more than this collective cloud of knowledge developed by the individual consciousness of all cells in the human body. Cells somehow knew to organize into large societies that then created internal organs. Internal organs then knew how to divide up responsibilities into specialties, which enable the human being to function. At each level of internal organization, there is an increasingly higher level of knowledge and awareness of the group. In this sense, even human awareness and knowledge may be said to arise from information generated from the microscopic entities and cells in our organs. The human's total consciousness is well beyond that of any individual cell in the body. The human mind, as it relates to the individual cells of the body, can be likened to God in relation to individual members of the human race. Like God, the mind knows everything, provides a collective purpose, and it does not exist anywhere in particular and yet exists within the soul of every person.

Many psychics achieve "impossible" feats and know information beyond their physical body when they connect with Spirit—or the Collective Consciousness. They generally must go into various types of trance states or twilight consciousness in order to retrieve this information because *conscious awareness is the master controller of the individual.* Our individual consciousness is dedicated to only understanding those sensory events that directly affect the individual.

This is why our five senses are louder, coarser, and more dominant than our psychic senses. Our five physical senses are only valuable to the individual member of the species. That's why we are so invested in their importance. When we are able to reduce our level of conscious awareness, our five senses become less important and our more subtle psychic senses are not blocked out by our regular senses. Our psychic senses receive information well beyond our physical space/time location because we have a reduced interest in our physical body. We gain access to this large, interconnected cloud of vibrational data that affects the entire human race in the same way that a single cell in the human body has access to knowledge about the entire body.

My definition of intuition explains why and how our understanding of the universe can be localized or remote. We can intuit the small universe of events that directly affect our bodies, or we can intuit events on the other side of the earth. The butterfly that flaps its wings in China may or may not contribute to the hurricane on this side of the earth. But if you can open your mind to that possibility, you may discover some interesting and seemingly impossible correlations. Prediction and prophesy, though they may sound like magical, mystical properties, are actually built-in components of human biology.

Ackerl, K., M. Atzmueller, and K. Grammer. "The Scent of Fear," *Neuroendocrinol Lett* 23 (2) (2002): 79–84.

Alleyne, Richard. "Black and White TV Generation Have Monochrome Dreams." *The Telegraph,* October 17, 2008.

"Barney Barnato's Suicide." *New York Times*, June 16, 1897.

Baron-Cohen, Simon, and John E. Harrison. *Synesthesia: Classic and Contemporary Readings.* Oxford, England: Blackwell Publishers Ltd., 1997.

Bartoshuk, L.M. "Sweetness: History, Preference, and Genetic Variability." *Food Technol*ogy. 1991 45(11): 108, 110, 112–113.

Bean, Bill. *Delivered.* Acton, Calif.: Richland Creek Publishing, 2010.

Beinfield, Harriet, and Efrem Korngold. *Between Heaven and Earth: A Guide to Chinese Medicine.* New York: Ballentine Wellspring/ Random House Publishing Group, 1992.

Bentov, Itzhak. *Stalking the Wild Pendulum: On the Mechanics of Consciousness*. New York: Bantam Books, 1981.

Bertoldi, Concetta. *Do Dead People Watch You in the Shower? And Other Questions You're All but Dying to Ask a Medium.* New York: HarperCollins Publishers, 2008.

Berthards, Betty. *Seven Steps to Developing Your Intuitive Powers.* Petaluma, Calif.: New Century Publishers, 2001.

Blavatsky, H.P. *The Key to Theosophy.* Pasadena, Calif.: Theosophical University Press, 2002.

Blum, Ralph H. *The Book of Runes.* New York: St. Martin's Press, 1983.

Bohart, Arthur C., and Leslie S. Greenberg. *Empathy Reconsidered: New Directions in Psychotherapy.* Washington, D.C.: American Psychological Association, 1997.

Boorstin, Daniel J. *The Discoverers: A History of Man's Search to Know His World and Himself.* New York: Vintage Books/Random House Inc., 1983.

Braden, Gregg. *Fractal Time.* Carlsbad, Calif.: Hay House, Inc., 2009.

Bragdon, Allea D., and David Gamon. *Brains That Work a Little Bit Differently: Recent Discoveries About Common Brain Diversities.* Bass River, Mass.: Brainwaves Books, 2000.

Brazelton, MD, T. Berry, and Joshua D. Sparrow, MD. *Touchpoints Three to Six: Your Child's Emotional and Behavioral Development.* Cambridge, Mass.: Perseus Publishing, 2001.

Brennan, Barbara Ann. *Hands of Light: A Guide to Healing Through the Human Energy Field.* New York: Bantam Books, 1988.

Brizendine, Louann. *The Female Brain.* New York: Morgan Road Books/ Random House Inc., 2006.

Brown, Tom. *The Tracker.* New York: Berkley Books, 1979.

Browne, Sylvia, and Antoinette May. *Adventures of a Psychic.* Carlsbad, Calif.: Hay House Inc. 1990.

Browne, Sylvia, and Lindsay Harrison. *Sylvia Browne's Book of Dreams.* New York: Signet/Penguin Group, 2003.

Bruyere, Rosalyn L. *Wheels of Light: Chakras, Auras, and the Healing Energy of the Body.* New York: Fireside/Simon & Schuster Inc., 1994.

Buchanan, Lyn. *The Seventh Sense: The Secrets of Remote Viewing as Told by a "Psychic Spy" for the U.S. Military.* New York: Paraview Pocket Books/Simon & Schuster Inc., 2003.

Burr, Chandler. *The Emperor of Scent: A Story of Perfume, Obsession and the Last Mystery of the Senses.* New York: Random House, 2002.

"Can Dogs Smell Cancer?" ScienceDaily. *www.sciencedaily.com/ releases/2006/01/060106002944.htm.* January 6, 2006.

Cappon, MD, Daniel. *Intuition: Harnessing the Hidden Powers of the Mind.* Toronto, Canada: Bedford House Publishing Corp., 1989.

Capra, Fritjof. *The Tao of Physics.* New York: Bantam Books Inc., 1980.

Carter, Rita. *Mapping the Mind.* Los Angeles: University of California Press, 1999.

Castaneda, Carlos. *The Fire From Within.* New York: Pocket Books/Simon & Schuster Inc., 1985.

Cayce, Edgar. *Auras: An Essay on the Meaning of Colors.* Virginia Beach, Va.: A.R.E. Press, 1973.

Cayce, Edgar Evans. *Edgar Cayce on Atlantis.* New York: Warner Books Inc., 1968.

Chalmers, David. *The Conscious Mind: In Search of a Fundamental Theory.* Oxford, England: Oxford University Press, 1997.

Cheetham, Erika. *The Further Prophesies of Nostradamus: 1985 and Beyond.* New York: Perigee Books/Putnam Publishing Group, 1985.

Chen, D. and J. Haviland-Jones. "Rapid Mood Change and Human Odors." *Physiology & Behavior*, 1999. 68 (1–2) , 241–250.

Choquette, Sonia. *Diary of a Psychic: Shattering the Myths.* Carlsbad, Calif.: Hay House Inc., 2003.

Clark, Glenn. *The Man Who Tapped the Secrets of the Universe.* St. Paul, Minn.: Macalester Park Publishing, 1951.

Cooper, J.C. *An Illustrated Encylopaedia of Traditional Symbols.* London: Thames & Hudson Ltd., 1978.

Cozolino, Louis. *The Neuroscience of Psychotherapy: Building and Rebuilding the Human Brain.* New York: W.W. Norton and Co., 2002.

Cytowic, MD, Richard E. *The Man Who Tasted Shapes.* New York: Jeremy P. Tarcher/Putnam Books, 1993.

Dalai Lama. *The Meaning of Life: Buddhist Perspectives on Cause and Effect.* Boston, Mass.: Wisdom Publications, 1992.

———. *The Universe in a Single Atom: The Convergence of Science and Spirituality.* New York: Morgan Road Books/Random House Inc., 2005.

Damasio, Antonio. *The Feeling of What Happens: Body and Emotion in the Making of the Consciousness.* San Diego, Calif.: Harvest Book/Harcourt, Inc., 1999.

Daniken, Erich von. *Chariots of the Gods.* New York: Berkley Books/Penguin Putnam Inc., 1999.

Davies, Rodney. *Psychic Development Workbook: How to Awaken and Use Your ESP.* New York: Sterling Publishing Inc., 1997.

Davis-Floyd, Robbie, and R. Suen Arvidson. *Intuition: The Inside Story—Interdisciplinary Studies.* New York & London: Routledge, 1997.

Day, Laura. *The Circle: How the Power of a Single Wish Can Change Your Life.* New York: Jeremy P. Tarcher/Penguin Putnam Inc., 2001.

———. *Practical Intuition for Success* New York: HarperCollins Publishers Inc., 1997.

DeBono, Edward. *Lateral Thinking: Creativity Step by Step.* New York: Harper & Row Publishers Inc., 1973.

Denning, Hazel M. *Intuition and Synchronicity: A Journey to Fulfillment.* Virginia Beach, Va.: A.R.E. Press, 2001.

Dispezio, Michael A. *Critical Thinking Puzzles.* New York: Sterling Publishing Co., Inc. 1996.

———. *Great Critical Thinking Puzzles.* New York: Sterling Publishing Co., Inc., 1997.

Dodanis, David. *Electric Universe: The Shocking True Story of Electricity.* New York: Crown Publishing Group, 2005.

Dossey, MD, Larry. *Prayer Is Good Medicine: How to Reap the Healing Benefits of Prayer.* San Francisco, Calif.: HarperSanFrancisco/ HarperCollins Publishers, 1996.

Douglas, John, and Mark Olshaker. *Mind Hunter: Inside the FBI's Elite Serial Crime Unit.* New York: Pocket Books/Simon & Schuster Inc., 1995.

Downer, John. *Supersense: Perception in the Animal World.* London: BBC Books, 1988.

Dresbold, Michelle, and James Kwalwasser. *Sex, Lies, and Handwriting: A Top Expert Reveals the Secrets Hidden in Your Handwriting.* New York: Free Presss/Simon & Schuster Inc., 2006.

Droscher, Vitus B. *The Magic of the Senses: New Discoveries in Animal Perception.* New York, Evanston, San Francisco, London: Harper Colophon Books/Harper & Row Publishers 1969.

Drosnin, Michael. *The Bible Code.* New York: Touchstone/Simon & Schuster Inc., 1997.

Dunne, J.W. *An Experiment with Time.* Charlottesville, Va.: Hampton Roads Publishing Co., Inc., 2001.

Eason, Cassandra. *The Illustrated Directory of Healing Crystals.* London: Collins & Brown/Anova Books Co. Ltd., 2003.

Ebon, Martin. *Psychic Warfare: Threat or Illusion.* New York: McGraw Hill Book Co., 1983.

Eden, Denna, and David Feinstein. *Energy Medicine.* New York: Jeremy P. Tarcher/Penguin Putnam Inc., 1998.

Edward, John. *One Last Time: A Medium Speaks to Those We Have Loved and Lost.* New York: The Berkley Publishing Group, 1998.

———. *What if God Were the Sun?* San Diego: Jodere Group Inc., 2000.

Edwards, Betty. *Drawing on the Artist Within.* New York: Simon & Schuster Inc., 1986.

Eich, Eric, John F. Kihlstrom, Gordon H. Bower, Joseph P. Forgas, and Paula M. Niedenthal. *Cognition and Emotion.* Oxford, England: Oxford University Press, 2000.

Emoto, Masaru. *The Hidden Messages in Water.* Hillsboro, Ore.: Beyond Words Publishing Inc., 2004.

Fenwick, Peter, and Elizabeth Fenwick. *Past Lives: An Investigation into Reincarnation Memories.* New York: Berkley Books, 2001.

Ferguson, Gail. *Cracking the Intuition Code: Understanding and Mastering Your Intuitive Powers.* Chicago, Ill.: Contemporary Books/McGraw-Hill Companies, 1999.

Fisher, Milton. *Intuition: How to Use it in Your Life.* Green Farms, Conn.: Wildcat Publishing Co. Inc., 1981.

Forman, Henry James. *The Story of Prophesy.* New York: Tudor Publishing Co., 1940.

"For Women, But Not Men, Religion May Aid Mental Health," *Social Psychiatry and Psychiatric Epidemiology,* Vol. 43, No. 1 (2008).

Franquemont, Sharon. *You Already Know What to Do: 10 Invitations to the Intuitive Life.* New York: Jeremy P. Tarcher/Penguin Putnam Inc., 2000.

Freud, Sigmund. *Leonardo da Vinci and a Memory of His Childhood.* New York: W.W. Norton & Co., Inc., 1964.

Gardner, Howard. *Frames of Mind: The Theory of Multiples Intelligences.* New York: Basic Books/Perseus Books Group, 2004.

Gardner, Martin. *Codes, Ciphers and Secret Writing.* Mineola, N.Y.: Dover Publications Inc., 1972.

Gawain, Shakti. *Developing Intuition: Practical Guidance for Daily Life.* Novato, Calif.: Nataraj/New World Library, 2000.

Gee, Henry. *Jacob's Ladder: The History of the Human Genome.* New York: W.W. Norton & Co., 2004.

Gerber, MD, Richard. *A Practical Guide to Vibrational Medicine.* New York: Quill/HarperCollins Publishers Inc., 2000.

"A Girl With an X-Ray Vision," Pravda.ru. *http://english.pravda.ru/science/tech/14-01-2004/4591-phenomenon-0/.* January 14, 2004.

Gladwell, Malcolm. *Blink: The Power of Thinking Without Thinking.* New York and Boston: Little, Brown & Co., 2005.

Goethe, Johann Wolfgang von. *Theory of Colors.* Cambridge, Mass. and London: The MIT Press, 1970.

Goldberg, Philip. *The Intuitive Edge: Understanding Intuition and Applying it in Everyday Life.* Los Angeles: Jeremy P. Tarcher, Inc., 1983.

Goode, Caron B. *Kids Who See Ghosts: How to Guide Them Through Fear.* San Francisco, Calif.: and Newbury Port, Mass.: Weiser Books, 2010.

Goode, Erica. "Experts See Mind's Voices in New Light." *The New York Times,* May 6, 2003.

Gosling, Sam. *Snoop: What Your Stuff Says About You.* New York: Basic Books/Perseus Books Group, 2008.

Gotfrit, M. "Range of human hearing." Zen Audio Project. *www.sfu.ca/~gotfrit/ZAP_Sept.3_99/new%20page.html.* 1995.

Grandin, Temple. *Thinking in Pictures: And Other Reports From My Life With Autism.* New York: Vintage Books/Random House Inc., 1995.

Granit, Ragnar. *Receptors and Sensory Perception.* New Haven, Conn. and London: Yale University Press, 1962.

Greene, Brian. *The Elegant Universe: Superstrings, Hidden Dimensions, and the Quest for the Ultimate Theory.* New York and London: W.W. Norton & Co., 2003.

Grinder, John, and Richard Bandler. *The Structure of Magic II.* Palo Alto, Calif.: Science and Behavior Books, Inc., 1976.

Gruber, Suzanne, and Bob Wasel. *Haunts of the Cashtown Inn.* Gettysburg, Pa.: Americana Souvenirs and Gifts, 1998.

Hall, Judy. *The Crystal Bible 2.* New York: St. Martin's Press, 1983.

Halliday, Robert, and Alan Murdie. *The Cambridge Ghost Book.* Ely, England: Fern House, 2000.

Harman, Willis, and Howard Rheingold. *Higher Creativity: Liberating the Unconscious for Breakthrough Insights.* New York: Putnam/Penguin Putnam, Inc., 1984.

Harner, Michael. *The Way of the Shaman.* New York: HarperCollins Publishers, 1990.

Hart, Matthew. *Diamond: The History of a Cold-Blooded Love Affair.* New York: Plume/Penguin Group, 2001.

Hauck, Dennis William. *Haunted Places: The National Directory.* New York: Penguin Books, 1996.

Hawkes, Joyce Whiteley. *Cell-Level Healing: The Bridge From Soul to Cell.* New York, London, Toronto, Sydney, and Hillsboro, Ore.: Atria Paperback/Beyond Words, 2006.

Hawking, Stephen. *A Brief History of Time (10th Ed.).* New York: Bantam Books, 1996.

Hay, Louise. *Heal Your Body: The Mental Causes for Physical Illnesses and the Metaphysical Way to Overcome Them.* Carlsbad, Calif.: Hay House Inc., 1984.

Hercz, Robert. "The God Helmet." *Saturday Night Magazine,* October 2002.

Hipskind, Judith. *How to Read Palms.* New York: Globe Communications Cop., 1998.

Hladik, L'aura. *Ghost Hunting New Jersey.* Cincinnati, Ohio: Clerisy Press, 2008.

Hogarth, Robin M. *Educating Intuition.* Chicago, Ill. and London: The University of Chicago Press, 2001.

Holland, John H. *Emergence from Chaos to Order.* New York: Basic Books/Perseus Books Group, 1998.

Holland, John. *101 Ways to Jump-Start Your Intuition.* Carlsbad, Calif.: Hay House Inc., 2005.

Holland, John, and Cindy Pearlman. *Born Knowing: A Medium's Journey— Accepting and Embracing My Spiritual Gifts.* Carlsbad, Calif.: Hay House Inc., 2003.

Holland, Dr. Julie A., and Kevin C. Riley, PhD, "Characterizing Hallucinations: An Aid in the Differential Diagnosis of Malingering." *Journal of the American Association of Emergency Psychiatry,* 1998, Vol 4, No. 1, pp. 3–5.

Holzer, Hans. *Beyond Medicine: The Facts About Unorthodox and Psychic Healing.* Chicago, Ill.: Henry Regnery Co., 1973.

————. *Ghosts: True Encounters With the World Beyond.* New York: Black Dog & Leventhal Publishers Inc., 2004.

————. *The Supernatural: Explaining the Unexplained.* Franklin Lakes, N.J.: New Page/Career Press Inc., 2003.

"How Scientists Proved That the Pain of Rejection Is All Too Real." *The Guardian.* October 10, 2003.

Hubbard, Whitney S., Raymond W. Werring, and Richard Brennan. *Psychic Criminology (2nd Ed.): A Guide for Using Psychics in Investigations.* Springfield, Ill.: Charles C. Thomas Publisher Ltd., 2002.

Johnson, Steven. *Mind Wide Open: Your Brain and the Neuroscience of Everyday Life.* New York: Scribner, 2004.

Jones, Marc Edmund. *Astrology: How and Why it Works.* New York: Penguin Books, 1976.

Jones, Marie D., and Larry Flaxman. *11:11 The Time Prompt Phenomenon: The Meaning Behind Mysterious Signs, Sequences and Synchronicities.* Franklin Lakes, N.J.: New Page Books/Career Press, 2009.

Jou, Tsung Hwa. *The Dao of Taijiquan: Way to Rejuvenation.* Scottsdale, Ariz.: Tai Chi Foundation, 2001.

Juan, MD, Stephen. *The Odd Brain: Mysteries of Our Weird and Wonderful Brains.* New York: MJF Books, 2006.

Jung, C.G. *Four Archetypes: Mother/Rebirth/Spirit/Trickster.* Princeton, N.J.: Princeton University Press, 1969.

————. *Psychology and the Occult.* Princeton, N.J.: Princeton University Press, 1977.

————. *Psychology of the Unconscious: A Study of the Transformations and Symbolism of the Libido.* Princeton, N.J.: Princeton University Press, 1991.

————. *Synchronicity: An Acausal Connecting Principle.* Princeton, N.J.: Princeton University Press, 1973.

Kahneman, Daniel. *Thinking, Fast and Slow.* New York: Farrar, Straus and Giroux, 2011.

Kaitz, M., A. Good, A.M. Rokem, and A.I. Eidelman. "Mothers Learn to Recognise the Smell of Their Own Infant Within Two Days." *Developmental Psychobiology*, Nov. 1987; 20(6): 587–91.

Kaku, Michio. *Hyperspace: A Scientific Odessey Through Parallel Universes, Time Warps and the 10th Dimension.* New York: Anchor Books/Random House Inc., 1995.

————. *Visions: How Science Will Revolutionize the 21st Century.* New York: Anchor Books/Random House Inc., 1998.

Kaptchuk, Ted J. *The Web That Has No Weaver: Understanding Chinese Medicine.* Chicago, Ill.: Congdon & Weed Inc., 1983.

Kardec, Allan. *The Book on Mediums: Guide for Mediums and Invocators.* York Beach, Maine: Samuel Weiser, Inc., 1996.

Kay, Keith. *The Little Giant Book of Optical Illusions.* New York: Sterling Publishing Co., Inc., 1991.

Kirkpatrick, Sidney A. *Edgar Cayce: An American Prophet.* New York: Riverhead Books/Penguin Putnam Inc., 2000.

Kitei, MD, Lynne D. *The Phoenix Lights: A Skeptic's Discovery That We Are Not Alone.* Charlottesville, Va.: Hampton Roads Publishing Co., Inc., 2010.

Koestler, Arthur. *The Roots of Coincidence: An Excursion Into Parapsychology.* New York: Vintage Books/Random House Inc., 1972.

Korn, Joey. *Dowsing: A Path to Enlightenment.* Grovetown, Ga.: New Millenium Press, 1997.

The Amazing Kreskin. *How to be (a Fake) Kreskin: Mental Marvels, Feats and Stunts That You Can Do.* Self-published, 1996.

The Amazing Kreskin, and Bret Saxon. *The Amazing Kreskin's Future With the Stars.* Self-published, 2001.

Kueppers, Harold. *The Basic Law of Color Theory.* Woodbury, N.Y.: Barron's Educational Series Inc., 1982.

Kurland, Michael. *The Complete Idiot's Guide to Extraterrestrial Intelligence.* New York: Alpha Books/Simon & Schuster Inc., 1999.

Lake, Cather Ann. *Linking Up: How the People in Your Life Are Roadsigns to Self Discovery.* Norfolk , Va. and Virginia Beach, Va.: The Donning Company Publishers, 1988.

Laszlo, Ervin. *Science and the Akashic Field: An Integral Theory of Everything.* Rochester, Vt.: Inner Traditions, 2004.

LeClerc, Alexandra. *Seeing the Dead, Talking with Spirits: Shamanic Healing Through Contact With the Spirit World.* Rochester, Vt.: Destiny Books, 2005.

Ledoux, Joseph. *The Emotional Brain: The Mysterious Underpinnings of Emotional Life.* New York: Touchstone/Simon & Schuster, Inc., 1996.

Leonard, George. *The Silent Pulse: A Search for the Perfect Rhythm That Exists in Each of Us.* New York: Bantam Books, 1981.

Leshan, Lawrence. *How to Meditate.* New York: Bantam Books, 1981.

———. *The Medium, the Mystic and the Physicist: Toward a General Theory of the Paranormal.* New York: Ballentine Books, 1974.

Leudar, Ivan, and Philip Thomas. *Voices of Reason, Voices of Insanity: Studies of Verbal Hallucinations.* London and Philadelphia, Penn.: Routledge/Taylor & Francis Group, 2000.

Lewis, H.W. *Why Flip a Coin? The Art and Science of Good Decisions.* New York: Barnes & Noble Books/MTF Books, 1997.

Liaros, Carol Ann. *Intuition Made Easy.* Scottsdale, Ariz.: Cloudbank Creations Inc., 2003.

Lipton, Bruce. *The Biology of Belief: Unleashing the Power of Consciousness, Matter and Miracles.* Santa Rosa, Calif.: Mountain of Love/Elite Books, 2005.

Llinas, Rodolfo R. *I of the Vortex: From Neurons to Self.* Cambridge, Mass.: MIT Press, 2001.

"A Longitudinal Descriptive Study of Self-Reported Abnormal Smell and Taste Perception in Pregnant Women." *Chemical Senses*, June 2004, 29(5): 391–402.

Luria, A.R. *The Mind of a Mnemonist: A Little Book About a Vast Memory.* Cambridge, Mass. and London: Harvard University Press, 1998.

Lynn, Steven Jay, Irving Kirsch, and Judith W. Rhue. *Casebook of Clinical Hypnosis.* Washington, D.C.: American Psychological Association, 1996.

MacAfee, John. *Beyond the Siddhis: Supernatural Powers and the Sutras of Palanjali.* Woodland Park, Colo.: Woodland Publications, 2001.

Maharishi Mahesh Yogi. *Transcendental Meditation: Serenity Without Drugs.* New York: Signet/The New American Library Inc., 1968.

Malone, John. *Unsolved Mysteries of Science: A Mind-Expanding Journey Through a Universe of Big Bands, article Waves, and Other Perplexing Concepts.* New York: John Wiley & Sons Inc., 2001.

"Map Makers Can Avoid Confusing the Color Blind." ScienceDaily Website. *www.sciencedaily.com/releases/2000/04/000428082212.htm*. April 28, 2000.

Markert, Christopher. *Dan Tien: Your Secret Energy Center.* York Beach, Maine: Samuel Weiser, Inc., 1998.

McCormack, Kathleen. *Beginner's Tarot.* London: Quarto Publishing PLC, 2001.

McMoneagle, Joseph. *Remote Viewing Secrets: A Handbook.* Charlottesville, Va.: Hampton Roads Publishing Co., 2000.

"Men Do Hear—But Differently Than Women, Brain Images Show." ScienceDaily Website. *www.sciencedaily.com/releases/2000/11/001129075326. htm*. November 29, 2000.

"'Mind's Eye' Influences Visual Perception." *Science Daily.* July 4, 2008.

Mitchell, Janet Lee. *Out-of-Body Experiences: A Handbook.* Jefferson, N.C.: McFarland & Company, Inc. 1981.

Moir, Anne and David Jessel. *Brain Sex: The Real Difference Between Men and Women.* New York: Dell Publishing, 1992.

Motoyama, Hiroshi. *Theories of the Chakras: Bridge to Higher Consciousness.* Wheaton, Ill.: The Theosophical Publishing House, 1981.

Myers, David G. *Intuition: Its Powers and Perils.* New Haven, Conn. and London: Yale University Press, 2002.

Myss, Caroline. *Anatomy of the Spirit: The Seven Stages of Power and Healing.* New York: Three Rivers Press, 1996.

Nabokov, Vladmir. *Speak, Memory: An Autobiography Revisited.* New York: Vintage Books/Random House, Inc.

Nesbitt, Mark. *The Ghost Hunter's Field Guide to Civil War Battlefields.* Gettysburg, Pa.: Second Chance Publications, 2007.

———. *The Ghost Hunter's Field Guide: Gettysburg and Beyond.* Gettysburg, Pa: Second Chance Publications, 2005.

Netzley, Patricia D. *The Greenhaven Encyclopedia of Witchcraft.* San Diego, Calif.: Greenhaven Press Inc., 2002.

Nickerson, Colin. "Oscar, Cat with the Purr of Death." *The Sydney Morning Herald*, July 27, 2007.

Noorbergen, Rene. *Nostradamus Predicts the End of the World.* New York: Pinnacle Books Inc., 1982.

Nørratranders, Tor. *The User Illusion: Cutting Consciousness Down to Size.* New York: The Penguin Group, 1991.

Nurosi, Aki, and Mark Shulman. *Colorful Optical Illusions.* New York: Sterling Publishing Co., Inc. 2004.

Oatley, Keith. *Emotions: A Brief History.* Oxford, England and Malden, Mass.: Blackwell Publishing, Ltd. 2004.

Oberkamp, Frances. *Intuition: How to Use It.* Paradise, Calif.: Morgan Road Books/Random House Inc., 2006.

Orloff, MD, Judith. *Dr. Judith Orloff's Guide to Intuitive Healing.* New York: Three Rivers Press, 2000.

Ostrander, Sheila, and Lynn Schroeder. *Psychic Discoveries Behind the Iron Curtain.* Englewood Cliffs, N.J.: Bantam/Prentice-Hall Inc., 1981.

Oz, MD, Mehmet. *Healing From the Heart.* New York: Penguin Putnam Inc., 1999.

Page, George. *Inside the Animal Mind: A Groundbreaking Explosion of Animal Intelligence.* Charlottesville, Va.: Hampton Roads Publishing Co., 1999.

Page, R.I. *Runes.* London: The British Museum Press, 1987.

Pagels, Elaine. *The Gnostic Gospels.* New York: Vintage Books/Random House Inc., 1989.

Pagels, Heinz R. *The Cosmic Code: Quantum Physics as the Language of Nature.* New York: Bantam Books/Simon & Schuster Inc., 1983.

Pearce, Joseph Chilton. *The Biology of Transcendence: A Blueprint of the Human Spirit.* Rochester, VT: Crown Publishers/Random House Inc., 2002.

Peat, F. David. *Synchronicity: The Bridge Between Matter and Mind.* New York: Bantam Books/Random House Inc., 1988.

Peirce, Penney. *Frequency: The Power of Personal Vibration.* New York: Atria Books/Simon & Schuster Inc./Beyond Words Publishing Inc., 2009.

Piaget, Jean. *Play, Dreams and Imitation in Childhood.* New York: W.W. Norton & Company, Inc. 1962.

Pinker, Steven. *The Language Instinct: How the Mind Creates Language.* New York: HarperCollins Publishers Inc., 2000.

Playfair, Guy Lyon. *Twin Telepathy: The Psychic Connection.* London: Vega, 2002.

Pohl, Rudiger. *Cognitive Illusions: A Handbook on Fallacies and Biases in Thinking, Judgement and Memory.* Hove, UK: Psychology Press, 2004.

Polkinghorne, John. *Belief in God in an Age of Science.* New Haven, Conn. and London: Yale University Press, 1998.

Puharich, Andrija. *Uri: A Journal of the Mystery of Uri Geller.* New York: Bantam Books/Doubleday & Co., Inc., 1974.

Radin, Dean. *The Conscious Universe: The Scientific Truth of Psychic Phenomena.* New York: HarperCollins Publishers Inc., 1997.

Ramachandran, V.S., and Sandra Blakeslee. *Phantoms in the Brain: Probing the Mysteries of the Human Mind.* New York: Quill/HarperCollins Publishers Inc., 1998.

Randi, James. *The Truth About Uri Geller.* Amherst, N.Y.: Prometheus Books, 1982.

Randles, Jenny. *Strange and Unexplained Mysteries of the 20th Century.* New York: Sterling Publishing Co. Inc., 1994.

Rank, Otto. *The Trauma of Birth.* New York: Harper Torchbook/Harper & Row Publishers Inc., 1973.

Ratey, MD, John J. *The User's Guide to the Brain: Perception, Attention and the Four Theatres of the Brain.* New York: Vintage Books/Random House Inc., 2002.

Redfield, James. *The Tenth Insight: Holding the Vision.* New York: Warner Books, Inc., 1996.

Reed, Henry. *Edgar Cayce on Channeling Your Higher Self.* New York: Warner Books, Inc., 1989.

———. *Who Speaks? Angel or Daimon in Trance Channeling.* New York: Warner Books.

Reed, Henry, and Brenda English. *The Intuitive Heart: How to Trust Your Intuition for Guidance and Healing.* Virginia Beach, Va.: A.R.E. Press, 2000.

Rinpoche, Tezin Wangyal. *Healing With Form, Energy and Light: The Five Elements in Tibetan Shamanism, Tantra and Dzogchen.* Ithica, N.Y.: Snow Lion Publications, 2002.

Rivlin, Robert, and Karen Gravelle. *Deciphering the Senses: The Expanding World of Human Perception.* New York: Simon & Schuster Inc., 1984.

Roach, Mary. *Spook: Science Tackles the Afterlife.* New York and London: W.W. Norton & Co., Inc., 2005.

Robinson, Lady Steam, and Tom Corbett. *The Dreamer's Dictionary.* New York: Warner Books Inc., 1974.

Robinson, Lynn, and Lavome Carlson-Finnerty. *The Complete Idiot's Guide to Being Psychic.* New York: Alpha Books/Simon & Schuster Inc. 1999.

Ruiz, Don Miguel. *The Four Agreements: A Toltec Wisdom Book.* San Rafael, Calif.: Amber-Allen Publishing Inc., 1997.

Ruiz, Don Miguel, as recorded by Mary Carroll Nelson. *Beyond Fear: A Toltec Guide to Freedom and Joy.* Tulsa, Okla.: Council Oak Books, 1997.

Rushnell, Squire. *When God Winks: How the Power of Coincidence Guides Your Life.* New York: Atria Books, 2001.

Russell, Walter. *A New Concept of the Universe.* Waynesboro, Va.: University of Science and Philosophy, 1989.

———. *The Secret of Light.* Waynesboro, Va.: University of Science and Philosophy, 1994.

"Russian X-Ray Girl Natasha Demkina Still Uses Her Gift to Help Common People." Pravda.ru. *http://english.pravda.ru/science/mysteries/29-05-2008/105380-natasha_demkina-0/.* May 29, 2008.

Sacks, MD, Oliver. *An Anthropologist on Mars: Seven Paradoxical Tales.* New York: Alfred A. Knopf/Random House Inc., 1995.

———. *The Best American Science Writing 2003.* New York: HarperCollins Publishers Inc., 2003.

———. *The Island of the Colorblind.* New York: Vintage Books/Random Hounse Inc., 1998.

———. *A Leg to Stand On.* New York: Touchstone Book, 1984.

———. *The Man Who Mistook His Wife for a Hat: And Other Clinical Tales.* New York: Touchstone/Simon & Schuster Inc., 1985.

———. *Migraine.* Los Angeles: University of California Press, 1992.

———. *Uncle Tungsten: Memories of a Chemical Boyhood.* New York: Alfred A. Knopf, 2001.

Salam, Abdus. *Unification of Fundamental Forces: The First 1988 Dirac Memorial Lecture.* Cambridge, Great Britain: University of Cambridge Press, 1990.

Santulli, MD, Robert B. *The Upper Valley Memory Center Handbook.* Self-published, 2007.

Schulz, MD, Mona Lisa. *Awakening Intuition: Using Your Mind-Body Network for Insight and Healing.* New York: Three Rivers Press/Random House, 1998.

Schwartz, Gary E. *The Afterlife Experiments: Breakthrough Scientific Evidence of Life After Death.* New York: Atria Books/Simon & Schuster Inc., 2002.

———. *The Sacred Promise: How Science is Discovering Spirit's Collaboration with Us in Our Daily Lives.* New York and Hillsboro, Ore.: Atria Books & Beyond Worlds, 2011.

Schwartz, Gary E and Linda G.S. Russek. *The Living Energy Universe.* Charlottesville, Va.: Hampton Roads Publishing Co., 1999.

Schwartz, Gary E., and William L. Simon. *The Energy Healing Experiments: Science Reveals Our Natural Power to Heal.* New York: Atria Books/Simon & Schuster Inc., 2007.

———. *The Truth About Medium.* Charlottesville, Va.: Hampton Roads Publishing Co., Inc., 2005.

Seale, Alan. *Intuitive Living: A Sacred Path.* Boston, Mass.: Weiser Books, 2001.

Sechehaye, Marguerite. *Autobiography of a Schizophrenic Girl: The True Story of "Renee."* New York: Meridian/Penguin Group, 1951.

Shapiro, MD, Sanford. *Talking With Patients: A Self Psychological View.* Northvale, N.J.: Jason Aronson, Inc., 1995.

Sharp, Eleyne Austen. *Haunted Newport: Spectral Sights of the Nearly Departed.* Seekonk, Mass.: TCI Press, 1996.

Shbentsov, Yefin, and Barbara Gordon. *Cure Your Cravings.* New York: Perigee Book/Penguin Putnam Inc., 1998.

Sheldrake, Rupert. *Dogs That Know When Their Owners Are Coming Home: And Other Unexplained Powers of Animals.* New York: Three Rivers Press, 1999.

———. *The Sense of Being Stared At: And Other Unexplained Powers of the Human Mind.* New York: Crown Publishers/Random House Inc., 2003.

Shermer, Michael. *How We Believe: Science, Skepticism and the Search for God (2nd Ed.).* New York: Owl Books/Henry Hold & Co. LLC, 2003.

Silva, Freddy. *Secrets in the Fields: The Science and Mysticism of Crop Circles.* Charlottesville, Va.: Hampton Roads Publishing Co., Inc., 2002.

Silvestre, Colette. *Développer Son 6e Sens.* Paris, France: Éditions Trajectoire, 2005.

Sinclair, Upton. *Mental Radio.* Charlottesville, Va.: Hampton Roads Publishing Company, Inc., 2001.

Sloane, Paul, and Des Machale. *Pocket Puzzlers: Lateral Thinking Puzzles.* New York: Sterling Publishing Co.

Smith, Angela Thompson. *Remote Perceptions: Out-of-Body Experiences, Remote Viewing and Other Normal Abilities.* Charlottesville, Va.: Hampton Roads Publishing Co., 1998.

Smith, Gordon. *The Unbelievable Truth: A Medium's Guide to the Spirit World.* Carlsbad, Calif.: Hay House Inc., 2004.

Smith, Kalila Katherina. *New Orleans Ghosts: Voodoo and Vampires.* New Orleans: De Simonin Publications, 2007.

Smith, Paul H. *Reading the Enemy's Mind: Inside Star Gate America's Psychic Espionage Program*. New York: Tom Doherty Associate Book, LLC., 2005.

"Sniffer Dogs Can be Used to Detect Lung Cancer; Research Suggests." ScienceDaily Website. *www.sciencedaily.com/releases/2011/08/110817194548. htm*. August 17, 2011.

Solms, Mark and Oliver Turnbull. *The Brain and the Inner World: An Introduction to the Neuroscience of Subjective Experience*. New York: Other Press, LLC, 2002.

Steiner, Rudolf. *Agriculture: Fondements Spirituels de le Méthode Bio-dynamique*. Genève, Suisse: Éditions Atroposophiques Romandes, 1999.

———. *Colour*. Forest Row, England: Rudolf Steiner Press, 2001.

Stern K., and M.K. McClintock MK. "Regulation of ovulation by human pheromones". *Nature* 392 (6672): 177–9. 1998.

Stevenson, MD, Ian. *Unlearned Language: New Studies in Xenoglossy*. Charlottesville, Va.: University Press of Virginia, 1984.

Sugrue, Thomas. *The Story of Edgar Cayce: There Is a River*. Virginia Beach, Va.: A.R.E. Press, 1973.

Swami Panchadasi. *The Human Aura: Astral Colors and Thought Forms*. Desplaines, Ill.: Yoga Publication Society, 1940.

Swann, Ingo. *Natural ESP: A Layman's Guide to Unlocking the Extra Sensory Power of Your Mind*. New York: Bantam Books, 1987.

———. *Psychic Sexuality: The Bio-Psychic "Anatomy" of Sexual Energies*. Rapid City, S.D.: Ingo Swann Books, 1999.

———. *Purple Fables (Quartet)*. Norfolk, Va.: Hampton Roads Publishing Co. Inc., 1994.

———. *Reality Boxes: And Other Black Holes in Human Consciousness*. East Windsor Hill, Conn.: Ingo Swann Books, 2003.

———. *The Wisdom Category: Shedding Light on a Lost Light*. East Windsor Hill, Conn.: Ingo Swann Books, 2003.

———. *To Kiss Earth Good-Bye*. New York: Hawthorne Books Inc., 1975.

———. *Your Nostradamus Factor: Accessing Your Innate Ability to See into the Future*. New York: Fireside. 1993.

Tahan, Malba. *The Man Who Counted: A Collection of Mathematical Adventures*. New York: W.W. Norton & Co. Inc., 1993.

Tammet, Daniel. *Born on a Blue Day*. New York: Free Press, 2007.

Targ, Russell, and Harold E. Puthoff. *Mind-Reach: Scientists Look at Psychic Abilities*. Charlottesville, Va.: Hampton Roads Publishing Company, Inc., 2005.

Taylor, Eldon. *Mind Programming: From Persuasion and Brainwashing to Self-Help and Practical Metaphysics.* Carlsbad, Calif.: Hay House Inc., 2009.

————. *What If? The Challenge of Self-Realization.* Carlsbad, Calif.: Hay House, Inc., 2011.

Taylor, Marjorie. *Imaginary Companions and the Children Who Create Them.* New York & Oxford, England: Oxford University Press, 1999.

Thurston, Mark. *Understand and Develop Your ESP: Based on Edgar Cayce Readings.* Virginia Beach, Va.: A.R.E. Press, 1977.

Tiller, William A. *Science and Human Transformation: Subtle Energies, Intentionality and Consciousness.* Walnut Creek, Calif.: Pavior Publishing, 1997.

Tomkins, Peter and Christopher Bird. *The Secret Life of Plants.* New York: Perennia/HarperCollins Publishers Inc., 2002.

Treffert, Darold A. "Ellen: 'With a Song in Her Heart."Wisconsin Medican Society. *www.wisconsinmedicalsociety.org/savant_syndrome/savant_profiles/ellen.* 2001.

Turin, Luca. *Parfum: le guide.* New York: Penguin, 2008.

————. *The Secret of Scent: Adventures in Perfume and the Science of Smell.* New York: Ecco, 2006.

Underhill, Ruth. *The Papago and Pima Indians of Arizona.* Palmer Lake, Colo.: The Filter Press, 1979.

Upczak, Patricia Rose. *Synchronicity Signs and Symbols.* Nederland, Colo.: Synchronicity Publishing, 2001.

Upledger, John E. *SomatoEmotional Release: Deciphering the Language of Life.* Berkeley, Calif.: North Atlantic Books, 2002.

————. *Your Inner Physician and You: CranialSacral Therapy and SomatoEmotional Release.* Berkeley, Calif.: North Atlantic Books, 1997.

Van Praagh, James. *Reaching to Heaven: A Spiritual Journey Through Life and Death.* New York: Dutton/Penguin Putnam Inc., 1999.

————. *Talking to Heaven: A Medium's Message of Life After Death.* New York: Dutton/Penguin Group, 1997.

Vasiliev, L.L. *Experiments in Mental Suggestion.* Charlottesville, Va.: Hampton Roads Publishing Co. Inc., 2002.

Walker, Brian Browne. *The I Ching or Book of Changes.* New York: St. Martin's Griffin, 1992.

Walker, K.L. *Aphasia: The Architecture of a Gagged Throat.* Union, Ky.: Shekhem Publishing LLP, 2004.

Walton, Travis. *Fire in the Sky: The Walton Experience.* Snowflake, Ariz.: Skyfire Productions, 2010.

Warcollier, Rene. *Mind to Mind.* Charlottesville, Va.: Hampton Roads Publishing Company, Inc., 2001.

Watson, James D. *Avoid Boring People: Lessons From a Life in Science.* New York: Alfred A. Knopf/Random House Inc., 2007.

Watson, James D., and Andrew Berry. *DNA: The Secret of Life.* New York: Alfred A. Knopf/Random House Inc., 2006.

Weber, Nancy Orlen. *The Gift of Interspecies Communication: True Stories and Exercises for the Soul.* Denville, N.J.: Unlimited Mind Publications, 2002.

———. *Psychic Detective: True Stories and Exercises for the Soul.* Denville, N.J.: Unlimited Mind Publications, 2002.

"Weird Georgia A Tunnel to Hell." Brown's Guide to Georgia Website. *www.brownsguides.com.* 2012.

Weiss, MD, Brian L. *Many Lives, Many Masters.* New York: Fireside/Simon & Schuster Inc., 1988.

Williams, Marta. *Learning Their Language: Intuitive Communication with Animals and Nature.* Novato, Calif.: New World Library, 2003.

Williams, Val. *Two Worlds as One: A Medium's Life.* Blackburn, England: Red Wing Publishing, 2000.

Wiseman, Richard, and Robert L. Morris. *Guidelines for Testing Psychic Claimants.* Amherst, N.Y.: Prometheus Books, 1995.

Wood, Elizabeth A. *Crystals and Light: An Introduction to Optical Crystallography (2nd Revised Ed.).* New York: Dover Publications Inc., 1977.

Zukav, Gary. *The Dancing Wu Li Masters: An Overview of the New Physics.* New York: Bantam Books, 1989.

NANCY DU TERTRE is a trained psychic detective, spiritual medium, medical intuitive, energy healer, and paranormal investigator. She is known as "the Skeptical Psychic." She has appeared on radio and television, given lectures to paranormal groups and university psychology students, founded the New York and New Jersey Skeptical Psychic Societies, teaches workshops, and hosts a CBS radio show called "Hot Leads, Cold Cases." She is also an attorney specialized in securities litigation. She graduated *magna cum laude* from Princeton University and with honors from Pace University School of Law. Ms. du Tertre has owned several businesses and is the author of an art history book (*The Art of the Limoges Box*) and co-author of the memoirs of a NYC homicide detective *(Behind Criminal Minds)*. For more information, please visit *www.theskepticalpsychic.com*.

ABOUT THE AUTHOR